P9-BJK-070

Prefaces
to
The Experience of Literature

THE WORKS OF LIONEL TRILLING

UNIFORM EDITION

LIONEL TRILLING

PREFACES
to
THE EXPERIENCE OF LITERATURE

New York and London
HARCOURT BRACE JOVANOVICH

Printed in the United States of America

Library of Congress Cataloging in Publication Data

Trilling, Lionel, 1905–1975.
Prefaces to The experience of literature.

(The works of Lionel Trilling)
1. Literature—History and criticism—Addresses, essays, lectures.
I. Trilling, Lionel, 1905–1975, comp. Experience of literature. 1979.
II. Title. III. Series: Trilling, Lionel, 1905–1975. Works. 1977.
PN511.T77   1979   809   79–1850
ISBN 0–15–173915–3

First edition

B C D E

Foreword

IN 1979 it seems quaint to reflect that there was once a "war of anthologies," the phrase used in *Literary History of the United States* to describe the conflict to gain recognition between formalist and radicalist poets, between Lowell and Wilbur, say, and Allen Ginsberg. Except as reference works, "readers" or anthologies are no longer generally regarded as the most equitable mode of presenting literature to students or to the public, a popular opinion being that one ought to come upon poetry and drama and fiction without the inhibiting presence of a critic. Let Dante proceed without Virgil. But *in se* textbook anthologies are a remarkable part of contemporary literary criticism. Cleanth Brooks, Robert Penn Warren, Irving Howe, Mark Shorer, Howard Mumford Jones, W. H. Auden, Mark Van Doren, and Lionel Trilling among others who edited these books lent authority to the assumption that some writings are more serious and more adept than others, an assumption necessary to our recognizing, and qualifying, experience. Whether or not this is best gained by giving the reader a trustworthy guide to both past and recent literature, one cannot ignore that contemporary discourse often suffers from the existence of an accepted corpus of cultural references. This leads, in my opinion, to more didacticism rather than less.

Even if critics in editing textbook anthologies did not always give readers a salutary direction, they did manage to make criticism itself immediately understandable and relevant. Lionel Trilling's essays in the book *The Experience of Literature,* initially published in 1967 by Holt, Rinehart and Winston, reveal a first-rate mind making connections between literature and living. He saw as obvious, which takes an enormous effort in intellectual matters, that readers are best served when made conscious and responsive to what they read. Speaking of equity, it is proof of Lionel Trilling's intent that he should warn in the Introduction: "No special theory of literature or method of criticism informs what I have written." This is the disclaimer from the author of *The Liberal Imagination, Beyond Culture,* and *The Opposing Self*!

As a publisher of anthologies, I must express envy of *The Experience of Literature.* Trilling wrote a commentary to *each* of the fifty-two major selections of literature, all are here in *Prefaces,* and he was not content merely to describe traditional genres of literature or state a general critical doctrine—to hand a rope and pickaxe to the climbers of Parnassus. No, he stood by, neither pushing nor lifting, ready to indicate the faces and crevices above. In my own rereading of the *Prefaces,* I found that reading Lionel Trilling one feels himself to be very intelligent.

It needs, finally, to be said that Diana Trilling, who is Editor of *The Works of Lionel Trilling* published by Harcourt Brace Jovanovich in a Uniform Edition, discussed with me the possibility of including here an index of the various editions of those works commented upon by the commentaries. It seemed a helpful reference for the reader of this book, but we found too many readily available sources to note them all; and any list would perforce become soon outdated. If Lionel Trilling leads you to your bookshelf or to a bookseller or librarian, have a good trip!

WILLIAM JOVANOVICH

Introduction

THE introduction to a book that deals with literature in general might naturally propose the question of why we read literature, of what use it is in our lives. The question is as engaging as it is natural—it has the allure of all questions that cannot be answered, not really answered. For a satisfactory explanation of why we read literature, a truly adequate account of the purposes it serves, must amount to nothing less than a description of the whole nature of man.

Partial answers can of course be given. The practitioner of one or another of the so-called behavioral sciences—the psychologist, the psychoanalyst, the sociologist—will tell us that we read literature because we want to escape from a harsh or dull reality to a pleasant or interesting fantasy, or to justify unlicensed hidden impulses, or to gain a measure of relief from or control over these impulses. The humanistic educator tells us that certain good things happen if we read literature, and he makes this the ground for saying we *should* do so—because we will be rewarded by an increased awareness, a heightened sensibility, a finer moral perception.

All this is true and worth saying. And the list of reasons could go on to be much longer, for literature serves all kinds of purposes, varying with different cultures, with different groups in the same culture, with individuals in the same group, with the age and emotional circumstance of individuals. Yet in the end the sum of all reasons that might be adduced does not really give us an entire explanation. Just so we do not understand why people engage in a sport when we have enumerated the benefits their activity is commonly said to bring. That it keeps one fit, that it distracts the mind from its troubles, that it affords an opportunity for the harmless release of aggressive and competitive impulses, that it gratifies pride—none of these, nor all of them together, come anywhere near suggesting why the skier is drawn to the slopes, the fisherman to the stream, the tennis-player to the court. In each case the attraction is finally gratuitous, lying beyond the reach of explanation. The same is to be said of artistic creation. If we were to ask, say, a poet why he engages in his enterprise and if he were to consent to answer (as perhaps he would not, finding the question absurd), he might grant that the love of fame or the hope of money or the wish to advance a certain view of life had some part in what he did, but the only answer that would seem to him to make sense was that he wrote poetry because he was a poet.

And to the question of why we read literature we must give a cognate answer, which is no answer: because we are human. Especially when we have it in mind that in every stage of culture, down to the simplest that we know, men make and experience what in our culture is called literature, that no aboriginal tribe, not the most primitive, is without its stories and poems to which a considerable value is assigned, we must recognize that the making and the experience of literature is what the zoologists call a species-characteristic trait of mankind.

But if this is so, another question at once proposes itself. If literature is that natural why need it be taught and studied? It is a question that is often put with some asperity, out of the sense that the processes of teaching and study, whether they go on in the classroom or in writing and reading literary scholarship and criticism, have the effect of interfering with the simple act of reading, that they make abstract and all too self-conscious what should of its nature be spontaneous and immediate. If the experience of literature is in fact what I have called it, a species-characteristic trait of mankind, then surely the pedagogical or scholarly or critical discourse that goes on about it is not necessary.

The objection has its cogency. And a teacher of literature may be quite as disposed to make it as anyone else; there are moments when it seems to him—when it seems to me—that all the discourse that goes on in the classroom and in essays and books is beside the point, that all this secondary activity is obtruding itself upon the primary activity of reading literature, and getting in its way. But although it is true that discourse about literature can on occasion become excessive and have the effect of dulling and obscuring what it is intended to illuminate, it is also true that talking about literature is as natural as producing and reading it. The literary experience is communal—it asks to be shared in discourse. In any developed culture the urge to say things about what we have read and to take account of what others say about it is no less natural than the creation and enjoyment of the art. The Florentines of the fifteenth century were not exactly a people given to abstractness or pedantic intellectuality, yet when they wanted to honor their most famous local poet fifty years after his death, they thought that the most appropriate way to do this was to institute a series of public discourses on his great poem, and the person they invited to lecture on Dante's *Divine Comedy* was not a university professor—at that time Florence did not have what we would call a university—but Boccaccio.

We find a pleasure that seems instinctual not only in the emotions that are aroused by what we read but also in communicating them to each other, in trying to understand why we feel as we do, in testing our emotions by those that others tell us that they have, in discovering what we might possibly feel beyond what we do feel. And discourse leads to dialectic: we disagree with others in observation and response and in the general principles that we and they have been led to formulate. This activity, in itself interesting and pleasant, increases the interest and pleasure of our private experience.

This will explain why in this anthology, with each of the plays and stories and certain of the poems, I have provided commentaries in the form of brief essays. They have one purpose only—to make it more likely that the act of reading will be an experience, having in mind what the word implies of an activity of consciousness and response. They try to suggest that the work of literature is an object that may be freely touched and handled, picked up, turned over, looked at from this angle or that, and, at least in some sense, possessed.

No special theory of literature or method of criticism informs what I have written. In some of the commentaries the emphasis falls on formal and technical matters—such as imagery, tone, point of view, versification, diction, and so on—that the reader ought to be aware of. Others deal with literary conventions that, whether because they are old or because they are new, the reader might not be familiar with. I have felt free to discuss the overt or implicit meanings of a work and to pursue (and sometimes to question) its moral or social or religious ideas. Where I have thought it useful to refer to critical theories or standards of taste of the past, I have done so. Although my concern is always with the work itself and not with the biographical or historical circumstances in which it was written, if a circumstance of biography or history seems to be to the point, I have adduced it. In short, I have availed myself of any of the elements of literary discourse that I have thought relevant to the work and likely to make it more accessible or interesting to the reader.

The commentaries could hardly say all there is to be said about the works to which they address themselves; and I have tried to have them say no more than might suggest to the reader how he could come into a more active connection with what he has read. It will be seen, I think, that they do not impose themselves as anything like doctrine, or limit in any way the reader's autonomy of response: they will not have failed of their purpose—on the contrary!—if they arouse the reader to disagreement.

Literature is a continuous enterprise and in choosing the works to be included in this anthology I have included on an equal footing both the traditional and the new. I have preferred those works that I thought would prove memorable to the reader by reason of their momentousness or their force of dramatic or intellectual energy. That a work has already proved memorable to many is always a special recommendation: not all the works I have chosen are "great" but I have made preponderant those to which the adjective might be applied.

The examples of each genre are arranged chronologically, although there are a few violations of this order for particular indicated reasons. The plays and stories have been drawn from several literatures, with due regard to the accuracy of the translations in which they appear. Because the adequate translation of poems is a virtually hopeless enterprise, the poems included are all English and American.

L.T.

1967

Contents

1 · DRAMA

2 · FICTION

Contents

3 · POETRY

Contents

1·DRAMA

Oedipus Rex

SOPHOCLES
496–406 B.C.

THE PLOT of *Oedipus Rex* is at once the most ingenious and the most terrible that has ever been conceived. It can be thought of as a detective story in which the detective, secure in his own virtue and in the consciousness that he is doing his duty, undertakes to discover the identity of the person who has committed a crime of great seriousness and is forced by the evidence he turns up to recognize that the criminal is none other than himself. And more than this is in store for him. As he pursues his investigations further, he learns that the criminal act, because it was he who committed it, is immeasurably worse than at first it had seemed.

Summarized even in this abstract way, the story of Oedipus is calculated to disturb us in our deepest and most private emotions, for most of us live with the sense of a guilty secret, although what the secret is about we do not know. And of course the play haunts and disturbs us the more because of the peculiar heinousness of what Oedipus has done. He has committed not merely terrible crimes but terrible sins, violating not only the law of society but of the gods. And even the idea of sin does not comprehend the horror of a man's having killed his father and married his mother. These acts are, as we say, unthinkable; the human mind can do nothing with them.

Our disturbance is not lessened but increased by the consideration that Oedipus did not commit his awful acts by intention. Of all the circumstances of the hero's fate, this is the one that most teases, baffles, and terrifies. It is reasonable to say—it has been said—that Oedipus is not accountable for what he did, that he had not really incurred guilt in killing his father and marrying his mother because he had not meant to do these things; on the contrary, once he had heard the awful prophecy, he had bent all his effort toward not doing them. This exculpation of Oedipus is based upon Aristotle's doctrine, set forth in his *Ethics*, to which assent is given by law and morality throughout the Western world, that for an act to have ethical significance, for good or bad, the person who commits it must have done so with consciousness and will. It is in these terms that Oedipus argues for his blamelessness in *Oedipus at Colonus*, the play that Sophocles wrote thirty years later. Worn out with suffering and on the point of death, the aged Oedipus, in a moment of bitterness and self-pity, says that he should not have been adjudged guilty because he had had no intention of wrong-doing. But in *Oedipus Rex* he makes no such claim to innocence. He does not justify himself; his mind is wholly given over to horror and self-loathing. We feel this response to be appropriate. The rationality of Aristotle's doctrine of intention seems quite inapplicable to the emotion evoked by Oedipus's situation, which occurs at a depth to which reason cannot penetrate. It is from the disclosure of this primitive depth that the play derives its terrible power, leading us to recognize that a man may incur guilt, and of an ultimate kind, even though a rational ethic might pronounce him innocent; we are brought to confront the possibility that reason can be superseded by darker modes of judgment. The security that a rational ethic had seemed to afford is taken from us.

An engaging question often raised about *Oedipus Rex* is whether or not it is a tragedy of fate. Much ingenuity has been expended to show that it is not. Some critics feel that the play becomes less interesting and impressive if it is taken as a tragedy of fate, for the protagonist then lacks the dignity that we associate with the possession of free will; he becomes, as we say, a puppet in the hands of destiny. Those who hold this position believe that they have an ally in Aristotle, who, in his *Poetics,* says that the protagonist of a tragedy should be a man worthy of respect and admiration but having some discernible weakness or fault of character to which his tragic disaster may be attributed. In some important sense, that is, he is to be thought responsible for what befalls him.

Aristotle's prescription would certainly seem to be satisfied by the character of Oedipus. He is admirable for many qualities. He is wise and courageous; it was he who, when everyone else stood helpless before the Sphinx that ravaged Thebes, answered her riddle and destroyed her, thus freeing the land of which he then became the ruler. As a king he is virtuous and conscientious. To be sure, he is called *tyrannos,* which, although it is not to be translated as "tyrant," means a king who rules by his own power, as distinguished from *basileus,* a king by legal right. Yet he is in no way arbitrary or repressive; he admits his wife to equal rule with him and allows her brother Kreon to stand almost on a parity with the royal couple. As husband and father he is dutiful and loving. He is not lacking in piety; although he speaks contemptuously to the great seer Tiresias, the protégé of Apollo, he holds the gods in due awe and is quick to undertake what Apollo's oracle at Delphi tells him should be done to rid the city of plague.

One fault, however, Oedipus does have, that of pride, and he is quick to anger when his pride is offended. His slaying of his unknown father Laïos at the crossroads had been the outcome of this trait. And it is his choleric pride, amounting to arrogance, that prevents him from heeding any word of caution when he is pursuing his search for the killer of Laïos, with the result that he is forced to confront the truth that he himself is the killer—and, of course, something more than that.

Yet no matter how fully we take account of Oedipus's fault of character, we have no ground for saying that the tragic disaster is brought about by this personal flaw and not by the predestination announced in the prophecy. That the fault detonates the disaster is of course true, but the explosives have been laid by what, in the nature of the prophecy about Oedipus, we can only call fate. The young hero's hot-blooded response to Laïos' insult and show of violence did indeed lead him to kill *a man,* and, what is worse, a king; but it was the fated ignorance of his parenthood and the unsought but destined occasion of the meeting between father and son that led him to kill *his father.* Any other proud and hot-blooded man who had done what Oedipus did would have committed an act that was to be deplored and condemned: for Oedipus alone the act was immitigable, and the more so because it led to an act yet more horrifying, his marriage to his mother.

If we take the line that Oedipus brought about his tragedy by refusing to heed the advice to be cautious in his search for Laïos' killer, we find ourselves in the position of supposing that all would have been well if he had prudently given up his investigation and settled to live in contented ignorance with his wife and children in plague-ridden Thebes. Of course we can suppose no such thing. Nor would we have any satisfaction if any such thing came about. To be sure, we are impelled to cry out a warning to the impetuous man not to call upon *that* witness, not to ask *that* question; we are fearful of the moment when the full dreadful knowledge will come to him of who he is and what he has done. But we do not want Oedipus to remain oblivious of the truth about himself. An Oedipus who prudently gave up his search would be an object of condescension, even of contempt: the Oedipus who presses on to the conclusion that destroys him compels our awed respect.

In short, then, whatever it may also be, the story of Oedipus must certainly be called a tragedy of fate. Yet to say this is, after all, not to say much. Something of what must be added if we are to account for the peculiar power of *Oedipus Rex* is suggested by a comparison of the story of the play with a well-known tale of similar purport. In the city of Ispahan, in Persia, a certain man's servant came to him and said, "I was in the market place and there I saw Death and he made a threatening gesture to me." The man said, "Let us flee," and he and his servant set out posthaste for Samarra. No sooner had they entered that city than they encountered Death, to whom the man said, "Why did you threaten my servant in the market place in

Ispahan?" Death replied, "My gesture was not one of threat but of surprise, for I had an appointment to meet you in Samarra, and I was surprised to learn, from seeing your servant, that you were still in Ispahan." In its barest outline, the story of Oedipus is no different from this—a man, fleeing his fate, encounters it. But the wry little parable of fatalism evokes no other response than an ironic shrug; the mind does not engage it, there is really nothing in the tale for the mind to engage. The implied generalization, that all men must submit to what is ordained for them, that some fulfil their fate by the very intention of evading it, may win from us a certain assent but not much interest. We respond very differently when a man such as Oedipus fulfils his fate by seeking to evade it—a man whose pride, courage, and intellect suggest an ideal of mankind, and whose particular destiny it is to experience on so great a scale the peculiarly human pain of remorse and self-reproach. The man who flees from Ispahan to Samarra is indeed without dignity, a mere puppet in the hands of destiny; the joke is on him, fate has made a fool of him. But Oedipus, who is unable to save himself by intelligence and right intention and who is subject to an order of things which does not proceed by human rules and is not susceptible to human understanding, is enhanced in stature by his doom.

Aristotle's *Poetics* is chiefly devoted to a discussion of tragedy, and it is obvious that among all the Athenian achievements in this genre the author gives his highest admiration to *Oedipus Rex.* One cannot resist the speculation that he held the play in especial regard because it so deeply challenges and so successfully baffles the rational intellect, of which he was the great exemplar, and that he loved this play because it proposed the existence of forces inscrutable to human reason. If his spirit was as large as his mind, he may well have found pleasure in contemplating an order that did not yield its secrets to the demands of rational intellect.

Oedipus at Colonus, the play that Sophocles wrote in the year of his death at the age of ninety, also speaks of an order that baffles reason. Oedipus is now very old; he has been wandering the earth, an outcast, attended only by his two daughters. Although he is feeble and foredone, his quickness to anger has not diminished, and now his rage is directed toward his two sons because they have permitted him to continue in the exile to which he had doomed himself. He is bitter at his fate and he insists on his blamelessness—he is not, it is plain, an endearing person. Yet word has gone out that the city will be blessed which gives this accursed outcast his last resting place and buries him with honor. And when death comes to him at Colonus, a suburb of Athens, it is not death as ordinary men know it, but apotheosis: by divine agency he is carried off from earth to live as a demigod. This end is not granted Oedipus in compensation for his suffering but in recognition of some power of his nature that approaches the divine. We are left to ponder how it is that this cursed man became a blessing and why this guilty man should have been so supremely rewarded.

The Tragedy of King Lear

WILLIAM SHAKESPEARE
1564-1616

O F THE supreme achievements of the creative mind with which *King Lear* is usually compared, it is perhaps the only one that seems to issue in hopelessness. Our conception of greatness in art inclines to set special store by the tragic vision, and our highest admiration most readily goes to those works that have some large element of darkness and dread. But when we bring to mind the masterpieces of art, and not only of literary art, with which *King Lear* is commonly ranked—the *Iliad, Oedipus Rex, The Divine Comedy*, Michelangelo's *Last Judgment*, Bach's *B-Minor Mass*, Beethoven's *Fifth Symphony*—we perceive that in all of them the dark elements are countered by strong affirmative emotions and attitudes. If in any of these works hope is not fully ascendant, it at least holds in balance the elements that might make for despair.

We do not necessarily feel this of *King Lear*. Here is a pre-eminently great work in which the positive expectations of life are considerably outweighed by the horrifying circumstances that are put before us. It is true that at the end of the play the evil-doers have been destroyed, the good are in control of the kingdom, and order and justice are soon to be restored. But the concluding scene speaks less of peace, let alone of hope, than of an ultimate weariness. Again and again in the course of the play the goodness and meaningfulness of life have been brought into question, and now, as life is about to resume its normal course, it can show little of the energy that might dispel the doubts that have been raised. In his last speech Kent refuses Albany's invitation to share the rule of the realm, giving as his reason that his death, which he desires, is near at hand. And Edgar's concluding words seem so charged with fatigue that they can scarcely get themselves uttered:

> The weight of this sad time we must obey;
> Speak what we feel, not what we ought to say.
> The oldest hath borne most; we that are young
> Shall never see so much, nor live so long.

No other of Shakespeare's tragedies ends on anything like the note of exhaustion sounded by these gray monosyllables. The closing speeches of *Hamlet, Macbeth,* and *Antony and Cleopatra* move to a music that summons the future into being.

Perhaps nothing can better suggest the uniquely despairing quality of *King Lear* than Keats's sonnet "On Sitting Down to Read *King Lear* Once Again." The young poet confronts with anxiety the experience he has freely chosen to undergo. He speaks of the play as "the fierce dispute / Between damnation and impassion'd clay." It is not a dispute from which he can stand apart, a passive listener; he must be involved in it, and with a painful intensity—he must, as he says, "burn through" it. This burning-through is not only painful but dangerous, and Keats is impelled to address a prayer to Shakespeare and the "clouds of Albion," asking their protection in the ordeal to which he is about to submit himself:

> Let me not wander in a barren dream,
> But when I am consumed in the fire,
> Give me new Phoenix wings to fly at my desire.

Keats's fear lest his experience leave him "barren" suggests how far *King Lear* may be from conforming to Aristotle's belief that tragedy fulfils a hygienic or therapeutic function. By inducing in the spectator emotions that are kept under strict control by its circumstantial or formal elements, a tragic play is said to bring about the discharge of such distress as habitually besets the mind and to establish an emotional equilibrium that sustains the vital energies. But Keats, from his previous readings of *King Lear,* anticipates that this particular tragedy may have exactly the opposite effect upon him.

His anxiety is not hard to understand; we share his apprehension of the destructive power the play might exert, for it seems to have the avowed intention of *assaulting* us. The storm in Act III, which is described as being more violent than any storm in memory, figures in the minds of many readers as the epitome or emblem of a play that batters and overwhelms us. One incident, the blinding of Gloucester, is so painful to read, let alone see on the stage, that doubts of its propriety as art have been expressed even by critics who are reluctant to admit that Shakespeare can ever be at fault. The murder of Cordelia in the face of our reasonable expectation that she will be rescued seems so gratuitous a blow to our hopes that the famous Shakespeare critic, A. C. Bradley, has actually defended, although not with entire seriousness, the eighteenth-century version of *King Lear* that revised the ending into a happy one.

One way in which the play manifests its intention of assault is by its refusal of artistic economy in favor of redundancy and excess. Thus, in representing filial disloyalty it is not content with the instance of Lear's two elder daughters but adds, what is no part of the traditional story upon which the play is based, Edmund's betrayal of Gloucester. One aged man wandering the world in misery is not enough: there must be two. As Lear's plight is paralleled by Gloucester's, so the overthrow of his mind is reiterated by the madness Edgar assumes, and this antiphony of significant irrationality is pointed up by the wild joking of the Fool. No play has ever had so many villains. Four of the leading characters, Edmund, Goneril, Regan, and Cornwall, are evil almost beyond belief, and they are appropriately served by the contemptible Oswald and the brutal captain who murders Cordelia. It has become almost a commonplace of critical analysis of *King Lear* to remark on its plethora of references to animals—133 references to 64 different animals—as if to press upon us a vision of humanity descending to brutishness.

The question of the governance of the world is often touched on in the play and always with the effect of reminding us either of its harshness or of its mysteriousness. The characters frequently appeal to or speak about "the gods," but from the things they say of them it is impossible to conclude what the divine disposition can be. Little ground is left for believing the gods beneficent. Gloucester calls them "ever-gentle" but in circumstances that lead us to take that epithet (and Gloucester's subsequent reference to "the bounty and the benison of Heaven") as ironical, the irony being intended not by Gloucester himself but by the play. Edgar says that the gods are "just," but the instance of the divine justice he cites, his father's having lost his sight in punishment for the "darkness" of the illicit sexual episode in which he begot Edmund, disgusts us with its agents and alienates us from the person who remarks it. The characterization of the gods that we are likely to remember best speaks of their affinity with the devils who are so often mentioned in the play:

> As flies to wanton boys, are we to the gods,
> They kill us for their sport.

"Nature" is frequently referred to in *King Lear* as a governing principle, but we can never be sure what "nature" means. It is invoked by Edmund as his "goddess," a deity who will provide the "law" that justifies his machinations. Lear calls it to witness the wrong that have been done him, but to no avail. If nature is sometimes portrayed as normative and beneficent, it is also shown to be indifferent or hostile. The assaulting storm, after all, is a phenomenon of nature. If nature may at one moment represent a principle of order, duty, and innocence, at another it is the principle of those animals, almost always regarded with aversion, which haunt the play.

That *King Lear* raises very dark thoughts indeed is denied by no one. The question debated by critics is whether the play in its whole and final effect is one of unrelieved pessimism or whether from the darkness some new light is born, possibly the brighter for the blackness from which it shines. One party to the debate takes its stand on the Aristotelian paradox of tragedy, that from dire events emerges some sensation of peace or reconciliation, some new readiness to accept life's pain, and not in passive acquiescence but in augmented strength of soul, and even with something like hope. To which the opposing party rejoins that, whatever tragedy is supposed to do and whatever in general it may do, this particular tragedy does not conform to type.

In the end the party of hope is forced to rely upon specious reasoning. It argues that the experience of Lear and Gloucester comprises not only their terrible sufferings but also the spiritual changes they undergo as a result of their agony. These changes are said to amount to regeneration—at the end of the play Lear and Gloucester are better men than they were at the beginning, they have been redeemed through suffering. A universal order that permits this redemption to take place is to be regarded as hopeful, as making no occasion for pessimism. In his introduction to *King Lear* in the Cambridge *New Shakespeare,* G. I. Duthie formulates the position thus: "The gods are merciful. If, after all their agony, Lear and Gloucester died uneducated, unregenerate, then we should indeed have to speak of pessimism. But both, as they die, are wise and redeemed. 'Nothing is here for tears'—unless we weep for the means that conduces to the end, for the dreadful cost of the salutary outcome. We must do so; and the conclusion of the play has indeed a sober colouring. Yet the unassailable fact remains that the gods, in benignity, permit Lear and Gloucester to die in a state of spiritual health. Their sufferings are redemptive. There is no ultimate ground for pessimism here."

One must wonder what special meaning this writer assigns to "merciful" and what sort of "benignity" it is that "permits" the two old men to die in the state of "spiritual health" they have so grimly won. In the *Book of Job* one of Job's friends advances the idea that suffering, because it can serve to discipline and enlighten man's spirit, is to be understood as an instance of God's benevolence; but

Job will have none of this facile defence of the divine order, and the Voice that speaks out of the whirlwind, God's own voice, says that Job is right to reject his friend's view as a mere rationalization. Some three thousand years later Mr. Duthie proposes the same view. It is perhaps possible to find comfort in the idea that the world is a school in which the soul is "educated" or a sanitorium in which it may regain "spiritual health"; yet we must inevitably remark that the authorities who govern these two institutions charge quite exorbitant fees for their redemptive services. Mr. Duthie himself speaks of the "dreadful cost of the salutary outcome" over which we might understandably shed tears. A cost dreadful indeed: so very dreadful that tears scarcely seem adequate to it, rather some awful cry, such as Lear's "Howl, howl, howl." Or, if tears at all, then those that Lear wept on his "wheel of fire," that "do scald like molten lead."*

As against arguments of the kind that Mr. Duthie advances, the opposite position accords more closely with our usual human experience of the play. The formulation which in our time has commanded most attention is that the Polish critic Jan Kott in his influential book, *Shakespeare Our Contemporary*. Professor Kott says that *King Lear* has never been dealt with in a direct and unembarrassed way, that "the cruelty of Shakespeare's world" has never been fully confronted. He finds the clue to this failure in the lack of appreciation of the mode of the *grotesque* which is salient in the play. The mode of the grotesque, he says, is crueller than the tragic mode, and the critics have ignored the extent of its presence in *King Lear,* occupied as they have been with finding justification for their belief

---

* It is oddly tactless of Mr. Duthie to quote the famous "Nothing is here for tears" from Milton's *Samson Agonistes*. The line refers to Samson's death. Samson has died in a moment of triumph, performing an act that serves his God and his people. Having sinned against the divine gift of his superhuman strength, he had been betrayed by his Philistine wife, who cut off his long hair, in which lay his power, and delivered him to his Philistine enemies. After a period of humiliation, suffering, and repentance as a slave of the Philistines, Samson finds his strength returning as his hair grows again. On a religious festival of his heathen masters, he brings down the roof of the temple in which the Philistine nobility is gathered, knowing that he too must perish. He dies not only as a man redeemed but as a victorious hero, the savior of his people. It is indeed true that nothing is *here* for tears, but how different is his situation from that of King Lear!

that the play makes the traditional "affirmation" of tragedy, such justification as may be found in the idea that "suffering ennobled Lear and restored his tragic greatness." And he undertakes to demonstrate the affinity of *King Lear* with the so-called theatre of the absurd, that strong and often impressive tendency of contemporary drama to represent, by the grotesque or by "black" comedy, the metaphysical pointlessness of human life.

Professor Kott does not do justice to the awareness of the pessimistic force of *King Lear* that has in fact prevailed; as for the element of the grotesque in the play, its importance was demonstrated in elaborate detail in a well-known essay by G. Wilson Knight as long ago as 1930.* Yet perhaps no critic has been so uncompromising as Professor Kott in insisting on the pessimism of *King Lear*. Indeed, pessimism scarcely describes what he tell us Shakespeare is propounding, which is nothing less than nihilism, the view that there is no meaning to be discovered in the universe, and, in consequence, but little in human existence.

Professor Kott reminds us that the basic assumption of traditional tragedy was that the universe, or, as he calls it, the absolute, was informed by a transcendent reason variously thought of as the gods, or God, or Nature, or History understood as a process. Because this transcendent reason was inscrutable, never available to human understanding, man was likely to be out of step with it and, in consequence, all too susceptible to defeat and suffering. But the downfall of the tragic hero was the means by which tragedy affirmed the existence of a transcendent reason. Such affirmation is no longer possible—in our time the assumption that a transcendent reason exists has lost virtually all its old force. Reason may be thought of as an attribute of man but not as an attribute of the universe; and man's suffering, which once could be supposed to have meaning because of its relation to the universal reason, can now be thought only grotesque. "In the world of the grotesque," Professor Kott says, "downfall cannot be justified by, or blamed on, the absolute. The absolute is not endowed with any ultimate reasons; it is stronger, and that is

* *"King Lear* and the Comedy of the Grotesque," in *The Wheel of Fire*.

all. The absolute is absurd." It is in the light of this modern conception of absurdity that *King Lear* must be understood—only thus, Professor Kott says, can we comprehend the full extent of the cruelty of its world, a cruelty that it is not possible to explain because it is wholly without meaning.

There can be no doubt that *King Lear* gives us ground for thinking the universe absurd. Again and again it proposes the idea of some ineluctable contradiction between the universe and man. Man's existence proceeds in circumstances so painful that we may well think of them as arranged by a hostile power which is the more terrible because no purpose can be ascribed to its enmity nor any order discerned in its behavior. Against this irrational animus there is no defence—all that men can do is endure. And the despair that King Lear embodies is concentrated in the line in which Edgar says what it is that they must endure, their "going hence, even as their coming hither"—it is surely a despairing imagination that proposes the bitterness of dying in terms of the bitterness of being born. The phrase that follows, "Ripeness is all," does not qualify the sentiment, for "ripeness" here does not mean richness or fulness of life but readiness for death, the only escape from absurdity.

But the incompatibility between rational man and an absurd universe is only one of the two explanations of human suffering suggested in *King Lear*. The other holds man himself accountable for his pain, either through his self-deception or through the cruelty of other members of the race. The play makes no hard and fast distinction between the two explanations. Nevertheless we can scarcely doubt that it requires us to see that the immediate cause of any man's suffering is his fellow man: the cruel will of nonhuman powers is put into execution by evil men. The intensity of the suffering is such and the bitterness over man's destiny of suffering is such that they can find adequate expression only by crying out to heaven. But at the quiet heart of the whirling speculations about the universe or the absolute there lies the idea of human justice and human mercy. When it is said that Lear is "regenerated" and "redeemed," the change that is being remarked upon in the aged king is his new consciousness of man's inhumanity to man, of the general failure of justice: his mind becomes obsessed with justice, he is filled with disgust at those human traits that stand in the way of its being done—greed, lust, pride, and the hypocrisy that masks them. And with the new consciousness of justice goes a new sense of the need for *caritas,* which is not "charity" in our usual modern sense, but "caring," the solicitude of loving-kindness:

> Poor naked wretches, wheresoe'er you are,
> That bide the pelting of this pitiless storm,
> How shall your houseless heads and unfed sides,
> Your loop'd and window'd raggedness, defend you
> From seasons such as these? O, I have ta'en
> Too little care of this! Take physic, pomp;
> Expose thyself to feel what wretches feel,
> That thou mayst shake the superflux to them,
> And show the heavens more just.

Although Lear does touch upon the cruelty of the universe, this is far less the object of his new consciousness than the failure of man's governance of himself, his falling short of what is required of him in doing justice and in loving mercy.

If we speak of a "failure" and a "falling short," we suggest not merely a thing to be desired, but also a standard or norm. I have said that we never know just how to understand the word "nature" as it is used in *King Lear.* But we cannot fail to recognize that among its several meanings is that of a normative principle. And one element of the human norm it implies, one term of the definition of man, is a certain degree of moral virtue, or at least the propensity for conduct which, if it departs from virtue, does not do so beyond a certain point. The play offers abundant evidence that human beings are capable of going well beyond that point. Yet the supposition that man's nature is to be defined in moral terms is not thereby denied.

Our commitment to the idea of the normative virtue of man is apparent in our language, as in our use of the word "humanity" to mean kindness or at least compunction in dealing with other members of the race, or with animals. Burns's famous lines, "Man's inhumanity to man / Makes countless thousands mourn," which everyone understands, would be nonsense were we not to take normative virtue for granted, for what could it possibly mean to speak of human beings acting in an inhuman fashion unless the *idea* of being human implied a degree of goodness, whatever the *actuality* of being human may mean? Bradley has remarked on the frequency with which the idea of monstrosity appears in *King Lear;* the play, he says, is replete with "beings, actions, states of mind, which appear not only abnormal but absolutely contrary to nature." In the degree to which people are good, they are felt to be natural, Kent and Cordelia being obvious cases in point: we are aware of their naturalness as a positive quality of their being, expressing itself in their manner and mode of speech. But Goneril and Regan are said by Lear to be "unnatural hags." Cornwall's blinding of Gloucester is an unnatural act, and an especially moving moment of the play represents the natural response to the monstrosity of this deed: one of Cornwall's servants cannot endure it and, knowing that he risks his life, draws his sword to prevent it. To Shakespeare's contemporary audience, this action must have been even more momentous that it is to us, for to the Elizabethans the idea of a servant confronting his master with a show of force would have been shocking, even unnatural. The Elizabethan judgment is underscored by Cornwall's crying out amazed, "My villain!" (using the word in its old sense of farm servant), and by Regan's exclamation, "A peasant stand up thus!" To the feudal lord and lady it was as much a shattering of the natural order for their servant to defy them as Lear felt it to be when his daughters rejected him. Shakespeare quite shared the opinion of his time; he believed that the deference given to superiors was in the order of nature. But in this instance his sympathy is given to the peasant who flares into hopeless rebellion at the hideous deed, who, though he break the "natural" bonds of society, does so because he recognizes a claim yet *more* natural, that of his humanity, of justice and mercy.

An awareness of the Elizabethan feeling about the naturalness of the social order will lead us to a more accurate judgment of the act out of which all the horrors and misfortunes arose, Lear's division of his kingdom. To this no Elizabethan, and surely not Shakespeare himself, would have responded with indifference. Again and again in his plays, Shakespeare speaks in praise of unity, of the organic interrelation of the parts of a polity. To divide a kingdom, to treat a realm as if it were not a living organism, was worse than imprudent, it was unnatural. It may have been unavoidable in view of Lear's failing strength and the lack of a male heir, but still it went against nature; its consequences could only be bad.

In short, *King Lear* raises moral, social, and even political considerations that mark out an area in which human life is not wholly determined by nonhuman forces, in which the absurdity of the universe is not wholly decisive. Although this area is not coextensive with man's existence, it is of very large extent. One hesitates to speak of it as an area of freedom, if only because any one individual is so little likely to be free within it. Yet it is the precinct in which mankind as a whole, with due regard to the well-being of its individual members, has the possibility of freedom. To be aware of this possibility will scarcely dispel all the dark thoughts that the play induces. But it does qualify the view that human suffering is to be referred only to an absurd dispensation.

Some large part of the human condition is, however, imposed upon man and makes a fate that is as grotesque as it is inescapable. Lear must grow old, his powers of body and mind must wane and fail. Nothing can save him from this destined end. Yet this in itself is not the root of his suffering as the play represents it. What maddens the old man is the loss of what might sustain him in his decline, the honor and dignity he had assumed to be his inalienable right. To grow old is a hard destiny. But to grow old in honor and dignity is not unendurable, while to grow old shorn of respect is a nightmare, the very essence of the grotesque. Respect is sometimes regarded as a sort of social fiction because it is expressed through signs and outward forms, such as the manner and tone in which the respected person is addressed, or the appurtenances of life that are bestowed upon him. Lear himself defines the symbolic nature of respect in his great reply to Regan's statement that he has no "need" of his train of knights:

> O, reason not the need! Our basest beggars
> Are in the poorest thing superfluous.
> Allow not nature more than nature needs,
> Man's life is cheap as beast's. Thou art a lady;
> If only to go warm were gorgeous,
> Why, nature needs not what thou gorgeous wear'st,
> Which scarcely keeps thee warm.

He says in effect that man creates his own needs—and that these are even more imperative than those of biology. The meanings and "values" that social man invents for himself are presented as of transcendent importance not only in this speech of Lear's but throughout the play, most notably in all that Kent and Cordelia say to the old man and all they do for him, in the one short time when they have him in their loving charge, to assure him that he has been restored to his kingliness and to the respect that befits it.

Of all that is implied by the play's intense awareness of that area of life in which human conceptions and conduct are prepotent, Professor Kott takes no account in his effort to demonstrate the nihilism of *King Lear*. "The theme of *King Lear*," he says, "is the decay and fall of the world." And so in part it is, but in part only—the full theme of *King Lear* is the decay and fall of the world as a consequence of a decay and fall of the human soul. It is indeed true that the vitality of the meanings and values created by man depends to some extent on a belief in a transcendent reason, and that to doubt the existence of such reason puts all in doubt. This would seem to be the animating idea of the theatre of the absurd in which Professor Kott finds such strong affinities with *King Lear*. But the dramatist of the theatre of the absurd takes for granted a metaphysical negation which has the effect of destroying the old human meanings and of making human life grotesque, whereas such a causal sequence was not conceived by Shakespeare. He took for granted a rational and moralized universe but proposed the idea that this universal order might be reduced to chaos by human evil.

Speaking in praise of *King Lear,* the English novelist Iris Murdoch said, "Only the very greatest art invigorates without consoling. . . ." That *King Lear* does not console is plain enough. If we ask how, in the face of its dire report of life, this play can be said to invigorate, the answer is that it does us the honor of supposing that we will make every possible effort of mind to withstand the force of its despair and to understand the complexity of what it tells us about the nature of human existence: it draws us into more activity than we had thought ourselves capable of.

The Wild Duck

HENRIK IBSEN
1828–1906

IN T. S. Eliot's *Murder in the Cathedral,* the Archbishop Becket
utters a sentence which has become famous—"Human kind,"
he says, "cannot bear very much reality."* The sad dictum may
serve to summarize the purport of *The Wild Duck.* And the play
goes on to suggest that it is wicked for one person to seek to impose
upon another a greater amount of reality than can comfortably be
borne. That this should be the "message" of a play by Henrik Ibsen
came as a great surprise—indeed, a shock—when *The Wild Duck*
was first presented in 1884.

And even now it is likely to startle any reader or playgoer
acquainted with the author's characteristic early work. For Ibsen
was an outstanding figure in the movement of modern art and
intellect that subjected all existing institutions, and the conventions
of thought and feeling, to relentless scrutiny in the interests of
truth; it was the stern judgment of this movement that society is a
contrivance to mask or evade or distort reality. The effort to dis-
criminate between what is real and what is illusory is of course not
a new endeavor for literature. But in the modern epoch it has been
undertaken with a new particularity and aggressiveness, and by
none more than by Ibsen. He had made his reputation with four
plays—*Pillars of Society, A Doll's House, Ghosts,* and *An Enemy*

---

* The sentence also appears in the first section of Eliot's "Burnt Norton."

of the People—and in each of them he had pressed home the view that falsehood, whether in the form of social lies and hypocrisy or of self-deception, weakens the fabric of life and deprives human kind of its dignity. Expectably enough, his work had met with resistance by the larger part of his audience, that is to say, the more conventional part. But by the same token, the "advanced" minority, a growing force in European culture, received him as a master of truth. In his lifetime and for many years after his death, people spoke of "Ibsenism," by which they meant the radical questioning of all established and respectable modes of life and the unyielding opposition to sham and pretense. It can therefore be imagined with what bewilderment and dismay the Ibsenites received a play which said that truth may be dangerous to life, that not every man is worthy to tell it or receive it, and that the avoidance and concealment of the truth, or even a lie, may have a vital beneficence.

In speaking of the fate of Oedipus, I remarked that although we feel apprehension as Oedipus approaches closer and closer to the knowledge that will destroy him, and although we may wish to warn him against continuing his investigation, we do not really want the dreadful truth to stay hidden from him. As I put it, "we do not want Oedipus to remain oblivious of the truth about himself. An Oedipus who prudently gave up his search would be an object of condescension, even of contempt. . . ." This is of course pretty much the feeling on which Gregers Werle proceeds when he resolves to bestow on Hjalmar Ekdal the terrible gift of reality. Hjalmar does not know that his wife had once been secretly the mistress of the elder Werle and that he is not in point of biological fact the father of his daughter. Gregers discloses the true state of affairs because he wants Hjalmar to "face reality" in order to gain the dignity which is presumed to follow upon that disagreeable confrontation. Why, then, do we blame Gregers for making the revelation?

The answer is that Hjalmar is not Oedipus, as poor Hjalmar himself well knows until he is tempted to believe otherwise. Perhaps no moment in the play is more bitterly affecting than that in which, after the disclosure has been made, Hjalmar says, "Do you think a

man can recover so easily from the bitter cup I've just emptied?"
Gregers replies, "Not an ordinary man, no. But a man like you—!"
And Hjalmar desperately and feebly tries to accept the moral heroism
that has been ruthlessly thrust upon him: "Good Lord, yes, I know
that. But you mustn't be driving me, Gregers. You see, these things
take time."

It may indeed be true that people cannot bear very much reality,
but some can bear even less than others. Hjalmar is one of those who
can bear scarcely any at all. Yet it might be said that in his weakness there is a kind of strength. Whatever his announced claims for
himself may be, in his heart of hearts he estimates himself fairly accurately. Until Gregers comes into his life with high talk of what the
"summons to the ideal" ought to mean to "a man like you," Hjalmar
knows that in order to get through life he needs all the help that
illusion can give him, and he takes all the help he can get. It is
plain enough that Hjalmar does not really believe he will vindicate
the family honor and rehabilitate his old father by making a fortune
as an inventor, but the double pose of righter of wrongs and of
lonely man of genius sustains and comforts him. We can scarcely
suppose that the truth about his wife and daughter had all these
years lain very far from his consciousness; if he had wanted to grasp
it, he could have reached out for it long ago. He had no such desire,
and in consequence he is established in a small but cozy way of life,
provided with an affectionate wife who cheerfully performs not only
her own tasks but his, and an adoring daughter; he lives in such
self-esteem as may arise for the uncontradicted assertion of his natural superiority. In the light of his wife's goodness of heart, it is not
of the least importance that this simple woman was once another
man's mistress; in the light of his daughter's boundless affection and
trust, it is of no consequence that he had not actually engendered
her; and Hjalmar had seen to it that what did not matter was never
allowed to come into his consciousness. But once the explicit truth is
forced upon him, it does its destructive work. We may feel that it
should not have had the effect upon the poor man that it does have;
we comment on the pettiness of his pride, on how accomplished he

is in nursing his grievance. Yet if we consider the sexual ethos of his time, we recognize that only a saint or a philosopher could have received the revelation with magnanimous good sense. The fact that Hjalmar is neither saint nor philosopher does not decisively distinguish him from most men.

The device by which Ibsen suggests the possible beneficence of illusion is a charming one, and also deeply moving, even more in actual presentation on the stage than on the printed page—it is always an electrifying moment for the audience when the forest in the garret is first revealed to view. There is something strangely affecting in a fiction, a mere fancy, that stands before us as a palpable actuality, to be seen and entered into; and the actuality of the forest is made more than palpable by its being inhabited by the beautiful and tragic wild duck. When first the sliding door is pushed back to reveal the moonlit scene, we have the sense that we have been permitted to look out through Keats's "magic casements, opening on the foam / Of perilous seas, in faery lands forlorn."

For the Ekdals, this fictive forest is a source not only of pleasure but of life itself. It calls forth their best emotions. Toward it, especially toward its most notable denizen, the wounded wild duck, Hedvig directs the natural grace of her spirit, and it is the means by which old Lieutenant Ekdal reconciles himself to his ruined old age. Even Hjalmar rises above his uneasy self-regard and surrenders to a childlike innocence when he comes under the spell of this avowed illusion, which so touchingly binds the family together. The little wilderness is a mere game which the Ekdals play, but into all the activities of human kind, even the most serious and practical, some element of the game is introduced; "make believe" and "as if" do not come to an end with childhood. And the "let's pretend" of play is the very essence of one of man's most characteristic and important activities, that of art.

Hjalmar's father, Lieutenant Ekdal, the simple-minded old hunter, who in his best days had been the mighty killer of actual bears, plays the forest game with the perfectly clear consciousness that it is a game, even though it is also, for him, life itself; and Hedvig plays it as a child, with an absolute commitment to it but with no real confusion of the fancy with reality. And when Hjalmar plays it, he too knows it for what it is. But there are illusions from which some people in *The Wild Duck* cannot detach themselves. Hjalmar must have some rôle which will conceal from his own perception and that of the world the fact that he is a man of no talent or distinction. In school he had been known as a great declaimer of poetry and therefore as a person of notable sensibility and high ideals, and it is partly the illusioned memory of Hjalmar as he was in the past that leads Gregers to intervene on behalf of his friend's moral dignity; Gregers accepts without question Hjalmar's claim to being a wronged man and an unfulfilled genius. Molvik, the former theological student, is a feckless drunkard but he takes heart from the rôle that Dr. Relling invents for him, that of a "demonic" character, a personality which manifests its power in the "wildness" of a supernal intoxication. As for Gregers himself, we can scarcely fail to see that his behavior as the uncompromising idealist is dictated not only by his grievance against his robust father but also by his desire to acquire a moral status that will mask the emptiness of his unloving heart.

People like these, living by illusions of personal distinction, did not always exist. Like the bereaved doctor of Chekhov's "Enemies" and Gabriel Conroy of Joyce's "The Dead," they are the creatures of modernity, especially of that aspect of modernity which Hegel, in his *Philosophy of History,* called the "secularization of spirituality." What Hegel meant by that phrase is suggested by the authority that Ibsen himself achieved and the means by which he achieved it. Where once the moral life of human kind had been chiefly in the keeping of the Church, it was now, by Ibsen's time, increasingly in the charge of playwrights, novelists, poets, and philosophers. Where once life had been relatively simple under the Church's guidance or direction, it was now complex in response to the questioning of writers. Where once it had been concerned with the fulfilment of the duties that were appropriate to one's station in life, it was now concerned with the fulness of a person's life as an individual, with its integrity and dignity, with the proud, vexed commitment to the ideal, that new moral and spiritual sanction which would have been quite incomprehensible a century or two earlier. Ibsen had done much to forward the "secularization of spirituality" and to advance the new self-consciousness, demanding that people be heroes of the spirit. *The Wild Duck* was written in a moment of brilliant self-doubt. This was perhaps induced by the disaffection from his disciples that any master may feel when he perceives how his own hard-won ideas are distorted by those who make easy use of them. But this turning of Ibsen upon himself cannot be attributed merely to his desire to discomfit his Ibsenite followers and to detach himself from the doctrinaire conception of what he had done. It came also, we feel sure, from a magnanimous mind's awareness of the difficulty of life and the impossibility of forcing upon it any single rule, even that of reality.

The Three Sisters

ANTON CHEKHOV
1860–1904

THREE SISTERS is surely one of the saddest works in all literature. It is also one of the most saddening. As it draws to a close, and for some time after Olga has uttered her hopeless desire to know whether life and its suffering have any meaning, we must make a conscious effort if we are not to be overcome by the depression that threatens our spirits. The frustration and hopelessness to which the persons of the drama fall prey seems to be not only their doom but ours as well. For between ourselves and those persons in *Three Sisters* with whom we sympathize there is remarkably little distance, certainly as compared, say, with the distance that separates us from Lear. Apart from the difference in nationality, nothing stands in the way of our saying that they are much like ourselves and our friends. They are decent, well-intentioned people, not extraordinary in their gifts but above the general run of mankind in intelligence and sensitivity, well enough educated to take pleasure in the arts and to aspire to freedom, the enjoyment of beauty, and the natural development of their personalities, all the benefits to which we give the name of "the good life."

And in fact, apart from their recognizability, these people are made especially easy for us to come close to because Chekhov, in representing them, takes full account of an element of human life that the tragic dramatists were not concerned with. Sophocles and

Shakespeare represented life in terms of character and fate. Chekhov proposes the part that is played in our existence by environment. There is nothing that more readily fosters our intimacy with other people than an awareness of the actual and particular conditions in which they live their lives from day to day.

Character, in the sense in which we use it of the creations of the great tragic dramatists, means the way in which a person confronts the things that happen to him, a number of which may come about as a consequence of his characteristic behavior. Fate is the sum of the decisive things that happen to a person, whether as the result of his characteristic behavior, or fortuitously, or at the behest of some transcendent power. Environment signifies those material and social circumstances in which an individual leads his existence, in particular those that make for his well-being or lack of it and that seem to condition his character and fate.

Since all events take place under nameable conditions, environment is an integral element of all dramatic genres, including tragedy. In the story of Oedipus, for example, it is clearly of consequence that Oedipus is king of Thebes, not of Athens, and that he lives as befits a king and not, say, a merchant. But we are not asked to be aware of these circumstances except in a general way. Our imagination of Oedipus in his regal life does not include particularities such as the boring ceremonial a king must endure, the strain of being always in the public eye, his exasperated sense of the frivolity of the innumerable palace servants, whose gossip and petty intrigue are a perpetual nuisance . . . and so on.

The modern literary imagination almost always conceives environment as adverse, as comprising those material and social conditions of life which constrain and hamper the protagonist and thwart his ideal development and which, more than anything that might happen to him in a sudden dramatic way, make his destiny. The habit of thinking about a human life in relation to its environment is of relatively recent growth. It began, roughly speaking, in the eighteenth century. Since then it has achieved an importance that can scarcely be overestimated.

This sense of the influence of environment on character and fate has deeply changed the traditional way of thinking about morality and politics. It enables us to believe in an essential quality of humanity, about which predications can be made, usually to the effect that it is by nature good, and then to go on to judge whether a particular circumstance in which an individual is placed is appropriate or inappropriate to his essential humanity. It thus serves as a principle of explanation in the personal life, and as a ground of social action. Few people can hear the contemporary phrase "juvenile delinquent" without immediately thinking of the family and neighborhood circumstances—the environment—that fostered the undesirable behavior of the young person. And in our view of ourselves we have learned to give great significance to the conditions of our lives, those that made us what we are and those that keep us from being what we might wish to be.

The awareness of environment is, as I have said, salient in our response to *Three Sisters*. We are never permitted to forget that the people in Chekhov's play are required to live in a certain way—far from the metropolis, Moscow, in a dreary provincial city; possessing the tastes and desires of a certain social class yet lacking the money to fulfil their expectations of life; bored by and disaffected from their professions. Their desperate unhappiness is not the result of an event, of some catastrophic shock, but, rather, a condition of life itself, the slow relentless withdrawal of all that had once been promised of delight and satisfaction. To catastrophe we can sometimes respond by mustering up our energies of resistance or fortitude, but the unhappiness that Chekhov represents is that of people who, as the environment takes its toll of them, have fewer and fewer energies of resistance or endurance, let alone renovation. It is a state that few of us can fail in at least some degree to know from experience, and our knowledge of it makes us peculiarly responsive to the pathos of *Three Sisters*. We are not surprised to hear that when the manuscript of the play was read to the members of the Moscow Art Theatre who were to perform it, the company was so deeply moved that many wept as they listened.

Chekhov did not take their tears as a tribute. He told them that they had quite misconceived the nature of *Three Sisters,* which was, he said, a "gay comedy, almost a farce." This may well be the strangest comment on his own work that a writer ever made. And Chekhov did not make it casually or playfully, as a provocative paradox. He insisted on it. The famous head of the Moscow Theatre, Constantin Stanislavsky, who directed and championed Chekhov's plays, says in his memoirs that he can remember no opinion ever expressed by Chekhov that the author defended so passionately; he held it, Stanislavsky says, "until his dying day" and believed that his play had failed if it was understood otherwise. Yet he was never able to make clear what he meant by this strange idea. Another theatrical colleague, Vladimir Nemirovich Danchenko, who was even closer to Chekhov than Stanislavsky was, tells us that when the actors asked him for an explanation of such a view, he never could advance reasons to substantiate it.* To his friends in the theatre it was plain that Chekhov was not being perverse, that he truly believed that this saddest of plays was a comedy. But why he believed this they did not know.

And perhaps we cannot know. At the end of Plato's *Symposium,* when all the other guests at the great party have fallen asleep, Socrates sits drinking with the comic poet Aristophanes and the tragic poet Agathon, compelling them "to acknowledge that the genius of comedy was the same with that of tragedy, and that the true artist in tragedy was an artist in comedy also. To this they were constrained to assent, being drowsy and not quite following the argument."† How the argument ran was not reported and will never be known. And it may well be that Chekhov's reason for calling *Three Sisters* a comedy despite all its sadness will also never be known, even by inference.

But perhaps we today are in a better position to speculate about it than were the members of the Moscow Art Theatre. To the people

---

* I have derived this account of Chekhov's view of the play from *The Oxford Chekhov,* translated and edited by Ronald Hingley, Volume III, pp. 314–316.

† Jowett's translation.

of his own time, the new and striking thing about the plays of Chekhov was that they expressed so fully the pathos of personal aspiration frustrated by social and cultural circumstances. The latter part of the nineteenth century in Russia saw the rapid development of the class of intelligentsia, as it was called, people of sensibility and education, readily accessible to the influence of ideas and ideals, who could imagine and desire more in the way of fulness of life than they would ever achieve.* This discrepancy is common to similar groups in all nations, but what made it especially marked in Russia was the repressiveness of the Czarist government and the backwardness of the economy. A young Russian who undertook to live the life of intellect and art, or simply the good life in which intellect and art have their place, had fewer opportunities to do so than a young person elsewhere in Europe. His will, checked and baffled, lost its impetus and turned back upon itself in bitterness and self-recrimination. All Chekhov's plays are concerned with the defeat of delicate and generous minds, and the warmth of feeling that the Russian intelligentsia directed to Chekhov in his lifetime was in gratitude for his having made its plight so fully explicit and for having treated its pathos with so affectionate a tenderness. It is not too much to say that the intelligentsia of Chekhov's time received the pathos of his plays as a precious gift and cherished it dearly.

But what was new at the turn of the century is now fairly old. Although the theme of the adverse social or cultural environment is still central to our thought, by the same token it is pretty much taken for granted. The personal frustration that Chekhov's characters suffered is now no longer assumed to be the inevitable fate of

* "Intelligentsia" is the form in which the Russian word *intelligentsiya* came into English (about 1914). Although it is now an accredited English word, it is used rather less frequently than it formerly was, having been somewhat displaced by "intellectuals." But "intelligentsia" has a special usefulness because it implies not so much the actual use of the intellect as the prestige of living by ideas and ideals and in relation to the arts. There is thus an overtone of irony in the use of the word which is perhaps intended to appear in the definition given by the *Oxford English Dictionary:* "The class of society to which culture, superior intelligence, and advanced political views are attributed."

The Russian intelligentsia was recruited from several social classes, but most of the characters of Chekhov's plays derive from the minor aristocracy or gentry, usually more or less impoverished.

the members of the intelligentsia; today, at least in some countries, they can look forward to lives of considerable freedom and activity, even affluence and power. As a consequence, while we respond, and even deeply, to the pathos of Chekhov's plays, we are not likely to value it in the same degree that it was valued by the members of the Moscow Art Theatre.

This being so, it is easier for us than it was for his colleagues in the theatre to suppose that Chekhov himself did not want his audiences to feel only the sadness of *Three Sisters,* although it had of course been his purpose to evoke it and make it poignant and salient. He also had another and what might seem a contradictory intention: to lead his audience *away* from those very emotions in the play which they most cherished. When Chekhov said that *Three Sisters* was a comedy, even a farce, he was not talking to critics or theorists of literature but to actors, and he was trying to suggest what should be brought to the text by those who put it on the stage, a complexity of meaning which the text might not at first reveal. The meaning of a highly developed work of literature cannot ever be given in a formula, and Chekhov's plays resist formulation rather more than most. Chekhov did not undertake to solve life; he was averse to the propagation of ideas; his sole purpose, he said, was to represent life as it really is. But life cannot be seen without judgment of some kind, and throughout *Three Sisters,* as throughout his other great plays, Chekhov undertakes to influence our judgment in many ways, giving us ground for sympathy with one character, of antipathy to another, of contempt for yet another, of distaste for this or that circumstance of existence, controlling not only the direction of our feelings but their duration and intensity as well, so that contempt begins to give way suddenly to understanding, or admiration to irony. Much, then, of our sense of the meaning of *Three Sisters* when we see it performed depends upon the style of the performance—upon, that is, the ability of the actors to complicate its emotional communication.

Stanislavsky, we are told, had a tendency to produce all Chekhov's plays in a deliberate and dramatic style, which emphasized the moments of painful feeling and made the plays into what were called "heavy dramas." This method, which in effect invited the audience to self-pity before the hopelessness of life, was no doubt the loyal Stanislavsky's way of expressing his sense of Chekhov's seriousness and importance. But if *Three Sisters* is acted with the lightness and the rapid tempo of the comic style, or with some of the briskness of farce, the response of the audience is bound to be different. The play will not then offer an exactly cheerful view of things; it will still be saying that life is, in all conscience, hard and bitterly disappointing. But this will not be its sole judgment. The seeming contradiction between the sadness of the text and the vivacity of the style will suggest an inconclusiveness of judgment, inviting the audience not to the indulgence of self-pity but to a thoughtful, perhaps even an ironic detachment.

Whether or not we accept the play as a comedy, we cannot fail to see that there is comedy in it, and a performance in the comic style will give full recognition to its abundant humor of character. All the male characters, in one degree or another, provoke our laughter or at least our smiles—Vershinin by his compulsion to make visionary speeches about mankind's future happiness, Andrey by his fatness, Chebutykin by his avowed total ignorance of medicine, Solyony by his absurd social behavior, especially his belief that he resembles the great romantic poet Lermontov, Kulygin by his pedantry and silliness, even poor good Tusenbach by his confidence that he can solve the problems of existence by going to work for a brick company. It is an aspect of his gift that Chekhov is able to make us laugh at these people without allowing us to despise them. Our laughter is a skeptical comment on the facile belief that nothing but the circumstances of environment accounts for people's destinies, for what we laugh at is the self-deception, or the pretension, or the infirmity of purpose that in some large part explains their pain and defeat—and our own.

The three sisters themselves, however, appear in a light very different from that in which the male characters are placed. We cannot say of them, as we do of the men, that they have helped contrive their defeat; the situation of women being what it was when Chekhov was writing, there was virtually no way by which they might have triumphed over circumstances to avoid the waste of their lives. Each of the three girls had, to be sure, overestimated the chances of happiness, but what they had imagined and desired was not beyond reason. Such deceptions as they practice on themselves do not warp their personalities into comic eccentricity, as happens with all the men. In the sisters, we feel, life appears in its normality, rather beautiful: they are finely developed human beings of delicate and generous mind. And the end of the play finds each of them doomed to unfulfilment, bitterly grieving over her fate, despite the resolution to live out her life in courageous affirmation. That this final scene is intensely sad goes without saying. But it is an open question for the reader or the stage director whether the exaltation of fortitude and faith that the sisters muster up in the face of defeat is to be taken ironically, as a delusion which makes the sadness yet more intense, or whether it is to be understood as sounding a true note of affirmation. The answer to the question should perhaps be conditioned by the knowledge that the scene was written by a dying man.

Chekhov suffered from tuberculosis, at that time a disease not easily cured. A physician of considerable skill, although he had given up the practice of medicine, he was not likely to be under any illusion about his chances of recovery; he died four years after the production of *Three Sisters,* at the age of forty-five. His illness did not deprive him of all gratification. He worked, although against odds. His work was honored, and he was much loved. But he had to live in exile from Moscow, even from Russia; he was often in pain, physical activity became ever less possible; he was often separated from his young wife for long periods. It could not have been without thought of himself that he wrote such despairing speeches as the one in which Irina says, "Where has it all gone? Where is it? . . . life's slipping by, and it will never, never return. . . ."

Yet as we read Chekhov's letters of the last years of his illness, we find no despair in them, no bitterness, not even the sorrow we might expect to find. They are full of the often trivial details of travel, business, and work, of expressions of concern and affection for others, they address themselves to ordinary, unexceptional life, without tragic reverberations, even without drama. Perhaps an unwillingness to burden others with his darker thoughts in some part explains why Chekhov wrote as he did, but as one reads the letters alongside the plays, one feels that Chekhov was living life as the speeches at the end of *Three Sisters* suggest it must be lived: without the expectation of joy, yet in full attachment, and cherishing what may be cherished, even if that is nothing more than the idea of life itself. A man of affectionate disposition upon whom death had laid its hand would probably not be concerned with making a rational or prudential judgment upon life: more likely he would be moved to wonder if a transcendent judgment might not be made. And when Chekhov wrote that "it will be winter soon, and everything will be covered with snow," he may well have wished to suggest that in the cycle of seasons the spring will follow and that, sad as we may be over what befalls ourselves and others, life itself is to be celebrated. Over the centuries the attributes and intentions of comedy have been numerous and various. But one of the oldest of them has been to say that, appearances to the contrary notwithstanding, all will be well, the life of the earth will renew itself.

The Doctor's Dilemma

GEORGE BERNARD SHAW
1856–1950

S HAW called *The Doctor's Dilemma* a tragedy, but it is hard to believe that he meant the description seriously. In manner and tone the play is a comedy; this is scarcely contradicted by the fact that one of the persons in the play dies before our eyes, for Louis Dubedat's histrionic last moments make a scene that is affecting in no more than a sentimental way.

The oddity of the author's having called the play a tragedy has never engaged the kind of speculation that has long gone on about Chekhov's insistence that *Three Sisters* is a comedy. A few critics have attempted to affirm its seriousness by observing that Ridgeon undergoes a moral decline, to the point where he commits a quasi-murder; they identify this as the tragic element in the play. But although it is true that Ridgeon's moral nature deteriorates, this is hardly a tragic event; at most, it touches with a certain grimness the comedy in which it occurs. The likelihood is that Shaw had no other reason for applying the misnomer than the wish to be impudent, to amuse himself by confusing his audience.

And of course it is only if we take the play to be a comedy that we can accept the artificiality that is one of its salient features. Comedy has always claimed the right to treat probability with blithe indifference, and *The Doctor's Dilemma* takes full advantage of this ancient license. The events of the play are shameless contrivances, beginning with the terms of the "dilemma," the all too pat juxtaposition of the immoral genius and the virtuous mediocrity. Nowhere except in comedy could an eminent physician give a dinner party at which certain of the guests are co-opted to sit as a kind of investigating committee to help the host decide whether or not another of the guests deserves to receive the medical treatment that will rescue him from impending death. We are then asked to believe that the committee, once formed, cannot bring itself to disband, that three of the busiest doctors in London are so captivated by the moral situation that they find time to pursue their investigations at a meeting in Louis Dubedat's studio, and that all of them make a point of turning up at his deathbed.

But even more than by the unblushing high-handedness of its dealings with probability, the play is a comedy by its commitment to one of the oldest enterprises of the comic genre, the exhibition of the absurdity of doctors. How very old it is has been suggested by the English scholar F. M. Cornford, who traces the comic doctor through various examples of folk drama, such as the Punch and Judy shows and the medieval mummers' plays, back to the comedy of ancient Greece.* According to Cornford, Greek comedy had its roots in the primitive rituals of the winter solstice; the figure of the comic doctors descends from the once awesome medicine man who presided over the ceremonial representation of the death of the old year and the birth of the new. In the comedy of the Renaissance the doctor is a stock figure, mocked for his pretentiousness and pomposity. The tradition of doctor-baiting reached its climax and its classic form in the several plays in which Molière ridiculed the physicians of his day. To the traditional mockery he added an intellectual dimension by concentrating on the elaborate jargon of scholasticism by which the profession masked its invincible ignorance.

By the nineteenth century the tradition was on the wane, and now, in the popular drama of our time, no profession is accorded so much respect as that of medicine. The cinema and television seldom

* *The Origin of Attic Comedy.*

show the doctor as anything but virtuous and responsible, in his youth sternly dedicated to his unimpeachable profession, in his latter years endowed with a wisdom to which no layman can aspire. This change in the "image" of the doctor is connected with the advances that medicine made in the course of the nineteenth century. From our present perspective these may seem small, but they are significant because they were the result of the development of biological knowledge—medicine began to school itself in the sciences as it never had before and seemed on the point of making good the claims of its effectiveness that for so long had been empty.

It was in this period of not unjustifiable optimism, when the common opinion of the medical profession moved toward becoming what it now is, that Shaw mounted the elaborate attack, which, beginning in his youth, was to continue through the greater part of his life. *The Doctor's Dilemma* is but one of his innumerable writings on medical subjects. They have been accused of error, extravagance, and perversity, in part because of their polemic style, which is often intentionally outrageous. But they are remarkably well informed, and in the main they make excellent sense.

The essence of Shaw's indictment is that the medical profession turned every new idea it acquired into authoritative doctrine and then into dogma, with the result that even its most promising discoveries became barren and often dangerous. Other of its deficiencies also contributed to his viewing it as a "conspiracy against the public," but Shaw directed his most active antagonism toward that aspect of medicine which its practitioners had come to believe was its greatest strength, its reliance on scientific research. He held that exactly when medicine based itself most confidently on science it was most likely to prove unscientific, establishing orthodoxies which stood in the way of truth. If the charge has bearing even upon the medical situation in our day, when the acceleration of research condemns received ideas to a shorter expectancy of life than they once had, in Shaw's time its cogency was still greater. A case in point is the germ theory of disease as it was then formulated. This was of obvious value, yet it served as the ground for untenable conclusions (such as that virtually all diseases are caused by germs), mistaken beliefs (such as that vaccination provided permanent immunity from smallpox and was wholly without danger), and unsalutary practices (such as Lord Lister's use of surgical antisepsis, eventually abandoned because the antiseptic interfered with the healing process).

But the scientific inadequacy of its accepted theories was not the whole of the objection that Shaw made to the state of the medical profession. He was dismayed by what he took to be its philosophical or spiritual failure. Central to his thought was the doctrine of vitalism, which holds that the life of organisms is the manifestation of a vital principle distinct from all physical and chemical forces. It was a view that led him to deny categorically the first premise of the medical practice of his day, that the human body is a mechanism and that any malfunction it may show is to be dealt with in a mechanistic way. Shaw's belief in vitalism stood in close relation to his social views, for he held that disease is best understood as a result of adverse conditions in the environment, and that health depends on comfort and beauty, which society has the duty to provide.

Even this summary account of Shaw's dealings with medicine will suggest that he must have come to the writing of his comedy of doctors in a spirit quite different from that of his predecessors in the long tradition. It is not possible to attribute any propagandistic purpose to the earlier comic writers. They mocked doctors with no intention of exciting indignation, only laughter. Even Molière, whose satire so tellingly exposes the intellectual deficiencies of medicine, does not propose that anything in particular can or should be done about the bad state of affairs. As one critic puts it, comedy for Molière was not a means but an end. Shaw often said in the most explicit way that the opposite was true of him, that he intended his art not as an end in itself but as a means to an end, the betterment of human life. He proclaimed his pre-eminent concern with ideas, and with ideas that were "constructive" and practical, and his proudest boast was that he belonged to the company of what he called the "artist-philosophers," those men who, by means of their art, addressed themselves to bringing about a change in the condition of human life. He spoke scornfully of the "pure" artists, those who did not undertake to solve life's problems but were content to represent life as it is, for what merely pleasurable interest the representation might have. Among these he includes Shakespeare, whom he lovingly scolds because "he was utterly bewildered" by life and because his "pregnant observations and demonstrations of life are not co-ordinated into any philosophy or religion."

Yet if we take *The Doctor's Dilemma* quite by itself, without reference to its author's other writings about medicine,* and without regard to his characterization of himself as an "artist-philosopher," the effect of the play is really not different from that of a play of Molière's. Many of the specific ideas expounded in Shaw's polemical writings find expression in *The Doctor's Dilemma*, but we feel that they are there for the sake of the comedy rather than that the comedy was written to serve them. Such conclusions as we may draw from the play are not about medicine at all; they are, rather, about "life," and do not seem different in kind from the conclusions that Molière's plays frequently yield—that Nature and common sense are good and should guide our judgment; that committing oneself to a ruling idea goes against Nature and common sense and leads to error or defeat or ridicule, or all three; that a genial flexibility of mind is a virtue, and that intellectual pride is a vice; that thinking in the terms prescribed by one's profession leads to personal and intellectual deformation; that true morality transcends moralistic judgment; that affectionate and charitable emotions are to be cherished, self-seeking motives to be condemned. Comedy has traditionally permitted us to derive just such generalizations from its laughter. They have great charm, and no doubt they serve a good purpose in disposing us to virtue, but they cannot lay claim to great intellectual originality or force. They can scarcely be "co-ordinated into any philosophy or religion"; they are not what we expect of an "artist-philosopher."

* Notable among them is the lengthy preface which Shaw wrote for the play when it was published in 1911. The large canon of what Shaw wrote about medicine over his lifetime is fully reviewed in Roger Boxill's admirable *Shaw and the Doctors,* a Columbia University dissertation.

In short, *The Doctor's Dilemma*, although it advertises Shaw's ideas about medicine, does not propound them with any great didactic power. On this occasion, the "pure" artist in Shaw seems to have overcome the "artist-philosopher," and the latter cannot have put up a very determined resistance. He would appear to have been quite content to surrender into the hands of undidactic comedy all the ideas he took so seriously in his polemical writings: his doctors are menaces to the public welfare only secondarily and in a way that does not seem to matter or in some aspect other than the one in which they stand before us; we see them as on the whole rather pleasant-natured men, who are to be laughed at for comedy's usual reasons, because they are fools, or monomaniacs, or self-deceivers. And the "artist-philosopher" goes so far in conspiring in his own defeat as to make a hopelessly "pure" artist the spokesman for his cherished vitalism.

Louis Dubedat is the embodiment of an idea that had considerable interest for people at the end of the nineteenth century, as it still does—that art is not required to serve morality, that it exists for its own sake and is thus a paradigm of life itself, which is also said to exist for its own sake, for no other reason than to delight in its own energy and beauty. A corollary is that the artist is not necessarily a virtuous person, that indeed he is typically *not* virtuous and that his indifference or hostility to moral considerations is a condition of his creative power. There is no more truth in this than there was in Ruskin's assertion that only a good man can produce good art, but the new notion of the amoral artist, like the more general idea which it paralleled, served to liberate people from certain rather glum notions about art that prevailed in the Victorian age. Shaw, it may be supposed, stood in an ambivalent relation to the new conception of art and the artist. His moral temper, which he was willing to call Puritan, rejected it; yet at the same time he could respond to it affirmatively because it spoke of the energy, freedom, and beauty that life ought properly to have, and also because it outraged the merely respectable morality of the middle class, which, depressing in itself, stood in the path of ameliorating change.

As an example of the artist who stands outside the considerations of morality, Dubedat is in some ways not an altogether satisfactory creation. His infractions of the moral code are all on a small scale. Almost everything he does is touched with slyness or meanness; petty deceit is his natural medium. He can outdo the doctors themselves in conventionality: there is reason to believe that he is perfectly sincere when he mocks them for supposing that Jennifer is not married to him, for not seeing that she is "a lady" who carries "her marriage certificate in her face and in her character." He is a snob and a prig who can say of the girl he married under false pretenses that he could not stay with her long because she was "quite out of art and literature and refined living." And his stature as an artist is only little greater than as an immoralist; nothing that is said of his work leads us to believe that he is anything more than a brilliant and engaging but quite minor talent.

Dubedat's minuscule quality is in part dictated by the exigencies of comedy. If his stature were larger, if he enlisted our sympathies to a greater extent, his fate would be more moving than would have suited Shaw's purpose. As it is, his utterance of his "creed" on his deathbed creates an effect that, in its ambiguity, is quite in accord with the comic mode. When he folds his hands and affirms his belief "in Michael Angelo, Velasquez, and Rembrandt; in the might of design, the majesty of color, the redemption of all things by Beauty everlasting, and the message of Art that has made these hands blessed," the conscious pathetic eloquence of the speech is meant to mock itself, at least a little, and his subsequent question about the newspaper reporter is an obvious ironic comment on it. Yet for Shaw a creed is always momentous, especially one that speaks of redemption and a blessing, and Dubedat's deathbed avowal of faith makes the vitalistic affirmation of life that is meant to stand as the condemnation of Ridgeon and his mechanistic views.

The character of Ridgeon is puzzling almost to a fault. Upon first acquaintance we like him very much and from the description of him upon his entrance it is plain that Shaw meant that we should. The first check upon this approving opinion appears at the end of the second act, when, with the help of Sir Patrick Cullen, he is confronting his dilemma. Only for a short time is the dilemma allowed to be one of principle: whether to save the honest, decent, but not very useful doctor, Blenkinsop, or the "rotten blackguard" artist, Dubedat, "a genuine source of pretty and pleasant and good things." No sooner has the dilemma been stated in its interesting simplicity that Ridgeon introduces a complication that alters its nature: he discloses to Sir Patrick his desire to marry Dubedat's wife. This frankness we find admirable; by openly stating what he has to gain by allowing Dubedat to die, Ridgeon assures us that he is a man of wholly objective judgment. But our admiration cools when Sir Patrick says, "Perhaps she won't have you, you know," and Ridgeon answers, "I've a pretty good flair for that sort of thing. I know when a woman is interested in me. She is." There is of course no reason why Jennifer should *not* be "interested" in Ridgeon; a woman is likely to have some interested response to a man who is attractive, powerful, and drawn to her. And when, at the end of Act V, Jennifer, who is not exactly a girl, says that she had never been interested in him because he was too old—he is fifty —we may well feel that Shaw, in contriving this humiliation for Ridgeon, has made Jennifer trivial and undeveloped. Nonetheless, Ridgeon's answer to Sir Patrick, which is made "with a self-assured shake of the head," is vulgar and fatuous. The moral elevation that Ridgeon seemed about to gain by his frankness is no longer possible.

By the end of Act III, Ridgeon has become a sentimental self-deceiver, convincing himself that the motive for his decision to let Dubedat die is the noble desire to preserve Jennifer's illusions about her husband. In Act IV he speaks in a voice that Dubedat authoritatively describes as "devilish." But these manifestations of his moral decline do not carry conviction; they seem less the result of the character's inner life than of the author's manipulation.

Six Characters in Search of an Author: A Comedy in the Making

LUIGI PIRANDELLO
1867–1936

THE essence of the theatre, as everyone is quick to understand, is illusion. The theatre sets out to induce in an audience the belief that the things and events it presents are not what they are known to be. The man on the stage who wears a crown and a purple robe and stalks with so stately a tread is a salaried actor who will go home after the performance to a light supper, a glass of beer, and bed. The audience knows this to be so but consents to accept him as "the King" and it has appropriate emotions when, in the course of the play, his "sacred" person is assaulted. Of course these emotions are not the same as would be felt by actual loyal subjects witnessing an actual attempt upon the life of their ruler, but they are consonant with the actual situation and they are often intense.

The audience comes to the performance with good will toward the theatre's designs upon it, with every intention of submitting to such illusion as the theatre can produce. The theatre, for its part, undertakes to provide the audience with adequate ground for suspending or mitigating its ordinary common-sense knowledge. The range of means by which the theatre brings about a successful illusion is wide. It includes, among other things, the distance set between the audience and the actors, scenery and lighting-effects, costume and make-up, the mimetic skill of the actors, the kind of language the actors are given to speak. The number of such devices employed varies considerably from epoch to epoch. Some cultural periods require more of them, some less. Victorian audiences would have considered inadequate the bare stage with which the Elizabethans were quite content. In our own day, the theatre is eclectic in its modes of production, which sometimes are very elaborate, sometimes so sparse as to suggest that all the theatre needs in order to bring illusion into being is to show that it wishes to do so.

Yet in the degree that the theatre is devoted to illusion, it delights in destroying it, or in seeming to destroy it. The word *illusion* comes from the Latin word meaning "to mock" (*illudere*), which in turn comes from the word meaning "to play" (*ludere*), and a favorite activity of the theatre is to play with the idea of illusion itself, to mock the very thing it most tries to create—and the audience that accepts it. Sometimes, having brought the illusion into being, it seems to suggest that it has no belief whatever in its own creation.

An amusing example of this occurs far back in the history of the theatre. The ancient Athenian drama was sacred to the god Dionysus, and the only time plays were presented was at the festival in his honor. On these occasions the priest of the god's cult presided over the performance and sat in the audience in a place of honor close to the stage. In one of the comedies of Aristophanes, *The Frogs,* the chief character is the god himself; he is represented as an arrant coward, and at one point in the action, when threatened with a beating, the comic Dionysus runs from the stage toward the audience and throws himself at the feet of the presiding priest whose protection he claims. The priest would seem to have been visibly disconcerted by this unexpected turn of events, and the Dionysus-character mocked his blushes and other signs of embarassment.

No doubt the audience found the episode especially funny, and in a way that was different from the other comic moments in the play. The sudden destruction of the assumptions that the spectators had been making, the unexpected mingling of the world of the stage with the world of actuality, surely delighted the Athenians as similar shocks to their expectation have delighted all audiences since.

Nothing that the theatre does is more engaging than its disclosing its own theatricality, its opening to question the illusion it has contrived. When Hamlet discusses the art of acting with the strolling players who have come to Elsinore there is always a little stir of new attention in the audience as it receives this reminder that the Prince of Denmark is himself an actor, and the excitement increases when, in a succeeding scene, the players act before the royal court the beginning of a crude little drama called "The Murder of Gonzago." This play-within-a-play is much less "real" than the play that contains it and it is usually acted in a stilted, unrealistic manner to emphasize the difference. But it has the effect of recalling to us that *Hamlet* is itself "merely" a play. Part of our experience of *Hamlet* becomes the awareness of the theatre itself—and of the theatre's awareness of itself.

One reason why these awarenesses—ours of the theatre and the theatre's of itself—are so engaging is that they relate to a primitive tendency to question the reality of what is commonly accepted as reality, to speculate whether life itself is not an illusion. The tendency may justly be called primitive because it is so commonly observed in children, who often have moments of thinking that all that goes on around them is but a show devised (sometimes with the purpose of putting them to a "test" by some supernal agency. This supposition of the nonreality of the actual world is of great importance in philosophic thought. Plato conceived of all that we see and know as the simulacrum of a reality that is concealed from us, and the continued interest of philosophers in the question of whether what we know is consonant with what really is made possible Alfred North Whitehead's statement that all succeeding philosophy is but "a series of footnotes to Plato." That life is a dream has often been said. Sometimes life is spoken of as a game. It is also said to be a play, and this is perhaps the most common expression of the impulse to doubt life's literal reality. Jaques' famous speech in *As You Like It*, "All the world's a stage / And all the men and women merely players," sums up an idea that has established itself in our language—we naturally speak of the "part" a person "plays" in life or in some particular situation, and of the way in which he fulfils his "rôle." Indeed the very word *person* suggests the theatre, for the original meaning of the Latin word *persona* was the mask worn by the actors of antiquity.

Of all the theatre's many celebrations of its own mysterious power, of all the challenging comparisons it makes between its own reality and that of life, Pirandello's *Six Characters in Search of an Author* is the most elaborate and brilliant. It carries the fascinating contrivance of the play-within-a-play to the point where it becomes a play-about-a-play. One might say that its *dramatis personae* are the elements of the theatre itself, all of them, as the author himself observed, in conflict with one another. The Six Characters have been "rejected" by the author, or at least he has declared himself unwilling to present their drama. The director, who despises the plays of Pirandello which he is required to put on, consents, after some resistance, to show interest in the Characters, but he finds them difficult and eventually not very satisfactory. The actors who are to play the Characters are contemptuous of them and hostile to them, an attitude which is reciprocated by the Father and the Stepdaughter, both because the actors have no drama of their own and also because they falsify the essence of the characters they play. The illusion of the theatre is wholly negated: we are permitted—forced, indeed—to see the bare stage and the shabby "properties" that are used for its contrivance. Yet of course, in spite of the civil war taking place within it, the theatre realizes its familiar purpose. We of the audience do indeed believe in the reality of the Characters who are said to have been denied their existence by the author; we are fascinated and distressed by their painful situation and shocked by its outcome. The theatre as Pirandello represents it is very much like life itself, always at odds with itself, always getting in its own way, yet always pursuing and, in the end, having its way.

It is, of course, life itself that the Characters hope the theatre will give them, and they are not concerned with distinguishing between real life and theatrical life, between life as people and life as characters. "The drama is in us and we are the drama," says the

Father. "We are impatient to play it. Our inner passion drives us on to this." The Father's speech confirms—in this most un-Aristotelian play—Aristotle's idea that a drama is not the representation of a person but of an action.

Yet there is a distinction to be observed among the various ways in which the Characters think about the possibility of their realization. The Father and the Stepdaughter are fierce and explicit in their demand that they be permitted to come into existence through the acting out of their drama. Painful and shameful as their fate is, they insist upon fulfilling and demonstrating it; they may be said to love it as the means by which they attain life—they *are* their fate, they are the drama it makes. The Son, however, wants no part of the drama in which he is inextricably, although marginally, involved. It can only distress and disgust him. He is, he says, an " 'unrealized' character" and wishes to remain just that. And we, aware of the pale, thin censoriousness and self-regard that make him stand aloof from his ill-fated family, agree with his estimate of the quality of his existence, except that we take him to be personally rather than dramatically unrealized: to us he seems fully projected as the dramatic representation of an unrealized person, one whose being is in the control of his personal deficiencies. His refusal to take part in the drama as a Character is tantamount to refusing to be what in colloquial speech we call a "real person," someone whose force or courage or definiteness we necessarily perceive. Yet, for all his objection to being implicated in the drama, and despite his repugnance to the family's fate, he has had to come to the theatre as part of the family; and when, in a moment of indignation, he says that he is leaving the situation from which he is so alienated, he does not go, he cannot go. Whatever his desire may be, he is bound to the family fate and has his part in its drama; against his will, he is *in* life even though he does not occupy much space in it.

As for the Mother, she is incapable of conceiving herself as dramatic. She is wholly committed to her motherly functions and feelings and for her such ideas as "fate" and "existence," let alone "drama," have no meaning. She cannot conceive them because to do so requires a double vision that she lacks: the ability to stand off from her function and feelings and observe them. The Father, the Stepdaughter—and even, in his own dim way, the Son—have this capacity; they "see themselves" and they put a value upon what they see. But the Mother, who cannot see herself, sets no value upon herself. It is not merely that, like the Son, she objects to being in this particular drama; the very idea of drama, since it involves observation and a degree of conceptualization, is offensive to her: it belittles the actuality of life. She is, Pirandello says in his Preface to the play, realized as Nature, while the Father and the Stepdaughter (and in some degree the Son) are realized as Mind.

In the preface Pirandello speaks of "the inherent tragic conflict between life (which is always moving and changing) and form (which fixes it, immutable)." The conflict is not only tragic but ironic, for the "form" that Pirandello conceives of as the antagonist of "life" would seem to be brought into being by life itself for the furtherance of life. (A similar idea is central to Thomas Mann's story, "Disorder and Early Sorrow.") The Characters exist, they live, by reason of their fixity and immutability: the word *character* derives from the Greek word meaning to engrave, and it suggests the quality of permanence. The Father and the Stepdaughter are committed to repeat the situation that pains and shames them; they cannot move beyond it, yet it is through this compulsive reliving of the past, which denies a future in which they might move and change, that they achieve their reality of existence, their life. Realized as Mind, they are fixed by the form appropriate to Mind, their idea of themselves. The Mother, realized as Nature, is fixed by the form appropriate to Nature, her instinctual blind devotion to her maternal function of bringing life into being and preserving it.

Purgatory

WILLIAM BUTLER YEATS
1865-1939

T HE ghost or *revenant*—the spirit of a dead person returned to the world of the living and manifesting its presence in some physical way—has its established place in modern literature. But of course it is established only as a literary convention—few people actually believe in the existence of ghosts. The author of a ghost-story takes this for granted. He himself, in all likelihood, does not believe in ghosts, and all that he counts on in the reader is a readiness to make what Coleridge called a "willing suspension of disbelief." If the reader consents to suspend his disbelief and if the author is sufficiently skilful, he can lead the reader's imagination to entertain feelings similar to those that would attend an actual experience of a ghost. Reader and author enter into an agreement, as it were, to make believe—or to *make belief*—for as long as the story lasts.

But Yeats entered into no such argument with the reader when he wrote *Purgatory*. His attitude toward the ghosts in his play is wholly the opposite of what we expect from a modern writer. When *Purgatory* was first produced—at the Abbey Theatre, Dublin, in 1939—the author was present and was called to the stage to respond to the applause of the audience. In the course of his speech he said, "I have put nothing into the play because it seemed picturesque; I have put here my own conviction about this world and the next." He meant that he believed quite literally in life after death, in the actuality of the spirits of the dead manifesting themselves as they do in the play, and in the complex conditions of the after-life that the action of the play implies. And *Purgatory* is by no means his only expression of this belief in the occult and the preternatural—from young manhood on, it stood at the very center of Yeats's intellectual and creative life. It is affirmed in many of his plays and poems and in *A Vision,* the book in which he gives a systematic account of the relation of human life to supernatural forces.

To some readers this belief will seem so bizarre that they will scarcely credit Yeats's own affirmation of it. Indeed, some critics have denied that Yeats really held the ideas he enunciated, saying that they were an elaborate fiction which he deliberately maintained because it aided his poetic imagination. I do not share this opinion. It may be that there was some ambiguity in Yeats's belief in the supernatural, or a degree of irony, but I am certain, as are most students of Yeats, that he believed what he said he believed.

A person of extremely rationalistic temper might be alienated from Yeats's play by the occultism and preternaturalism that inform it. Such a reader might say that he was perfectly willing to be entertained, or even affected, by a ghost-play if the ghosts are conceived of in the usual modern way, as a literary convention, but that, because he cannot accept the actuality of ghosts, he can take no interest in a moral situation which is based on the assumption that ghosts exist. Most people, however, will not be so absolute. While they will perceive that Yeats's literalness of belief puts a demand upon them to believe as Yeats does, and although they will no doubt refuse this demand, the knowledge that Yeats literally believed what he set forth is likely to enhance rather than diminish the effect of the play. However much we may be attracted by those elements of a work which Yeats calls "picturesque," our response to what he calls his "conviction" is bound to be graver and solider. It is one thing to suspend our disbelief in improbable or, as most of us would say, impossible circumstances. It is quite another thing, and a far more momentous one, to suspend our disbelief in what to someone else is a conviction, especially if it is a conviction about the nature of man's destiny.

My own experience with *Purgatory* may be in point. When I read the play for the first time, I supposed it to be nothing more than "picturesque." I thought that Yeats had been chiefly concerned to contrive a situation which would allow the expression of an extreme—an ultimate—rage against life and disgust with it, emotions so intense that they would lead a man to destroy not only his own father but his own son, both the root and the fruit of his life. Taking this view of the play, I regarded the ghosts as a device for telling about past events in an immediate and vivid way. So understood, the play had considerable interest for me. The spareness of its verse, the harshness of its diction, and the violence of its action commanded my attention and engaged my curiosity. But when I read Yeats's statement about the literalness of his belief in life after death and then looked into the details of his conviction, I found that the play began to exert a new and more imperative power. And perhaps it will suggest how much greater this power was if I say that although, on my first reading of the play, its conscious reminiscences of *King Lear* seemed to me rather presumptuous, as did the reference to *Oedipus Rex* which we must inevitably suppose the action implies, these allusions seemed entirely appropriate after I had understood that I was confronting Yeats's "conviction about this world and the next." I saw *Purgatory* as being, like *Oedipus Rex* and *King Lear,* a tragic confrontation of destiny, less grand than its predecessors but not less intense.

Yeats's conviction about the life after death is given systematic expression in Book III of *A Vision,* a strange work which may be described as a theory of history and a theory of personality, a detailed statement of how things happen in the world and why people are as they are. It takes for granted the existence of supernatural forces and of personal entities apart from the flesh; it represents the human soul as going through a continuous cycle of birth, death, and purification, and describes this process in detail. How Yeats came into possession of this information is explained in the introduction to the volume, which tells how certain teacher-spirits undertook to instruct him and did so over a period of years, communicating with him through Mrs. Yeats by means of automatic writing.

According to *A Vision,* the career of the soul after death is complex, but to understand *Purgatory* it is enough to know that after the soul is separated from the body at death it is not separated from its passions, its pains, and—this is of particular importance to the play—from the consequences of its actions during life. In order to achieve freedom, the soul must purge away these elements of its fleshly existence that still remain in its imagination. It accomplishes this by returning to its fleshly experiences, seeking to understand them and to disengage itself from them. The process—it has something of the aspect of a spiritual psychoanalysis—can, Yeats tells us, go on for a very long time.* He says that where the soul has great intensity and where the consequences of its passions have affected great numbers of people, the process of purging its passion and its experience "may last with diminishing pain and joy for centuries." But in the work of liberation, the dead can be aided by the living, who are able, Yeats says, "to assist the imaginations of the dead."

Only when we are aware of all this can we begin to understand the Old Man's motive in murdering the Boy. He kills his son in order, as he says, to finish "all that consequence."

> I killed that lad because had he grown up
> He would have struck a woman's fancy,
> Begot, and passed pollution on.

He believes that, by bringing the "consequence" to an end, he will free his mother's spirit from her sexual passion so that it will be "all cold, sweet, glistening light," and for a moment, after the murder of his son, he supposes that he has accomplished his intention.

> Dear mother, the window is dark again,
> But you are in the light because
> I finished all that consequence.

---

* The Characters of *Six Characters in Search of an Author* are similarly compelled to re-enact the painful experiences that define their being, but not for the purpose of understanding them and of becoming detached from them.

But he hears the hoofbeats of his father returning to enact yet again the moment of his conception and he knows that he is "twice a murderer and all for nothing." Inevitably we ask why he failed. And so far do we go in our willing suspension of disbelief in Yeats's conviction that we speculate about the reason in terms of Yeats's own account of the process of the spirit's liberation. We find it possible to suppose, that is, that the Old Man's act of killing the Boy is itself a "consequence," that it is charged with the passion of hatred and contempt. And how, we ask, can the Old Man believe that he has "finished all that consequence" when he himself, a chief consequence, remains? In other words, we find ourselves—to our amusement—putting rational questions on the basis of a system of belief to which we deny rationality.

Galileo

BERTOLT BRECHT
1898–1956

O F THE circumstances of Galileo's career that are set forth
in Brecht's play, a great many are at variance with historical actuality. Thus, although it is true that the manuscript
of *Two New Sciences* had to be smuggled out of the country to be
published in Holland, this was done not by Andrea Sarti but by no
less a person than Prince Mattia de' Medici. As a matter of fact,
there was no Andrea Sarti in Galileo's life, and no Mrs. Sarti; they
are inventions of the author. During his last years on his little farm
at Arcetri, near Florence, Galileo was not attended by his daughter
Virginia; she died, at the age of thirty-four, just after he entered the
period of house arrest which was to end only with his death. And,
indeed, Virginia never lived with her father after her early girlhood
—Galileo had put his two illegitimate daughters into the convent at
Arcetri when they were very young and both had become nuns.
Virginia was nothing like the dull girl of the play. Remarkable both
for her intelligence and her saintly disposition, she adored her father
and he adored her, and despite her religious vocation, she approved
of his work and followed it eagerly.

Although Galileo at Arcetri was strictly supervised by the Inquisition, he did not live in complete isolation. Many distinguished
travelers came to pay him their respects; it was so much the thing

to do that one of Galileo's biographers notes it as strange that Descartes failed to make a call when he was in Florence. Among the visitors were John Milton and Thomas Hobbes from England, and Gassendi, the famous mathematician, from France. In 1639 a gifted young scientist of eighteen by the name of Viviani attached himself to the old master as an affectionate disciple and close companion; this precocious youth was later to become the leading mathematician of his age. Castelli, the Benedictine monk who had long been Galileo's favorite pupil, spent considerable time with him. Torricelli, the famous physicist, took up residence on the farm for a period and worked with Galileo on his theories of mechanics. So much for Brecht's representation of Galileo as doing his last work in snatched clandestine moments. So much, too, for the idea that Galileo was held in contempt by his pupils and fellow workers for having abjured his views under pressure from the Inquisition.

It is also worth observing that the intellectual position of the Church in its condemnation of Galileo was much less assured and positive than we might guess from what the play tells us; as one scholar says, the Church acted with "dogmatic timidity," for although it condemned Galileo's views, it did not venture to assert in a formal way a contrary view. Moreover, the position of the public in regard to the condemnation is inaccurately represented; we are given no adequate indication of the regard in which Galileo was held by people of all classes, including important sections of the aristocracy and the clergy. And Galileo himself was an altogether larger person than Brecht has chosen to show, more conscious, intelligent, and brilliant, more powerful and forthright in polemic, and more complex intellectually, for there is every evidence that, although anticlerical, he found no difficulty in being a sincere and devout Catholic. Even his fault of vanity was on a larger scale than the play suggests.

To remark on Brecht's departures from historical facts does not constitute an adverse critcism of *Galileo*. It has never been thought incumbent upon the author of a historical play to conform to the way things really were; Shakespeare, for an obvious example, plays fast and loose with history. The loyalty of the dramatist is not to fact but to dramatic effectiveness and such moral truth as drama may propose, and he has always had the privilege of omitting and altering circumstances to suit his artistic and moral purpose. But in this instance the playwright's departures from accuracy might seem to entail a sacrifice of advantage. As compared with the historical truth, the play's account of Galileo's career is less rich and complex, less charged with interest than the corresponding actuality, and the characters are less engaging than the real persons upon whom they were modelled. If this is so, it is because Brecht wished it to be so. He precisely did not want his play to be rich and complex. He did not want his characters to be engaging. His theory of drama dictated otherwise.

That theory is best understood through the political passions that give rise to it. Brecht, the son of a middle-class North German family, had experienced to the full the horrors of the First World War —he had served as a surgical orderly—and the extreme social disorders of his nation after its defeat. The bitter anger and contempt that he felt were directed not only upon the powerful classes he held responsible for these evils but also upon the artistic culture of the nation they dominated. In his adverse judgment of the national culture, Brecht had in mind not only those works of art that might be condemned out of hand as manifestly sharing the moral failure of the ruling classes but even that "high" culture whose idealism was commonly understood to be opposed to the crass self-seeking of the wealthy and the powerful. Like many European artists in the period after 1918, Brecht discredited virtually the whole humanistic tradition of art on the grounds that it was essentially, or objectively, an apology for the corrupt and vulgar society out of which it had arisen.

That Brecht became committed to Communism in his youth and maintained the commitment—although sometimes uneasily—until his death, undoubtedly bears upon his theory of the stage. Yet neither the theory nor the work that exemplified it met with the approval of the Communist Party.* Brecht shared with the Party the belief that art must serve a social function and advance the cause of revolutionary progress. But the official position on how this is to be done is notably conservative—the Party is opposed to experiment; its doctrine of "socialist realism," which requires the writer to inculcate a "positive" morality by stimulating strong, simple emotions on behalf of what is "right" and "good," might have been formulated, save for its name, by some mediocre Victorian aesthetician—and it could not countenance Brecht's radicalism in the theatre, which went so far in controverting traditional canons as to seem to subvert the very idea of art.

Brecht set himself implacably against the element of the theatre that has always been thought its very essence: he had nothing but contempt for illusion. He poured scorn upon the devices of composition and production which induce an audience to believe that it is experiencing an actual event to which it responds empathetically, with the emotions that follow upon making an "identification" with the protagonist. Brecht sought to produce the very opposite effect; he wanted his audience to be at a distance and disengaged from what happened on the stage. He spoke of this as the *Verfremdungseffekt,* literally the estranging or alienating effect. The audience is meant to see things, not as the hero sees them, but rather as it is led to see them through the activity of its own intelligence. Its estrangement or distance from the events occurring on the stage does not keep the audience from being interested in what takes place. But it is not to be even momentarily under the illusion that it is witnessing events of real life; it is to be always conscious that what it sees is "nothing but" a play, and one on which the intelligence is invited to exercise itself, and at the moment of performance rather than later, when the emotions have quieted. Brecht avowed it as his intention not to arouse feeling but to initiate thought. The theatre, he insisted at one point in his career, is not meant for enjoyment. By this he

* An important exception to the Communist resistance to Brecht is to be found in the success he achieved in the East German Republic. The theatre he founded in East Berlin is devoted chiefly to the production of his plays.

meant not so much that the theatre must be "serious" rather than "light" and "entertaining" as that the audience must not sit passive while the performance elicits emotions that, in one way or another, flatter its self-esteem.

In order to deliver his audience from the traditional bondage of illusion and bring it into activity, Brecht rejected many of the hitherto unquestioned criteria of dramatic art. So far from trying to achieve the firm coherence of structure that is regarded as a prime dramatic virtue, he avoided it for the very reason that it is usually valued, because it is instrumental in arousing and directing the emotions of the audience. His plays do not mount to a dramatic climax but tell a story in numerous discrete episodes that are connected only loosely. So far as possible, they avoid the dramatic in favor of the narrative mode; in *Galileo,* for instance, the verses sung at the beginning of each scene to summarize the action that is to follow and the display of quotations from Galileo's works are consciously nondramatic devices. Brecht's theoretical preference for the narrative as against the dramatic mode led him to speak of his plays as examples of the "epic" theatre. He had in mind the effect produced by an ancient bard chanting a poem to the warriors gathered in some king's feasting-hall: though interested in what they hear, the listeners are not overpowered by it; they are being *told* what has happened, not asked to believe that the event is taking place before their eyes.

The word "epic" is perhaps not a wholly fortunate expression of Brecht's meaning, for it carries connotations of heroic largeness and nobility which Brecht certainly did not intend. Quite the contrary, indeed. Brecht sometimes spoke of his plays as being "non-Aristotelian," a description which referred to their settled indifference to symmetry and coherence of structure and to their avoidance of the strong feelings that would produce what Aristotle called *catharsis* or purgation, a discharge of emotion leading to a state of psychic rest. It also referred to his distrust of whatever might suggest the heroic dignity and grandeur upon which Aristotle put so strong an emphasis in his discussion of tragedy. For Aristotle, tragedy was to a very considerable extent a matter of style; the tragic style depends on the elevation of the characters in the drama as expressed not only in their moral disposition and social status but also in their deportment and manner, above all in their language. Brecht's temperament as a dramatist is defined by nothing so much as his antagonism to the heroic or tragic style. His characters show no trace of it; his language, determinedly colloquial and popular, even "low," and as far removed from the literary language as possible, denies the very credibility, let alone any possible relevance to human affairs, of an elevated style.

A dramaturgy so antagonistic to established tradition naturally calls for its own style of acting. Brecht trained his actors to give up the ideal of impersonation in which they had been reared. Just as he did not want his audience to "identify" with the characters, he did not want his actors to "be" the persons they portrayed. The Moscow Art Theatre had carried the ideal of personification to the point of extravagance; its famous director, Stanislavsky, trained his actors to achieve an actually felt identity with the characters they played. For this method—which had, incidentally, a decisive influence on the Russian theatre and the Communist theory of the drama—Brecht had nothing but contempt. It was for him the extreme example of what he called "culinary" theatre, in which the audience sits passive while being serviced its meal of emotion. The actors of the "epic" theatre are required to make it plain that they are only actors. They are to speak not as though what they say had just occurred to them but as though they are reporting by quotation what the represented characters had said. And they are to indicate their consciousness of the presence of an audience and their awareness of the doctrinal intentions of the play, communicating the sense that they, like the audience, stand at a cool distance from what happens on the stage.

The theatre, it would seem, has autonomous powers which are not to be controlled by the theory of even so gifted a dramatist as Brecht. Despite his best efforts to achieve distance and estrangement, to circumvent the emotional response of his audiences by the negation of illusion, his plays, charged with the energies of his moral and political purposes, have the effect of enthralling and sometimes of deeply moving those who witness them.

Brecht's theory of the stage goes far toward explaining why *Galileo* departs from historical actuality in so many respects. Almost every manipulation of the real circumstances of Galileo's life is in the direction of making it simpler and more commonplace, by which means, we may suppose, it becomes the more readily available to the scrutiny and judgment of the audience. A Galileo who happens to have heard about a Dutch device of two lenses in a tube and who makes a little extra cash by giving the appropriated invention to the Venetian senate to manufacture and market, is, presumably, easier to judge than the real Galileo who, having contrived the notable improvements in the telescope that made it an effectual means of research, supplied carefully crafted instruments to the astronomers of Europe, the best that could be had at that time. A Galileo whose character is in part defined by his domestic arrangements, by a dull if dutiful daughter, a bustling housekeeper who tries to keep prudential considerations always to the fore, and assistants who are not notable for intellectual brilliance, is less likely to infect the audience with ideas of heroic dignity and charm than a Galileo who was loved by the remarkable person the real Virginia was, by princes and many dignitaries of the Church, and by younger colleagues whose range of scientific imagination make the invented Andrea and Federzoni look like mere laboratory technicians.

But one of Brecht's manipulations of history cannot be explained by reference to Brecht's theory of the stage. This is the representation of Galileo as having dishonored himself in not choosing death in preference to the abjuration of his beliefs. No modern scholar confirms the play on this point. One of the most authoritative students of Galileo's life, work, and times, Giorgio de Santillana, puts the matter unequivocally: "The abjuration itself is not at all the surrender and moral disgrace that self-appointed judges have made it out to be." We have seen that Galileo's colleagues and co-workers felt none of the scorn that Brecht finds appropriate to the situation.

As Professor de Santillana says, Galileo's recantation "was not considered a moral degradation. It was a *social* degradation, and it was as such that it broke the old man's heart." (Galileo was seventy at the time of his trial.) But although Galileo's heart may have been broken, his spirit, Professor de Santillana goes on to say, was not. He continued his work, and in *Two New Sciences* produced his greatest achievement. In his letters his contempt for those who had condemned him was manifest. His pride was no doubt sustained by the active sympathy of the public, for, to quote Professor de Santillana yet again, "pious believers who would never have touched a Protestant tract, priests, monks, prelates even, vied with one another in buying up copies of the *Dialogue* on the black market to keep them from the hands of the Inquisitors."*

The "self-appointed judges" who hand down their condemnation of Galileo do so on the grounds that he valued his life more than the truth. This is wholly to misconceive the situation. Everyone was aware that Galileo had really consented to abjure nothing but his right to publish the truth. For him to have sacrificed his life for this right, in the fact of the Church's long-established dominion over the intellectual activity of its communicants in matters that affected belief, would have been not a moral but a political act of a kind that the assumptions of the time did not comprehend. There were, to be sure, men whose religious beliefs led them to renounce the Church and oppose its authority. Such men often suffered martyrdom for their faith. But Galileo was not put on trial for a matter of faith. He himself would have corrected us for speaking of the "beliefs" which he abjured: he did not hold the *belief* that the earth moved around the sun, he possessed the *knowledge* that this was so. It was a fact that did not require the witness of his martyrdom. He felt this the more because to him it was not so much the Church that had condemned him as a successful faction of the clergy and because he knew to what lengths of legal trickery it had had to go in order to secure his condemnation. He also knew how much weight his demonstrations carried with the learned among the

---

* Giorgio de Santillana, *The Crime of Galileo,* pp. 320–325 *passim.*

higher clergy and understood the significance of the Pope's not making the issue one of dogma, and he could therefore suppose that the Church would eventually reverse itself, as in fact it did a century later.

Opinion will differ as to whether or not Brecht went beyond the legitimate privileges of the historical playwright in representing Galileo as a man who had betrayed the cause of truth. But whichever way opinion goes, it must remain a matter for curiosity why Brecht so grossly distorted the story of Galileo's life, when there were such strong reasons why he might have hesitated to do so.

For one thing, the harsh simplicity of the play's moral judgment violates Brecht's Marxist creed. Marxism is nothing if not historical, and strict in its historicity, and it is one of its essential tenets that conduct cannot be judged by absolute timeless standards but only by reference to the cultural conditions that prevail at a given historical moment. To project backward into the past the standards of the present, as Brecht does, and to condemn Galileo by the criteria of a modern social and political morality is a violation of this idea.

Then, in the light of his almost obsessive desire for an active, thinking audience, it must be wondered why Brecht leads the audience of *Galileo* so simplistically to the conclusion that the protagonist is to be condemned. In the last dialogue between Andrea Sarti and his master, Sarti proposes the idea that Galileo is blameless, for he perceives that in having refused martyrdom the old man had preserved himself to advance the great cause of science by the composition of his last work. But Galileo himself refuses this exculpation; his own condemnation of his conduct is the last word on the matter and the one that the audience is expected to accept, for it has been given no ground for a contrary view. In this instance at least, Brecht is not solicitous for the intellectual activity of his audience; on the contrary, he remorselessly holds the audience in bondage to the historical data he has chosen or invented. And he insists on this conclusion out of what must seem sheer wilfulness. Eric Bentley, who has translated many of Brecht's plays and whose sympathetic criticism has done much to establish the dramatist's reputation, is uncompromising on this score. "One cannot find," Professor Bentley says, "within the boundaries of the play itself, a full justification for the virulence of the final condemnation."*

The wilfulness and the virulence of the final condemnation are especially puzzling in the light of Brecht's earlier views of moral and political intransigence both in his work and in the conduct of his life. One of Brecht's characteristic moral positions is that in circumstances of oppression a man does well to check the impulse to forthright heroism and to seek to achieve his ends by cunning, concealing what he truly thinks or expressing it only obliquely, and biding his time. This was Brecht's own way of dealing with hostile authority—whoever writes about Brecht from knowledge of his life remarks on his unwillingness to expose himself to danger. "He knew how to take care of himself," Professor Bentley says and goes on to specify the occasions on which Brecht had cannily considered his safety or comfort rather than the demands of heroic idealism. Yet here he represents Galileo as virtually a villain for doing what he himself had not only previously advocated but had also, in effect, actually done. An earlier version of the play had invited the audience to a quite considerable activity of judgment by requiring it to deal with a man whose cunning inevasion deserves admiration even though his cowardice deserves contempt. But in the published version, Galileo's refusal to be heroically intransigent can wake only a saddening scorn.†

One is inevitably drawn to the speculation that Brecht, in changing his view of Galileo, was changing his view of his own course of conduct, that the Galileo who hates and condemns himself for his abjuration represents the author's own judgment on himself. But the personal interpretation, although it recommends itself, can have but a minor part in our understanding of the moral doctrine of the play. Nor, perhaps, is it finally to our purpose that Brecht himself has explained the revision of his judgment of Galileo by his re-

---

* "The Science Fiction of Bertolt Brecht," the introduction to the Grove Press edition of *Galileo*, 1966, p. 21.

† The first version of *Galileo* has not been published. Professor Bentley has read it in manuscript and I take my account of its tendency from his essay.

sponse to the explosion of the atomic bomb, which induced him to take a more rigorous view of the responsibility of the scientist and of the intellectual in general. An author's testimony on why he wrote as he did must always be treated with respect, but it is not always as authoritative as it seems. If we ask why, in the second version of his *Galileo,* Brecht revised not only his earlier judgment on his protagonist but also the moral attitude of a lifetime, perhaps the satisfactory answer is that his protean mind, doctrinal but indifferent to the claims of doctrinal consistency, happened at this moment to be captivated by the idea of an absolute intransigent morality and the heroism it calls for.

2 · FICTION

My Kinsman, Major Molineux

NATHANIEL HAWTHORNE
1804–1864

THE essential situation of this baffling story is simple
enough, and it is familiar to us from scores of legends,
myths, and fairy tales. The hero, a very young man, a
youth, sets out on his travels to seek his fortune or to claim a birth-
right. His chief characteristic, apart from whatever bravery he may
have, is his innocence of the ways of the world. He has been brought
up in simple or humble circumstances, and now he enters a life far
more complex than any he had ever imagined, in which intrigue
and danger await him. A chief interest in all such tales is the young
man's passage from adolescence into maturity. This is accomplished
through acts of courage and ingenuity, although sometimes, as in
the story of Parsifal, the achievement is more complicated and involves the making of certain moral and intellectual choices. The
difficulties which the young man confronts suggest those trials or
tests that regularly form part of the initiation rites by which primitive peoples induct the youths of the community into the status of
manhood.

There can be no doubt that Robin's experience the night he comes
into Boston brings his youth to an end, and that his maturity begins
after he has identified himself with the wild insurrectionary crowd.
But what are we to conclude about the nature of this maturity?
Obviously, Robin's loss of his youth comes about through his loss

of innocence. But are we to be glad or sorry about the loss? Probably glad, since Robin's innocence was largely compounded of ignorance and a foolish confidence in his "shrewdness." And yet, when he leaves his innocence behind, we cannot be certain whether it is for something good or for something bad; we cannot make out what Hawthorne wants us to think.

This ambiguity has a variety of sources. One of them is the author's apparently double attitude toward the popular insurrection. Although the opening paragraph of the story does not carry a strong charge of emotion in favor of the Colony's right to govern itself, even a neutral statement of the political situation is bound to prejudice at least American readers in favor of the insurrectionists with whom Robin eventually makes common cause. Yet when Hawthorne describes the members of the conspiracy, he does so in ways that are scarcely sympathetic, and he is at some pains to suggest that their leader is perhaps the devil himself.

We are also in considerable doubt about the moral meaning we are supposed to assign to Major Molineux, the victim of the successful machinations of this devil-leader. Major Molineux, for all that he is on the "wrong" political side, has a nobility that no member of the popular party can claim. "He was an elderly man, of large and majestic person, and strong, square features, betokening a steady soul. . . ." The account of his degradation is shocking in the extreme; Robin is surely right in thinking that his kinsman could never endure to see him again after he had been witness to the dreadful humiliation of tar-and-feathers. And yet, although Hawthorne speaks of the disgrace as "foul," because it deprives the Major of all semblance of humanity, making him a ghastly object of ridicule, he represents his young hero as being warmly associated with the Major's tormentors, eventually joining in the hideous laughter of the mob at its victim's plight.

It is of course Robin's participation in the mob's laughter that makes the shocking climax of the story. At the sight of his degraded kinsman, Robin's first emotions had been "pity and terror"—the feelings which, as Aristotle tells us, are aroused by tragedy. But these "classic" emotions, as we might call them, quickly yield to a "be-wildering excitement." When Robin hears the laughter of the crowd begin again, first the laughter of all the figures who represent the life of worldliness—the police officer, the harlot, the innkeeper, the substantial citizen, the barber—and then the laughter of the general mob, he joins in with an especial gusto: "every man shook his sides, every man emptied his lungs, but Robin's shout was the loudest there." Hawthorne abates nothing in his characterization of. the wild mob in which the young hero, once so gentle, submerges himself: "When there was a momentary calm in that tempestuous sea of sound, the leader gave the sign, the procession resumed its march. On they went, like fiends that throng in mockery around some dead potentate, mighty no more, but majestic still in his agony. On they went, in counterfeited pomp, in senseless uproar, in frenzied merriment, trampling all on an old man's heart." The cruel and savage act in which Robin enthusiastically shares has quite transcended its political origin. It has become one of those great primitive orgies in which the king is ritually slain. Whether or not Hawthorne was aware that such rituals did once actually take place, it is scarcely possible for anyone today to read the passage without having them in mind.*

Has Robin, then, by his burst of laughter at his kinsman's plight, taken sides with the devil? If he has, the story speaks no word of blame for his act. Nor, indeed, does the story say a word of blame of the presumptive devil himself. The gentleman who befriends Robin seems genuinely kind, truly virtuous and wise, yet when Robin asks him about the satanic ringleader, he replies by saying nothing more than that he does not know him "intimately" and asking, "May not a man have several voices . . . as well as two complexions?" The description of this leader as he rides at the head of the procession makes him out to be fierce and terrible, but not malign or disgusting. He is clad in military dress and bears a drawn sword, and, with his face half red, half black, he is said to look

---

* See "The Killing of the Divine King," Chapter xxiv of Sir James Frazer's *The Golden Bough.*

like "war personified." But if he is war personified, we must recall that Major Molineux is himself a soldier and derives his dignity from his military character.

The final words which the friendly gentleman addresses to Robin condone, even approve, the youth's conduct. After urging Robin not to return home immediately, he says, "If you prefer to remain with us, perhaps, as you are a shrewd youth, you may rise in the world without the help of your kinsman, Major Molineux." Possibly, of course, the gentleman is wicked despite his seeming to be a man of simple good will, and means to lead Robin into ways of corruption and cynicism. But if, as seems reasonable, we take him to be good and his speech to be sincere, then the story would seem to be saying that Robin is well rid of his kinsman, that he is the better for no longer depending on his help. This being so, the story makes the judgment that Robin's cruel deed of turning upon his kinsman in ridicule was a necessary step in his coming of age.

It is a strange idea to contemplate. Yet in what other way are we to resolve the ambiguities of the story? Freud says somewhere that every young man must learn that the reality of the world is the way the neighbors say it is, not the way his parents say it is—we have to learn, that is, that life does not conform to the idealism which the family tries to teach us. This is the lesson that Robin learns, not intellectually or abstractly, but by the experience of the expressed impulses that his gentle, virtuous upbringing did not recognize and would not countenance.

It is exactly his gentle, virtuous upbringing that he repudiates by his laughter. But actually Robin had already repudiated his rearing even before joining in the mob's mockery of his kinsman—at the moment, just before the climax, when he has his intense vision of his home and family. As the vision comes to its end, he sees all the members of the family going into the house, "and when Robin would have entered also, the latch tinkled into its place, and he was excluded from his home." We have had no hint that Robin harbors resentment at having been sent out into the world while his elder brother is kept at home in the bosom of the family, but clearly just such resentment announces itself here, and in very forthright terms. And it is now, after this vision of his virtual expulsion from the family, that he is carried away by the laughter of the crowd. Major Molineux, his father's cousin, is his father's surrogate and representative; when Robin laughs at the degradation of this man, his laughter is in effect directed at his father and at all the virtues that his father stood for and to which he had assented.

But how can Robin's conduct not be blamed? How can it be condoned, and even approved, as the story may very well be doing? Can we suppose that a man like Hawthorne, a man notable for his gentleness, is saying that the dark and evil impulses of the savage mob have some beneficent part in the young man's development? Can he be telling us that the experience of evil is necessary to the understanding and practice of good, or that what is thought bad by gentle and pious people is not really, or not wholly, bad?

The questions that press upon us cannot be answered with any assurance that we are responding with precise understanding to what the author means. Yet, however we do answer, we cannot fail to recognize our relief that Robin, having capitulated to his cruel impulse and having repudiated authority and dignity, need never again utter the phrase, "my kinsman, Major Molineux." From this time on, he will at least travel under his own name and in his own right.

Bartleby the Scrivener: A Story of Wall Street

HERMAN MELVILLE
1819-1891

IN A letter he wrote to Hawthorne in 1851, Melville, speaking of his friend in the third person, offered him this praise: "There is the grand truth about Nathaniel Hawthorne. He says NO! in thunder; but the Devil himself cannot make him say *yes*. For all men who say *yes*, lie. . . ." Melville was referring to Hawthorne's relation to the moral order of the universe as it is conventionally imagined, but his statement, which has become famous, is often read as Melville's own call to resist the conformity that society seeks to impose. It was taken in this way by one of the notable students of Melville, Richard Chase, who quotes it at the beginning of an account of Melville's attitude toward the American life of his time and goes on to say that "although Melville was not exclusively a naysayer, his experiences and his reflections upon the quality of American civilization had taught him to utter the powerful 'no' he attributes to Hawthorne. He learned to say 'no' to the boundlessly optimistic commercialized creed of most Americans, with its superficial and mean conception of the possibilities of human life, its denial of all the genuinely creative or heroic capacities of man, and its fear and dislike of any but the mildest truths. Melville's 'no' finds expression in the tragic-comic tale of 'Bartleby the Scrivener.' "*

* "Herman Melville" in *Major Writers of America*, edited by Perry Miller, Volume I, p. 880.

But although this great story tells of a nay-saying of a quite ultimate kind, perhaps the first thing we notice about Bartleby's "no" is how far it is from being uttered "in thunder." And exactly its distance from thunder makes the negation as momentous as it is; the contrast between the extent of Bartleby's refusal and the minimal way in which he expresses it accounts for the story's strange force, its mythic impressiveness. Whether he is being asked to accommodate himself to the routine of his job in the law office or to the simplest requirements of life itself, Bartleby makes the same answer, "I prefer not to"—the phrase is prim, genteel, rather finicking; the negative volition it expresses seems to be of a very low intensity. Melville is at pains to point up the odd inadequacy of that word *prefer* by the passage in which he tells how it was unconsciously adopted into the speech of the narrator and his office staff, and with what comic effect.

Actually, of course, the small, muted phrase that Bartleby chooses for his negation is the measure of his intransigence. A "no! in thunder" implies that the person who utters it is involved with and has strong feelings about whatever it is that he rejects or opposes. The louder his thunder, the greater is his (and our) belief in the power, the interest, the real existence of what he negates. Bartleby's colorless formula of refusal has the opposite effect—in refusing to display articulate anger against the social order he rejects, our poor taciturn nay-sayer denies its interest and any claim it may have on his attention and reason. "I prefer not to" implies that reason is not in point; the choice that is being made does not need the substantiation of reason: it is, as it were, a matter of "taste," even of whim, an act of pure volition, having reference to nothing but the nature of the agent. Or the muted minimal phrase might be read as an expression of the extremest possible arrogance—this Bartleby detaches himself from all human need or desire and acts at no behest other than that of his own unconditioned will.

It is possible that Melville never heard of Karl Marx, although the two men were contemporaries, but Melville's "story of Wall Street" exemplifies in a very striking way the concept of human alienation which plays an important part in Marx's early philosophical writings and has had considerable influence on later sociological thought. Alienation is the condition in which one acts as if at the behest not of one's own will but of some will other (Latin: *alius*) than one's own. For Marx its most important manifestation is in what he called "alienated labor," although he suggested that the phrase was redundant, since all labor is an alienated activity. In Latin *labor* has the meaning of pain and weariness as well as of work that causes pain and weariness, and we use the word to denote work that is in some degree enforced and that goes against the grain of human nature: a culprit is sentenced to a term of "hard labor," not of "hard work." By the same token, not all work is alienated; Marx cites the work of the artist as an example of free activity, happily willed, gratifying and dignifying those who perform it.*

In undertaking to explain the reason for the alienated condition of man, Marx refused to accept the idea that it is brought about by the necessities of survival. Man, he said, can meet these necessities with the consciousness of free will, with the sense that he is at one with himself; it is society that alienates man from himself. And Marx held that alienation is at its extreme in those societies which are governed by money-values. In a spirited passage, he describes the process of accumulating capital in terms of the sacrifice of the free human activities that it entails: "The less you eat, drink, and read books; the less you go to the theatre, the dance hall, the public-house; the less you think, love, theorize, sing, paint, fence, etc., and the more you *save*—the greater becomes your treasure which neither moth nor dust will devour—your *capital*. The less you *are,* the more you *have;* the less you express your own life, the greater is your *externalized* life—the greater is the store of your alienated being."†

---

* Perhaps sport provides a more immediately cogent example of a free and therefore highly valued activity. Many sports require a submission to the most gruelling discipline in training and a quite painful expenditure of energy in performance. Those who engage in them take this for granted and, it would seem, even find that it contributes to the gratification they experience. If the same activity were not freely chosen but enforced, the discomforts would be felt as cruelty and degradation.

† Quoted by Robert Tucker in *Philosophy and Myth in Karl Marx*, Cambridge University Press, 1961, p. 138.

This describes the program for success in a money society; it was followed, we may note, in his early days by John Jacob Astor, who commands the ironized respect of the narrator of "Bartleby the Scrivener," and no doubt to some extent by the narrator himself. Those members of a money society who do not consent to submit to the program are, of course, no less alienated, and they do not have the comforting illusion of freedom that the power of money can give.

It can be said of Bartleby that he behaves quite as if he were devoting himself to capitalist accumulation. He withdraws from one free human activity after another. If "the theatre, the dance hall, the public-house" had ever been within his ken, they are now far beyond it. If there had ever been a time when he delighted to "think, love, theorize, sing, paint, fence, etc.," it has long gone by. He never drinks. He eats less and less, eventually not at all. But of course nothing is further from his intention than accumulation—the self-denial he practices has been instituted in the interests of his freedom, a sad, abstract, metaphysical freedom but the only one he can aspire to. In the degree that he diminishes his self, he is the less an alienated self: his will is free, he cannot be compelled. A theory of suicide advanced by Sigmund Freud is in point here. It proposes the idea that the suicide's chief although unconscious purpose is to destroy not himself but some other person whom he has incorporated into his psychic fabric and whom he conceives to have great malign authority over him. Bartleby, by his gradual self-annihilation, annihilates the social order as it exists within himself.

An important complication is added to the story of Bartleby's fate by the character and the plight of the nameless narrator. No one could have behaved in a more forbearing and compassionate way than this good-tempered gentleman. He suffers long and is kind; he finds it hard, almost impossible, to do what common sense has long dictated he should do—have Bartleby expelled from the office by force—and he goes so far in charity as to offer to take Bartleby into his own home. Yet he feels that he has incurred guilt by eventually separating himself from Bartleby, and we think it appropriate that he should feel so, even while we sympathize with him; and in making this judgment we share his guilt. It is to him that Bartleby's only moment of anger is directed: " 'I know you,' " says Bartleby in the prison yard, " 'and I want nothing to say to you.' " The narrator is "keenly pained at his implied suspicion" that it was through his agency that Bartleby had been imprisoned, and we are pained for him, knowing the suspicion to be unfounded and unjust. Yet we know why it was uttered.

Bartleby's "I prefer not to" is spoken always in response to an order or request having to do with business utility. We may speculate about what would have happened if the narrator or one of Bartleby's fellow-copyists, alone with him in the office, had had occasion to say, "Bartleby, I feel sick and faint. Would you help me to the couch and fetch me a glass of water?" Perhaps the answer would have been given: " 'I prefer not to.' " But perhaps not.

The Grand Inquisitor

FËDOR DOSTOEVSKI
1821–1881

O F "The Grand Inquisitor" it can be said almost categorically that no other work of literature has made so strong an impression on the modern consciousness or has seemed so relevant to virtually any speculation about the destiny of man. The peculiar interest it arouses is not hard to explain. With extreme boldness and simplicity Dostoevski brings into confrontation the two great concepts that preoccupy the modern mind, freedom on the one hand, happiness and security on the other. These concepts he embodies in characters of transcendent stature: the person who does all the talking in the story imposes his authority upon us not merely because he is very old, powerful, and intelligent but because he is Satan himself; and the silent person is divine. No other modern literary work has speculated on human fate in terms so grandiose.

To the reader of the present day, the knowledge that Dostoevski wrote "The Grand Inquisitor" in 1879 may come as a surprise. For the story takes for granted a form of social organization that we know nowadays from actual experience but that Dostoevski did not know, the totalitarian state. The history of the last decades can be told in terms of this kind of society, for Hitler's Third Reich, Mussolini's Fascist Italy, Soviet Russia, and China are salient examples of it. By means of its police powers the totalitarian state exercises control over the actions of its citizens; it also attempts, with a considerable degree of success, to win their acquiescence and attachment by providing (or promising) material and social benefits that will relieve them of care and anxiety. It represents itself in a paternal guise, as taking responsibility for the well-being of its people, on condition that they delegate—actually surrender—to the government their will and initiative. There are, of course, genuinely democratic states which make the welfare of their citizens a chief aim of their existence—Sweden is the example most often cited—and it may be said that, to one extent or another, the ideal of welfare plays a part in the theory of all highly developed social organizations today. But even in democratic societies, and even by people who are advocates of the view that it is the duty of governments to underwrite the security and contentment of their citizens, the fear is often expressed that such a program, if carried far enough, might seduce men into conformity and passivity, leading them to give up the freedom of individual will which we believe makes people fully human. And it is just this surrender of freedom that the Grand Inquisitor regards as a necessary condition of the peace and happiness of mankind and that he confidently expects will be brought about by the development of the all-powerful, all-providing state.

The historical prescience of "The Grand Inquisitor" is indeed remarkable, but we need not be astonished by it, as if it were visionary. It derives from Dostoevski's willingness to take seriously the social and political speculations which were current in the intellectual life of his day, and from his ability to believe that what at the moment existed only in theory and desire would eventually come to exist in fact. He had but to project his bitterly adverse interpretation of the ideals of socialism and imagine them carried out to their furthest possibility to conceive most of the characteristics of the Grand Inquisitor's state. Its remaining traits were provided by the hostility that Dostoevski, an impassioned communicant of the Greek Orthodox Church, the national church of Russia, felt toward Roman Catholicism.

There is really nothing new in the criticism that Dostoevski directs against the Church of Rome. Even his bizarre idea that Roman

Catholicism is an agency of state socialism is a new and imaginative version of an old charge directed against the Roman Church—that it seeks to establish its worldly power at the cost of its allegiance to spirit and truth, that it has departed from the way of Jesus to follow the way of imperial Caesar. Any non-Catholic Christian who makes this accusation is likely to draw its terms from that episode in the life of Jesus known as the Temptation in the Wilderness, in which Jesus was offered temporal power by the devil and refused it. For having made that refusal the Jesus of Dostoevski's story is rebuked by the Grand Inquisitor. Here is the Gospel account of the episode as given by St. Luke (4:1–13):

And Jesus being full of the Holy Ghost returned from Jordan, and was led by the Spirit into the wilderness, being forty days tempted of the devil. And in those days he did eat nothing: and when they were ended, he afterward hungered. And the devil said unto him, If thou be the Son of God, command this stone that it be made bread. And Jesus answered him, saying, It is written, That man shall not live by bread alone, but by every word of God.

And the devil, taking him up into an high mountain, shewed unto him all the kingdoms of the world in a moment of time. And the devil said unto him, All this power will I give thee, and the glory of them: for that is delivered unto me; and to whomsoever I will give it. If thou therefore wilt worship me, all shall be thine. And Jesus answered and said unto him, Get thee behind me, Satan: for it is written, Thou shalt worship the Lord thy God, and him only shalt thou serve.

And he brought him to Jerusalem, and set him on a pinnacle of the temple, and said unto him, If thou be the Son of God, cast thyself down from hence: for it is written, He shall give his angels charge over thee, to keep thee: and in their hands they shall bear thee up, lest at any time thou dash thy foot against a stone. And Jesus answering said unto him, It is said, Thou shalt not tempt the Lord thy God.

And when the devil had ended all the temptation, he departed from him for a season.

Dostoevski's use of the episode is subtle and brilliant. The story in its Gospel form, although its high significance is unmistakable, has relatively little reverberation. Jesus resists each of the temptations with no difficulty whatever, with no indication that he is really being tempted. As why should he be?—for if what Satan offers him is, as it would seem to be, for his own gratification only, this can scarcely be a temptation to a being of his divine perfection. If, however, what the devil proposes is not for the sake of Jesus himself but for the sake of mankind, then it constitutes a temptation indeed. For then Jesus knows that in refusing the powers that are offered him, the powers of material sustenance, authority, and miracle, he is condemning mankind to hardship, strife, and doubt. And he imposes this hard destiny upon men for the sake of a mere intangible thing which does not promise even eventual happiness on earth, that is to say, for the sake of freedom—the freedom to know good and evil and to choose between them, and to seek salvation. When Jesus chooses not to seek dominion over men's hearts and minds by means of worldly power exercised on behalf of human contentment but only through their freely given faith, he knows that he subjects mankind to a heavy burden, a great trial. Thus understood, the temptation that he endures is surely a real one, and his choice may well be thought difficult even for a divine being—for a divine being whose divinity expresses itself in the entireness of his love for mankind.

And once we comprehend the nature of Jesus' temptation in Dostoevski's story, we are implicated in it—we too must choose between passive security and freedom. And the choice, as we confront it in the terms that Dostoevski contrives, is by no means simple, for the Inquisitor argues his case with the force of rationality and humaneness very much on his side. In his statement, "Feed men, and then ask of them virtue," must we not see both good sense and human sympathy? Do not all enlightened people incline to believe nowadays that "there is no crime, and therefore no sin; there is only hunger," that all antisocial behavior, as we have learned to call it, is to be explained by the circumstances that forced it on the person who is condemned as a criminal or a sinner? We are readily drawn to the belief that intelligent political and social organization can obviate public and personal tensions and thus make for peace and decent behavior on the part both of nations and individuals.

In short, on intellectual and moral grounds that we understand

and respond to, the Grand Inquisitor offers us what we want, what we feel we properly should have, and might well have, a social arrangement that points to the possibility of the Earthly Paradise. Why, then, do we reject it, as of course we do?

One way of answering the question is to recall two striking phrases that were coined some hundreds of years ago. Both refer to the loss of the original Paradise through Adam's eating the fruit of the Tree of Knowledge, the knowledge being that of good and evil. Adam's sin was called *"felix culpa,"* the happy sin; the fall of man in which the sin resulted was called "the fortunate fall." The reason why the sin was said to be "happy" and the fall "fortunate" was that they made the occasion for Jesus to undertake the redemption and salvation of man, bringing him to a yet nobler condition than before his loss of innocence. It is not necessary to accept the religious implications of this idea to respond to what it says about the nature of man—that man is not all he might be unless he bears the burden of his knowledge of good and evil, and the pain of choosing between them, and the consequences of making the wrong choice. The Grand Inquisitor speaks of man's surrendering his freedom in exchange for happiness, and he means exactly the freedom to know good and evil and to choose between them, even though with pain. The whole intention of his Earthly Paradise is to relieve man of the pain that freedom entails. We reject what he offers because its acceptance means the loss of the dignity of freedom.

Dostoevski, we can scarcely doubt, wishes us to go beyond this rejection; he would have us believe that with each rational step a polity takes toward material well-being its people are carried that much nearer to passivity, dependence, and spiritual extinction. He is at one with his Devil-Inquisitor in offering us only extreme courses, either a life of spiritual freedom in the "wilderness" or a life of slavery in society. The spell of his art is strong indeed, and while we are under its influence it needs an effort of mind to reflect that humanity is not in reality confronted with alternatives so unmodified and, we may say, so simple in their absoluteness.

The Death of Ivan Ilych

LEO TOLSTOI
1828–1910

W E ALL fear death and our imaginations balk at conceiving its actuality. We say readily enough that "all
men are mortal," but like Ivan Ilych in Tolstoi's story,
we say it as an abstract general proposition and each one of us finds
it hard to believe that the generalization has anything to do with
him in particular—with him personally, as we say. And literature
tends to encourage us in our evasion. Not that literature avoids dealing with death—on the contrary, there is probably no subject to
which it recurs more often. But even very great writers are likely to
treat it in ways which limit its fearsomeness. The death of the hero
of a tragedy, for instance, seldom seems terrible to us; we often think
of it as making a moment of peace and beauty, as constituting the
resolution of distressing conflicts. Literature inclines to soften death's
aspect by showing it as through a veil, or by suggesting that it is
sad and noble rather than terrifying, or by asking us to "accept" it
as part of life.

This tendency is wholly reversed by "The Death of Ivan Ilych."
Tolstoi does not try to reconcile us to the idea of our extinction and
he does not mask the dreadfulness of dying. Quite the contrary—not
only does he choose an instance of death that is long drawn out and
hideously painful, and dwell upon its details, but he emphasizes the
unmitigated aloneness of the dying man, the humiliation of his help-

lessness, and his abject terror at the prospect of his annihilation, as well as his bitter envy of those who still continue in existence while he is in process of becoming nothing.

Tolstoi is explicit about these aspects of death as no writer before him had ever been, and the effect is excruciating. Perhaps no work of fiction is so painful to read as this story.

Why is this vicarious torture forced upon us? We can scarcely feel that the author's purpose was purely literary, that Tolstoi chose his subject as any writer chooses a subject, because it is interesting in and for itself. We cannot doubt that his intention was other than artistic, and we conjecture that it might well be religious, for religion often tries to put us in mind of the actuality of death, not in its terrors, to be sure, but in its inevitability, seeking thus to press upon us the understanding that the life of this world is not the sum of existence, and not even its most valuable part. And the circumstances of Tolstoi's life at the time he wrote "The Death of Ivan Ilych" confirm our sense of the story's religious inspiration.

Some eight years before writing "Ivan Ilych," Tolstoi experienced a great spiritual crisis which issued in religious conversion and altered the whole course of his life. He abandoned the ways of the aristocratic class into which he had been born and undertook to live as a primitive Christian, committing himself to an extreme simplicity of life and to the service of mankind, especially the poor and the humble. He repudiated art and his own great achievements as a novelist and proposed the doctrine that artistic creation was justified only when it led men to morality and piety.

The particular nature of his crisis is most relevant to "The Death of Ivan Ilych." At the age of fifty, Tolstoi was thrown into a state of despair by his insupportably intense imagination of mortality. It was not a new problem that he confronted—even in his youth he had known periods of black depression because he felt that the inevitability of death robbed life of all meaning. In *Anna Karenina,* the great novel he had completed shortly before the onset of his crisis, Prince Levin, who closely resembles Tolstoi, cannot endure the thought that "for every man, and himself too, there was nothing but suffering, death, and oblivion." Death, he feels, makes life "the evil jest of some devil," and he must either learn to see human existence in some other way or commit suicide. Levin is able to pass beyond this terrible alternative; he overcomes his despair and accepts life for what good he may find in it. For a time it lay within Tolstoi's power to make a similar decision, but the period of calm was not of long duration; the horror of death again became unbearable and could be coped with only by the help of a religious faith.

And yet, despite this much ground for supposing that Tolstoi had an overt religious purpose in writing "The Death of Ivan Ilych," it is not easy to show that the story itself supports the hypothesis. If we search it for religious doctrine, we find none. Nor can we even discover in it any significant religious emotion. Although it is true that the conclusion, the moment of Ivan Ilych's escape from pain into peace and even into "light," is charged with feelings and described in metaphors that are part of the Christian tradition, the passage can scarcely be taken as a genuinely religious affirmation or as effectually controverting the thoughts that the dying man has had about "the cruelty of God, and the absence of God."

On the contrary, it might well seem that Tolstoi, by his representation of death, is trying to win us not to the religious life but, rather, to a full acceptance of the joys of the life of this world. From the Christian point of view, his intention might even seem to be open to the charge of paganism. It was an ancient pagan custom to seat a human skeleton at a feast as *memento mori,* a reminder of death, to urge upon the revelers the idea that life is short and that the fleeting hours must be snatched; just so does Tolstoi use Ivan Ilych's death to shock us into awareness of what it means to be alive.

And it is not the virtuous life that Tolstoi has in mind or the pious life—he means life in any actuality, any life that is really lived. Ivan Ilych is remorseful not for the sins he committed but for the pleasures he never took. "Ivan Ilych's life had been most simple and most ordinary and therefore most terrible," says Tolstoi in the famous opening sentence, and as the reader follows Ivan Ilych's career as a "successful" person, he cannot but conclude that even if the poor man's taking of pleasure had involved his sinning, his life would have been less "ordinary" and therefore less "terrible."

And this would indeed seem to be a pagan conclusion. But perhaps it is not only pagan—perhaps it is also to be understood as Christian. For without life there cannot be a spiritual life, without the capacity for joy or delight there cannot be the conception of the happiness of salvation. The first inhabitants of Hell whom Dante meets on his journey are the Neutrals or Trimmers, the people who had lived "without disgrace and without praise"—those who, as Dante says of them, "were never alive." It was thus that Ivan Ilych had lived, without disgrace and without praise, as one who was never alive. In his maturity only three things had afforded him pleasure—his official position and the power over other men that it gave him; the decoration of his pretentious and conventional home; and playing whist. He had never known the joy of loving or of being loved. He had never felt the sting of passion or the energy of impulse. He had never experienced the calm pleasure of moral satisfaction such as might come from the consciousness of having been loyal or generous. He had never admired anyone or anything; he had never been interested in anything or anyone, not even, really, in himself. He had never questioned or doubted anything, not even himself.

Indeed he had lived without any sense that he had a self or was a self. He had assumed all the roles that respectable society had assigned to him: he had been a public official, a husband, a father. But a self he had never been, not between the time of his childhood (when there had been a little glow of pleasure and affection) and the time of his dying. Only at the point of his extinction is selfhood revealed to him. The means by which the revelation is effected are agonizing; it comes through pain and fear, through self-pity, through a hopeless childlike longing for comfort and love. Yet in his his awful dissolution, Ivan Ilych is more fully a human being than he had ever been in the days of his armored unawareness of himself. And it is when he has been tortured into an awareness of his own self that he can at last, for the first time, begin to recognize the actuality of other selves, that of the young peasant Gerasim and that of his poor sad son.

The Treasure

WILLIAM SOMERSET MAUGHAM
1874-1966

No reader will fail to see, and without needing to give much thought to the matter, that "The Treasure" is different in kind from all the other stories in this volume. The difference can be stated quite simply: the other stories are serious, this one is not. It does not undertake to engage our deeper feelings or to communicate anything new about the nature of human existence. It proposes to do nothing except entertain.

Among people to whom literature is important, there are various ways of responding to writing of this kind, and one of them is exemplified by an opinion expressed by the philosopher George Santayana. In his old age Santayana had a lively appetite for contemporary fiction and a considerable openness of mind toward it. But he said that he found it impossible to read Somerset Maugham. In a letter to a friend, after mentioning that someone had given him several volumes of Maugham's stories, he went on to remark that what he chiefly felt about them was "wonder at anybody wishing to write such stories." He continued: "They are not pleasing, they are simply graphic and plausible, like a bit of a dream that one might drop into in an afternoon nap. Why record it? I suppose to make money, because writing stories is a profession. . . ."

This strikes me as doing rather less than justice both to Maugham's accomplishment and to the kind of pleasure one may take in a story like "The Treasure." Maugham does not sound our depths or invite us to sound his, and quite possibly he has no depths to be sounded. Perhaps he invites us to respond to nothing save his lively if limited intelligence and his cool mastery of his craft. But if this is not a high enterprise, it is not an ignoble one, and to some it will be engaging exactly because it has no designs upon their profound and serious selves.

Another philosopher, the French theologian and aesthetician Etienne Gilson, is more lenient than Santayana in his judgment of nonserious art, and, I think, more instructive. Gilson draws a distinction between "real painting" and what he calls "picturing," and as an example of the latter he cites the pleasant amusing scenes of American life that used to appear on the covers of *The Saturday Evening Post*. These, he says, are obviously not to be evaluated by the standards we apply to the work of a Rembrandt or a Cézanne; they nevertheless have appropriate standards of their own and they evoke from us a pleasure appropriate to their intention. They are not inferior or failed examples of another and higher art, and it is mere aesthetic snobbery to judge them as if they were and to refuse what pleasure they offer.

By analogy with Gilson's "picturing," we may think of certain kinds of fiction as "storying" and judge them within their own categories. Detective and spy novels and science fiction undertake to engage our interest by virtues that are peculiar to them, and there are discriminations of an appropriate sort to be made among them— they are good or bad or mediocre according to their own canons. Some readers find it impossible to respond to their attractions, or decide that they do not have time for them—it seems a pity!—but only a priggish and captious reader will condemn them because they do not match Hawthorne or Tolstoi in moral and spiritual power.

And indeed we cannot fail to observe of "The Treasure" that, despite its refusal to be serious and to propose any greater awareness of the actualities of existence, it does after all touch upon a subject which has pertinence to our real interests. It refers to our sense of the high value of natural impulse and the absurdity of social convention. What amuses us in the story is Harenger's intense relief that his episode of sexual intimacy with his efficient parlor-maid is not going to change their established relationship and that the ordered elegance of his life is not to be threatened. We find it comical that a man whose sexual impulse was at least strong enough to overwhelm him on one occasion, and presumably in a happy way, should set more store by his narcissistic love of comfort and orderliness than by his erotic satisfaction. The pleasures of habitual comfort are not to be despised, but our partisanship with nature and impulse is quick to pass adverse judgment on a man who prefers these to the passional pleasures. Our laughter over Harenger's choice announces our option—at least for the moment—in favor of "life."

An incidental charm of "The Treasure" is its representation of a vanished mode of life which, especially to American readers, might well seem quaint, even improbable. America has never had a servant class or the kind of class system which codifies the relationship between master and servant, nor has it countenanced for men the life of elegant comfort and self-regard that is so important to Harenger. And even in England the attitudes that the story takes for granted exist nowadays only in vestigial form. At least from a strictly literary point of view it is possible to regard this as something of a loss, for the master–servant relationship was one of the best subjects of comedy.

Duchoux

GUY DE MAUPASSANT
1850-1893

IN violation of the chronological order in which the stories of this volume are arranged, I have put "Duchoux" after "The Treasure" because I think that something is to be gained by reading the stories in this sequence. I said of "The Treasure" that it was unlike all the other stories in the volume in that it was not serious, and it seems to me that it may be enlightening to try to discover why Maugham's story fails of seriousness while Maupassant's achieves it.

The comparison has cogency because the two stories address themselves to the same theme. Each is about a man of extreme self-centeredness who is drawn to another person only to retreat from the relationship because it threatens his established mode of life. In both instances, the self-regard of the man is expressed in his attachment to a certain *style* of living—Harenger in "The Treasure" and the Baron in "Duchoux" are committed not only to comfort but to elegance.

Yet despite this virtual identity of theme, the two stories are very dissimilar in effect. If ever an author wrote stories, as Santayana says Maugham did, "because writing stories is a profession," it was Maupassant. And "Duchoux" has indeed the air of having been written only to amuse. Yet we can scarcely fail to see that Maupassant's story has a weight of meaning that Maugham's cannot claim.

The difference may in some part be explained by the kind of personal relationship each story describes. We think it odd of Harenger, and funny, that after a gratifying sexual experience, he has no wish to repeat it because to do so would interfere with the fussy arrangements of his life. He supposes, no doubt correctly, that it will make an impossible situation to have a servant who is also his mistress (marriage, of course, is not in question), and he has no difficulty in deciding that it is the servant he prefers. We smile at his choice and think him rather poor-spirited for having made it. Yet of course we know that sexual connections are often made only to be broken, that an erotic episode is nothing but a fortuitous event unless strong feelings are permitted or invited to intervene. But the relation between a father and a son is of a far more exigent kind. Literature treats it much less frequently than the sexual relation in any of its forms, but whenever it does touch upon it, the effect is likely to be grave and somberly moving. In the Bible, for example, no stories approach in tragic or pathetic import those of Abraham and Isaac, of Jacob and Benjamin, of David and Absalom. Especially if the father is advanced in years, the connection that he feels with his son is unspeakably intense, for it is, we suppose, the connection with life itself, with futurity and hope.

This being the traditional and, as it were, ideal paternal feeling, our expectations suffer a comic jolt when the Baron, coming to inspect the son he has never seen, rejects him out of hand because he dislikes his appearance, manner, and style of life. The Baron is in every way a deficient father, and of course he displays an absurd effrontery in thinking that he has the right to intrude himself into his son's life at this late date, as well as a monumental stupidity in fancying that he could possibly find happiness in his son's home. Yet despite his selfishness, arrogance, and stupidity, our sympathy, such as it is, goes out to the Baron—certainly to him rather than to his son.

How is this response to be explained? The Baron's rejection of his son is a very drastic action—for a father to "disown" a son, even for weighty reasons, is, we feel, a violation of nature. Our sense of this is so strong that it extends, as in the present instance, even to a father's disowning an illegitimate son whom he is seeing for the first time. We expect that "nature" and "blood" will assert themselves, that across the gulfs of their separate lives, something in each man will respond to the other; at least that the father, who is aware of the connection, will feel it strongly when in the presence of the son. Our piety prepares us for that moving dramatic event, the scene of recognition, and of course we fail to get it. And yet, cheated of our expectations though we are, we take pleasure in the Baron's decision not to disclose the relationship. The Baron, we feel, could not do otherwise than conclude that he was not, after all, a father if it was M. Duchoux who was his son. And we experience a certain satisfaction as our instinctual pieties are checked and challenged by our skeptical intelligence, which poses the question, What is a son?

It is a question that has been asked, in a very memorable way, by William Butler Yeats in one of his finest poems, "Among School Children." As Yeats puts the question, it refers not to a father's but to a mother's idea of what a son is, but its force is the same. The poet is visiting a girls' school in an official capacity and as he stands among the little pupils, he becomes conscious of his age, of his being "a sixty-year-old smiling public man," and he asks whether this could possibly have been what his mother envisioned when she conceived him in delight, bore him in agony, and reared him in hope.

> What youthful mother, a shape upon her lap [,]
> . . . .
> Would think her son, did she but see that shape
> With sixty or more winters on its head,
> A compensation for the pang of his birth,
> Or the uncertainty of his setting forth?

The implication is that the mother would have lovingly imagined the son as a baby, as a little boy, as a youth, as a young man, with the charm or beauty appropriate to each age, but that she would scarcely be entranced by the thought of him in old age.

Yeats puts the question in a high, poignant way; Maupassant puts it comically and with a touch of cynicism. What is a son? Whatever else he may be, for a parent of any imagination at all, he is not merely a person in his own right but the fulfilment, in some degree, of the right way for a man to be. Whatever he may be, it is clear what a son cannot be—a short, plump, fidgety man, who, when he talks of business, wags his round head in satisfaction, who has embraced middle age before his time, whose mind gives no sign of being able to rise above real estate deals and a sordid, garlicky domesticity. Such a man denies anyone's idea of a son—M. Duchoux himself would be dismayed by a son in his own image!

Enemies

ANTON CHEKHOV
1860–1904

WHOEVER tries to account for the peculiar charm of Chekhov's work will sooner or later touch upon a certain personal trait of the author which is suggested by his stories and plays. If we try to give this quality a name, we may call it *modesty*. Chekhov is a writer of the very highest distinction. He set great store by art, insisted on the importance of its function in our lives, and was jealous for the status of the artist in society. But in everything he wrote he seems to be saying that he does not claim for himself the brilliant dominating powers that are often thought to be the essence of artistic genius. He was a physician, although he eventually gave up medicine for literature, and in his conception of himself as a writer there is something of the self-effacement we like to think is appropriate to a good medical practitioner, subordination of himself to the case he deals with and a gentle deference to the suffering he observes.

His modesty is to be seen not only in his manner but in his choice of subjects. Chekhov does not try to achieve the intensities of Tolstoi and Dostoevski, his great compatriots of the generation before his own. He was one of the most intelligent of men, and we may suppose that there was nothing in the Russia of his time of which he was unaware, but he did not undertake to confront the high issues of politics, religion, and morality that play so decisive a part in the work of the two pre-eminent Russian novelists; his stories and plays do not deal directly with grandiose public concerns or with transcendent intentions of good or evil. His expressed sense of the nature of human existence refers to muted passions, frustrated hopes, affronted self-esteem, the boredom and listlessness that overtake once-aspiring spirits, the dull pain of isolation and alienation. It is as if he were telling us, with characteristic compassion, that the life of a man as it was lived in his time in Czarist Russia is too restricted and hampered to admit the possibility of conduct and emotions which could achieve that grandeur we call heroic.

His implicit denial of the possibility of the heroic mode does not make Chekhov unique in his time, or ours. On the contrary, it brings him into one of the most important general tendencies of literature of the past three or four centuries, the adverse questioning of the heroic mode.

In the sense in which the word is most likely to be used in the history of literature, the heroic is not in the first place a category of morality but, rather, a category of style. In everyday speech we use the word to convey the idea of courage of a striking kind and its significance does not go beyond this. But in the traditional literary conception of the heroic character, although courage is indeed an essential element, it is not in itself definitive. It was essential because a person without courage cannot possibly be a person of dignity, and what is definitive of the heroic character is his dignity. Dignity, however, is not in itself a moral quality—it is a quality of appearance, of style or manner.

Not every tradition of heroic literature in Europe was directly influenced by the requirements laid down by Aristotle for the classical hero of tragedy, but all traditions have required the hero to be a person who commands our respect by reason both of his exalted social position and the qualities of temperament that are presumed to accord with this position. He was also expected to have an appearance and manner appropriate to his princely rank and temperament. Aristotle described the heroic mode only in connection with a certain kind of poetic composition, tragedy; and he understood tragedy not merely in terms of the catastrophic fate it represented but also in terms of its style, every element of which—every detail of language, music, deportment, and costume—must suggest loftiness and grandeur. Ancient tragedy made no pretensions to what we call realism. As Aristotle said by way of definition, it shows men as nobler than they really are, by which he meant more dignified and impressive than they really are. On the stage, the tragic hero indicates his nobility by the style in which he speaks and comports himself, and it is on the stage, we must remember, that the hero really has his being. An authority on the Greek theatre, Professor Margaret Bieber, reminds us of this when she says, "The hero is an actor." And the late Robert Warshow, in a brilliant essay on "Western" movies, says much the same thing when he defines the hero of a "Western" as "a man who looks like a hero."

The literary and histrionic nature of the heroic mode does not keep it from having its effect upon actual life. Indeed, it suggests an ideal to which men may actually aspire—the qualities that engage men in poetry and on the stage do so because, in one way or another, they seem desirable in our daily lives. Dignity is of course a quality of style or manner, but it has substantial and obvious moral and social implications as well; it implies the right to respect, which an American poet has called, with a curious courage of simplicity, "the ultimate good."* At the same time, exactly because the heroic mode is so essentially literary and histrionic, and so much concerned to transcend the actuality of the commonplace, it is open to adverse judgment. We feel that it celebrates form above content, appearance above reality; we therefore accuse it of being false, pretentious, and highfalutin. At all times, even among the Greeks themselves, the idea of the heroic has been subject to satire and burlesque. In the sixteenth century the mockery of the heroic becomes, in fact, one of the great themes of literature. Shakespeare in *Troilus and Cressida* flatly denied the dignity of the warrior princes who were the heroes of Greek epic and tragedy. In *Henry IV* he questioned the heroic ideal even more memorably in the opposition

* John Berryman, "The Statue," in *The Dispossessed*.

of Hotspur and Falstaff, the former ready to sacrifice his very life for the dignity of his honor, the latter mocking honor and dignity as mere words. By the end of the century, criticism of the heroic mode was in full cry. The first great novel, Cervantes' *Don Quixote* (1605–1615), begins as a satire on the heroic idea; and it is remarkable how many of the major novelists, from Fielding in the eighteenth century to James Joyce in the twentieth, make comedy out of the contrast between life as it appears in the literature of the heroic tradition and life as it really is.

But however much the writers of the last three hundred and fifty years may burlesque the heroic ideal, their preoccupation with it suggests that its power over the human mind is still very great. If, with many of our novelists, we take intense note of the dull and trivial circumstances in which we live our daily lives, and call this "reality," we do so with a degree of resentment, under the shadow, as it were, of our sense of the heroic. The realistic novel, we might say, is haunted, if not by the presence, then by the absence, of the heroic idea.

Certainly this is true of the work of Chekhov. His best plays and stories represent the pathos of lives from which the possibility of the heroic has been removed even while the conception of it remains— in the recollection that life once promised a dignity it has since denied; in the memory that people once commanded a respect that can no longer be won either from others or from themselves.

The story "Enemies" is an especially subtle and sad and comic treatment of this omnipresent preoccupation with the heroic mode. Aboguin, the deceived husband, thrusts a photograph of his unfaithful wife at the doctor, the bereaved father, who cries out in passionate revulsion, "I don't want your trivial vulgar secrets. . . ." By the contemptuous adjectives that spring to his lips, the doctor lays claim to the heroic status. Triviality and vulgarity—these are the two qualities that, above all others, constitute the negation of the heroic ideal. And the bereaved father will have none of them. He thinks of his grief as conferring dignity upon him, as giving him a spiritual status which can compete with Aboguin's superior social position. His sorrow validates his existence as what he calls "a real man," and in a passion of pride he resents the intrusion of Aboguin's less noble pain.

Up to the moment when Dr. Kirilov uses his grief to assert his dignity, both grief and dignity have been very real indeed. Stricken and silent, so worn out by sorrow that he is scarcely able to move, facing the end of all hope, almost of all life, yet grimly consenting to discharge his duty, the doctor stands before us with a kind of rigid nobility, demanding both our sympathy and our respect in the highest degree. But when he asserts his right to be thought heroic and tragic because of his suffering, when he says that he must not be involved in a "vulgar comedy" or a "melodrama," and uses his terrible loss to belittle Aboguin and gain moral advantage over him, his grief becomes less compelling and his stature as a man is diminished.

Chekhov makes it as hard as possible for us to withdraw our moral approval from Dr. Kirilov. Our sympathies on his behalf are engaged by his profession, his social circumstances, his devotion to his wife, his age, and the nature of his loss. His antagonist—one might say his competitor in grief—is clearly a person of far less seriousness, sincerity, and depth of feeling. We can scarcely fail to know that the wounded pride of Aboguin will soon heal and become a mere grievance against his faithless wife. The doctor, we are sure, will never have another son in his marriage, but Aboguin will undoubtedly acquire a new wife. But although Chekhov is quite aware of Aboguin's personal inferiority to Kirilov, it is upon the latter that the weight of his moral disapproval falls. What offends him is the doctor's bitter insistence on his superiority as a person and mourner, the fact that Kirilov puts his grief at the service of his social competitiveness.

It is often said of Chekhov that he, more than any other writer, has influenced the theory and practice of the modern short-story. This is true, yet it is worth remarking that there is one element of "Enemies" that must be called anything but modern. No writer of our day would permit himself the passages of generalization and moralizing with which the story ends. The modern theory of fiction, learned in considerable part from Chekhov himself, is that the events of a story must speak for themselves, without the help of the author's explicit comment. (Hemingway's "Hills Like White Elephants" is an extreme demonstration of this fictional technique.) In any course on the short story an enlightened teacher would surely instruct his students that they must not, as Chekhov does here, tell the reader about the bad effects of unhappiness upon the character, or prophesy what Dr. Kirilov's moral future will be. But I find this surrender of the artist's remoteness in favor of a direct communication with the reader refreshing as well as moving. The willingness of Chekhov to put himself on a level with the reader and to speak in his own person seems to me an instance of the charming modesty of his spirit.

The Pupil

HENRY JAMES
1843–1916

THE pathos of Morgan Moreen's fate is twofold, that of the
child and that of the genius. As a genius, Morgan is nobody's child—the great point of his curious existence is that
nothing has come to him from his parents. Henry James speaks of
the "mysteries of transmission" and of the "far jumps of heredity,"
speculating that the quality of Morgan's spirit can perhaps be traced
to some unknown remote ancestor. But he really means that Morgan's quality, like all great human endowments, cannot be explained.

If the quality of Morgan's spirit does indeed amount to genius,
it is not of the artistic kind. Rather, it is a genius of perception and
morality—Morgan possesses the rare gift of seeing things as they
really are and of judging them justly. He is thus at the opposite
extreme from his family, all of whom are committed only to the appearance of things. As the boy says in one of his moments of expressed misery, "All they care about is to make an appearance and
to pass for something or other." They are sunk in worldliness,
hopelessly bound to the hope of acquiring social standing. Their
whole view of life, we are told, is not only "rapacious and mean," but
also "dim and confused and instinctive," devoid of any trace of the
bright conscious intelligence that makes Morgan what he is.

In some sense Morgan is no less worldly than his family. For it is the world—the worldly world of "society," of social status and the petty scheming by which it is won—that makes the matter upon which his intelligence exercises itself. About the actualities of this world he knows far more than his family does. If we respond to him as a truly innocent person, it is not because he is ignorant of corruption, or naïve about it. His innocence derives from his gift of seeing things as they are and calling them by their right names.

The word *innocence* means, literally, harmless, being without sin or guilt. But certain additional meanings attach to it, of which one is *cleanness:* in our culture, white is the emblematic color of innocence and *spotlessness* its frequent synonym. And the idea of cleanness must often occur to us in the course of reading "The Pupil," in which moral deficiency is represented by a soiled shabbiness.

The note is struck in the first paragraph of the story, for nothing could be more precisely indicative of the moral life of Morgan's family than the condition of Mrs. Moreen's gloves, those "soiled *gants de Suède*." Thereafter James misses no opportunity to remind us of the slovenliness of the Moreen mode of life. Mrs. Moreen's handkerchief is as soiled as her gloves; she thinks nothing of having an interview with Pemberton in his bedroom in the morning, wearing a dressing gown and sitting on the unmade bed; her daughters are not likely to be presentably dressed except when company is expected; her husband has been seen shaving in the drawing room.

The disorder and sordidness of the Moreen household are not indicative of any moral depravity, only of a deficient sense of reality. Mr. and Mrs. Moreen are very much at ease in talking about high ideals of moral sensibility. This, to be sure, suits their purposes of fraud, especially in their dealings with poor Pemberton, but they are not wholly insincere, or at least they are not wholly conscious of their insincerity. In some part they are themselves taken in by what they say about delicacy of conduct. And it is just this easy self-deception that defeats them in their career of deceit. For these people have no talent whatever for the way of life they have chosen. Brother Ulick fancies himself a gambler, but it is usually he who is fleeced. Paula and Amy are never able to advance their plans for advantageous marriages. And the mother who aspires to marry one of her daughters to an English lord does not have sense enough to know that this is an enterprise that requires clean gloves and handkerchiefs.

It is only Morgan who comprehends the hopelessness of the family's undertaking and it is only he who perceives what it is that makes their failure inevitable—they lack the simple self-respect that is necessary for success even in a life of fraud. Nothing pains Morgan more than his family's deficiency of pride, which, as he sees, makes them the object of the world's contempt. And it offends his intelligence, his acute sense of reality, that because they lack pride they must scheme and cheat with no possible chance of success, that concerned as they are with appearances they do not know how they themselves appear to others.

James's condemnation of the Moreen "troupe" is open and unqualified. Yet he would have had no story if he had not given us the right to feel at least a little tenderness for Morgan's family. There would have been no story, that is, if Morgan did not love them, and he would not have loved them if they had not loved him. They do not love him enough, or wisely. But they do cherish him, or some idea of him; it was they who first perceived his "genius," which they respect without understanding. Their relation to Morgan is said to be possession rather than love, yet even possession is connection of a kind, and it is not until his parents surrender possession of him that Morgan dies.

And yet it is not the Moreens whom the story seems to hold accountable for Morgan's death. The blame falls upon Pemberton. We are naturally reluctant to observe this. For one thing, all through the story our censure has been directed to the Moreens; we have been trained, as it were, to hold them responsible for everything bad. And of course we have it well in mind how admirably Pemberton has behaved for four long years. We can grant that he is a rather passive young man who cannot think of a better way to make a living than as a private tutor and who is unable to insist on his rights; inevitably this somewhat diminishes the nobility we want to attribute to his devotion to Morgan. Yet even when these deductions are made, Pemberton still seems to stand as an example of that medieval loyalty of one person to another upon which Henry James, like Joseph Conrad, set the highest moral value.

Pemberton's loyalty, however, turns out to be fatally flawed. James gives no explanation of the change that has occurred in Pemberton to make him think so bitterly of the proposal that he take charge of Morgan's life, or none beyond the tutor's sense that "his youth [was] going and that he was getting nothing back for it." The idea of Morgan's going away to live with Pemberton had not originated, we recall, either with Morgan or the Moreens but with Pemberton himself—it was he who, in the first flush of his affection for Morgan, had suggested that the two "go off and live somewhere together." It had then been only a fantasy, although not without its seriousness. But now, when Pemberton returns to the Moreens after his period in England, he has the sense that Morgan is delivering the whole of his life into his care, and he can think of the responsibility only in an ugly way. Morgan's life presents itself to him as nothing but a "burden," and a burden which is not merely heavy but "blighting." What he had once seen as so bright and precious now figures in his mind as a "dreadful little life." Morgan, recovering from his crushing humiliation over his parents' sordid ruin, is enraptured at the prospect of going off with his friend, but the tutor, once so spontaneous in his affection, cannot meet the boy's rush of joy with anything more than the awareness that a warm response was called for. "When he [Morgan] stammered, 'My dear fellow, what do you say to *that?'* how could one not say something enthusiastic?" We are told that Morgan's seizure "immediately followed" Pemberton's response to Morgan's joy with nothing more than a recognition of the obligation to be enthusiastic. Mrs. Moreen's wail, "But I thought he *wanted* to go to you!" urges it upon us that Morgan's death "followed" not merely in point of time but as an effect follows a cause—the mother seems to see that the boy would not have died if he *had* wanted to go to Pemberton. We conclude that he no longer wanted to go because he was no longer wanted.

Throughout most of the story we have accepted Pemberton as not much more than the person through whose eyes we observe events. But as the story comes to its end, we must see him as something more, a moral agent. As such he fails. Out of his love for Morgan, he had given much, four years of his life. Yet it seems to be one of the paradoxes of love that the more one gives the more one commits oneself to give. But it is also true that, as Yeats says, "Too long a sacrifice makes a stone of the heart," even too long a sacrifice made in love. If we pass an adverse judgment on Pemberton, it must be with the awareness of how very difficult love is, with the understanding that only a saint or a genius of morality would have met the demands of the situation in which this poor young man was placed. Still, we cannot avoid judging him adversely: there are occasions when, if a man is not a saint or a moral genius, he is nothing at all.

The Secret Sharer

JOSEPH CONRAD
1857–1924

ONE of literature's most engaging themes is the initiation of a boy or a young man into a new stage of his development toward maturity. We have seen it strikingly handled in "My Kinsman, Major Molineux," and now we meet it again in "The Secret Sharer," which sustains comparison with Hawthorne's story in the subtlety and range of its psychological drama.

Some of the power of "The Secret Sharer" derives from the particular profession to which its young protagonist has devoted himself. It is a profession whose moral implications are large and manifest, for the captain of a ship exercises an authority unique in its extent, and he bears a proportionate responsibility. In the official language of maritime affairs he is called a *master*. The old-fashioned word has a double meaning. The captain is a master-mariner in the sense that once obtained when people spoke of a master-builder or a master-mason, meaning a craftsman who has been certified by his guild as knowing all that he should know of his craft or trade. A ship's captain is master of the whole art of managing a ship. Of all the ship's company, he is the man who knows most through experience and study, his knowledge having been certified by rigorous examination. (Conrad held a master's certificate in the British merchant service, and there was nothing in his life of which he was prouder.) But the captain is also master in the sense that, on the ship he commands, his word is law. The maritime code of every nation forbids his orders to be questioned, let alone disobeyed.

For any man, but especially for a man as young and as sensitive as Conrad's captain, the occasion of his taking his first command is crucial indeed. How significant is the phrase *to take command!* We say that a man is *given* the command of a ship, but the moment comes when he must *take* what he is given, when by his bearing and his conduct he must make plain his belief that he has the right to exercise the authority of his position. He does so at some cost, for by the nature and extent of his authority he is cut off from the rest of the ship's company and condemned to a lonely existence—one cannot be on familiar terms with those from whom one requires not merely cooperation but obedience, perhaps at the risk of their lives. When, in Conrad's story, the young captain says that he will stand the first watch himself, in part moved to do so by the knowledge that his officers and crew are fatigued from some days of hard work before his arrival, this unconventional behavior, his undertaking of a duty inappropriate to his status as a captain, raises uneasy questions in the minds of his subordinates; far from reassuring them of his good intentions, his act leads them to wonder about his capacity to command.

Their doubts of their captain are, of course, an echo of his own doubts of himself. He is by no means easy about his new status. He is conscious of being "the youngest man on board (barring the second mate)"; it is not easy for a young man of any degree of sensitivity to assume authority over his elders, even though they may be his inferiors in intelligence and education. This natural youthful diffidence is accentuated by his readiness to make large demands upon himself. Nothing is more characteristic of him than his concern over how he will meet the test he imposes on himself—to wonder, as he says, how far he would "turn out faithful to that ideal conception of one's own personality every man sets up for himself secretly." It is surely not true that *every* man sets up for himself an ideal conception of his personality such as this young man does and, of those who do, not many have controlling images of their best selves so rigorous as the young captain's, or so grandiose. "In this breathless pause at the threshold of a long passage," he says, "we [that is, he and his ship] seemed to be measuring our fitness for a long and arduous enterprise, the appointed task of both our existences to be carried out, far from all human eyes, with only sky and sea for spectators and for judges." It is no ordinary young man, no ordinary ship's captain, who thinks of his existence as having its "appointed task," the performance of which is to be watched and judged by no mere human eyes but by, as it were, the universe itself.

A young man in this relation to an ideal is in some sense a divided being—he stands apart from himself to take his own measure; he exists both as an actual self and as the self he aspires to be. The time will come when he will, as the phrase goes, "find himself," but until then his conduct may well be checked and hampered by the division in his being. In the captain's situation his state of mind is given a literal, objective form by the disconcerting presence of Leggatt, whom he speaks of as exactly his "other self," the "secret sharer" of his existence.

The secrecy with which Leggatt's presence on the ship must be enshrouded is not an innocent one. The salient fact about Leggatt is that he is a murderer. The word may seem harsh in view of the extenuating circumstances of Leggatt's crime and the sympathy that his personality evokes. Yet the ugly word conveys the simple truth—however understandable Leggatt's act may seem to the captain and to us, it would be severely condemned in a court of law and in all probability severely punished. Are we then to conclude that when the young captain commits himself to Leggatt, taking his admired guest to be the ideal conception of his own personality, it is Leggatt's fatal violence that constitutes the ideality to which he aspires? There appears to be some ground for this conclusion in the fact that Leggatt's crime makes the single point of real difference between the captain and his hidden guest, the one element of Leggatt's being which is not already matched by the captain's. In all other respects, as their immediate sympathy with each other suggests, the two young men are virtually the same person. They are scarcely distinguishable in appearance; they share memories of *Conway,* the school ship for merchant seamen on which both had been trained, although at different times; they are of the same social class, having the same degree of social superiority not only to the members of the crew but to all the officers, including the captain of the *Sephora;* and they are alike in their high devotion to the profession they have in common. There is only the crime of one of them to make a difference between them, and it would seem to lie within the logic of the story that what constitutes Leggatt's ideality for the captain is his having killed a man who stood in the way of his effectual exercise of command.

Certainly the captain is singularly unmoved by Leggatt's act. Even before he knows about the extenuating circumstances of the killing, he is disposed to make light of it. To Leggatt's declaration, "I've killed a man," he has an explanation which comes with startling readiness—"'Fit of temper,'" he "confidently" replies. And when he hears the details of the episode, he is quick to understand that "the same strung-up force which had given twenty-four men a chance, at least, for their lives, had, in a sort of recoil, crushed an unworthy mutinous existence." As the captain well knows, this is not at all the view of the case that would be taken by the men of his crew, and of course he knows, from Leggatt's account, that it is not at all the view that was taken by the crew and the captain of Leggatt's ship: any doubt he might have on this score is dispelled by the sentiments expressed by the search party from the *Sephora.* Leggatt himself takes the killing with considerably more seriousness than the captain. He speaks of it as an "ugly business"; he remembers how tenacious had been his grip on the man's throat; he does not palter with the fact that it had been his intention to kill; he is under no illusion that the act had been a *necessity* of command: he is quite clear that it had been committed in uncontrollable rage.

Yet although Leggatt regards the incident gravely enough, he too, like the captain, understands his murderous violence as "a sort of recoil" from the terrible energy needed to enforce authority in a desperate situation; he does not take it upon his conscience. He regrets his act but has no remorse over it. He and the captain are at one in by-passing the judgment of society, both its morality and its code of law. The two young men do not think of themselves as available to judgment by standards that are merely social—they submit only to the imperatives of a transcendent law, that of "sea and sky"; their sense of duty is defined not merely by their relation to society but by their relation to the universe.

If we try to make explicit what Conrad's story communicates symbolically, we may say that the disconcerting secret that the young captain undertakes to hide from the crew in hiding Leggatt is the coercive *force* that lies concealed at the heart of all authority. Yet it is not simply because Leggatt has revealed this grim ultimate truth about what it means to command that the captain recognizes in him the ideal conception of personality to which he must be faithful. Rather, what engages the captain's loyalty to his guest is that Leggatt had risked everything in the service of his lofty view of duty. In an extreme situation he had dared to call upon the coercive force that, lying concealed in all authority, ought never be exposed; in the use of this force, his passion for duty had over-reached itself by what we are asked to think of as a mishap of the emotions, with the tragic result that Leggatt is now forever barred from the exercise of command. In destroying that "unworthy mutinous existence" he had destroyed himself, or what he believes to be the best part of himself, his career as a ship's officer. The young captain's loyalty to Leggatt, his other and ideal self, takes the form of assuming a risk no less grave than Leggatt's and of the same kind. Knowing that all his future, "the only future for which [he] was fit," would in all likelihood be destroyed by any mishap to his ship, and in the face of the terrified astonishment of his officers and men, who think him quite literally insane, the captain sails dangerously close to shore to give Leggatt a chance to swim for his life. Leggatt drops over the side. The captain is at last alone and at one with himself, freed, we may say, of the guilty secret of command by his willingness to acknowledge it.

The Dead

JAMES JOYCE
1882–1941

"He died when he was only seventeen!" says Gretta Conroy when she tells her husband about Michael Furey. "Isn't it a terrible thing to die so young as that?" But no reader will give the answer that Gretta seems to expect from her husband. No reader upon whom the story has had its intended effect can fail to know that it is better to have died as Michael Furey died than to have lived after the fashion of Gabriel Conroy and all the other guests at the Christmas party. And this is the answer that Gabriel Conroy does indeed give when he lies down beside his sleeping wife. "Better pass boldly into that other world," he thinks, "in the full glory of some passion, than fade and wither dismally with age." The title of the story, we eventually understand, refers less to Michael Furey than to Gabriel Conroy, to the guests at the Christmas party, to all the people of Ireland as Conroy now perceives them. They, although still breathing, are the truly dead, and young Michael Furey, if only because he exists as he does in the minds of Gretta and Gabriel Conroy, is alive, a clearly defined personal entity, a strong energy.

"The Dead" is the last, the longest, and the most complex of the stories of James Joyce's first volume of fiction, *Dubliners*. Of this book Joyce said, "My intention was to write a chapter of the moral history of my country and I chose Dublin for the scene because the city seemed to me the centre of paralysis." What Joyce had in mind when he spoke of "paralysis" is suggested by an incident in "The Dead," Aunt Julia's singing. For a fleeting moment there is a remission of the "paralysis," for the old lady sings surprisingly well, and we are told that "to follow the voice was to feel and share the excitement of swift and secure flight." *The excitement of swift and secure flight:* here is life as the poets wish it to be, as we all at some time imagine it possibly can be. But in quoting the sentence, I have omitted a qualifying clause. The whole sentence reads: "To follow the voice, without looking at the singer's face, was to feel and share the excitement of swift and secure flight." If one did look at her face, Joyce is telling us, one saw the approach of death and the limitation of mind and spirit that marks not Aunt Julia alone but all the relatives and friends who are gathered around her. One saw the poverty of experience and passion, of gaiety, wit, intelligence— the death-in-life of a narrow, provincial existence.

Joyce writes of his own nation and city with passionate particularity. But when we consider the very high place that "The Dead" has been given in the canon of modern literature, and the admiration it has won from readers of the most diverse backgrounds, we must say that Joyce has written a chapter in the moral history not only of his own country but of the whole modern Western world. Gabriel Conroy's plight, his sense that he has been overtaken by death-in-life, is shared by many in our time: it is one of the characteristics of modern society that an ever-growing number of people are not content to live by habit and routine and by the unquestioning acceptance of the circumstances into which they have been born. They believe they have the right to claim for themselves pleasure, or power, or dignity, or fullness of experience; a prerogative which in former times was exercised by relatively few people, usually members of the privileged classes, and which now seems available to many people regardless of class. Yet almost in the degree that modern man feels free to assert the personal claims which are the expression of a heightened sense of individuality, he seems to fall prey to that peculiarly modern disorder so often remarked by novelists, psychologists, and sociologists—an uncertainty about who the person is who makes the claims, a diminished sense of his personal identity.

Identity is the word that Gabriel Conroy uses when he thinks about death: he sees "his own identity . . . fading out into a grey impalpable world." And his imagination of death provides the image of his life. All through the evening his identity had been fading out into the grey impalpable world of his aunts' party. All through his youth and his early middle-age his identity had been fading out into the grey impalpable world of Dublin society.

It is sometimes said that Gabriel Conroy is what James Joyce would have been, or what he supposed he would have been, if he had not fled Dublin at the age of twenty, with no resources but his talent and his youth, risking privation for the sake of achievement and fame. And certainly the juxtaposition of the author and his character helps us understand Gabriel Conroy. Joyce was one of an old and rare species of man: he was a genius, with all the stubborn resistance and courage, all the strong sense of identity, by which, in addition to great gifts, genius is defined. Gabriel Conroy is one of a new, and very numerous, kind of man whose large demand upon life is supported neither by native gift nor moral energy. He has the knowledge of excellence but cannot achieve it for himself; he admires distinction and cannot attain it.

Poor Conroy's deficiency manifests itself most saliently and sadly in his relation to his wife. Gretta is a person of rather considerable distinction; among the guests at the party she is the only woman who possesses beauty, charm, and temperament. She is vivacious and spirited, and, as her evocation of the dead Michael Furey suggests, she has a capacity for intense feeling. To this endowment her husband responds with admiration and love, but he has the dim, implicit knowledge that he cannot match it with qualities of his own. When his wife tells him the story of her girlhood romance, his inarticulate self-knowledge is suddenly made explicit and devastating. The sharp clarity with which Michael Furey has remained in Gretta's consciousness, his embodiment of will and passion, make plain to Gabriel Conroy how fully he himself has succumbed to his aunts' impalpable grey world of habit, respectability, and mediocrity.

The literary means by which Joyce represents the world of Conroy's friends and relatives are striking in their subtlety and diversity. If Joyce has an opinion about the people who gather at the old aunts'—and we know he has—he does not express it overtly. At times he seems to subordinate his own judgment to theirs, as when he gravely tells us about the serving maid Lily that she "seldom made a mistake in the orders, so that she got on well with her three mistresses. They were fussy, that was all. But the only thing they would not stand was back answers." Now and then he seems to yield to the spirit of the party and uses a prose which, in a fatigued way, takes on something of the consciously fanciful humor of Dickens in his scenes of jollification: "On the closed square piano a pudding in a huge yellow dish lay in waiting and behind it were three squads of bottles of stout and ale and minerals, drawn up according to the colours of their uniforms, the first two black, with brown and red labels, the third and smallest squad white, with transverse green sashes." For the most part, however, the tone of the prose is neutral and a little naive, as if Joyce has no point of view of his own, or as if he were saying that he has no wish to judge, let alone to blame— for how can one blame the dead for being dead?

Nothing could be more brilliant and subtle, or humane, than Joyce's management of his own—and our—relation to Gabriel Conroy. All the details of Conroy's behavior at the party contribute to our perception of his second-rateness. But we are never invited to despise him, we are never permitted to triumph over him. Joyce spares him nothing in making us aware of his mediocrity: we know all about his nervous desire to be liked and approved, his wish to be thought superior, his fear of asserting whatever superiority he may actually have, his lack of intellectual and emotional courage, his sulky resentment when he feels slighted, his easy sentimentality. But at the same time Joyce does not obscure Conroy's genuine intention of kindness, his actual considerateness, his demand upon himself that he be large-minded and generous. And he protects Conroy from our ultimate contempt by making plain the extent of his fairly accurate self-knowledge; there is little we discern to Conroy's discredit that the unhappy man does not himself know and deplore.

But self-knowledge cannot save Conroy from being the kind of man he is, and when we try to say what that kind is, we are bound to think of his commitment to galoshes. In the British Isles, much more than in America, the wearing of galoshes and rubbers is regarded as an excessive and rather foolish caution about one's health. The fact that Conroy makes such a great thing of wearing them himself and urges them on his wife—but on the night of the party she defies him—puts him in almost too obvious contrast with Michael Furey, who had died from standing in the rain to bid his love farewell. It is Conroy's sense of his vulnerability, his uneasy feeling that almost every situation is a threat, that makes him what he is. He has no valid reason to think that the servant girl is really angry with him; when she responds to his remark about her getting married, her "great bitterness" is directed not at him but at the conditions of her life, yet Conroy feels that "he had made a mistake," that he had "failed" with her, and he is extravagantly distressed. He is equally self-conscious and timorous in his half-flirtatious dispute with Miss Ivors, feeling that the nature of their relation makes it impossible for him to "risk a grandiose phrase with her." He does indeed achieve a moment of dignity when he is moved by desire for his wife, but even here he protects himself, resolving to postpone his wooing until he is certain of being fully responded to. And when he does at last speak, it is to make an irrelevant and banal remark that quite belies his emotion.

Conroy's own last adverse judgment on himself is extreme—he sees himself as "a ludicrous figure, acting as a pennyboy for his aunts, a nervous, well-meaning sentimentalist, orating to vulgarians and idealising his own clownish lusts, the pitiable fatuous fellow he had caught a glimpse of in the mirror." This extravagance of self-contempt is not only the outcome of self-knowledge; it is also the expression of Conroy's self-pity, an emotion which we are taught to despise. But Joyce does not despise it and he does not permit us to despise it. As Conroy lies in defeat and meditation beside his sleeping wife, his evocation of the sadness of life under the dominion of death is the climax of his self-pity, yet when his commiseration with himself reaches this point of intensity, the author's own emotion is seen to be in active accord with it. This sudden identification of the author with his character is one of the most striking and effective elements of the story. Joyce feels exactly what Conroy feels about the sadness of human life, its terrible nearness to death, and the *waste* that every life is; he directs no irony upon Conroy's grief but makes Conroy's suffering his own, with no reservations whatever. At several points in the story he has clearly regarded Conroy's language, or the tone of his thoughts, as banal, or vulgar, or sentimental. But as the story approaches its conclusion, it becomes impossible for us to know whose language we are hearing, Conroy's or the author's, or to whose tone of desperate sorrow we are responding. It is as if Joyce, secure in his genius and identity, were saying that under the aspect of the imagination of death and death-in-life there is no difference between him and the mediocre, sentimental man of whom he has been writing.

The Hunter Gracchus

FRANZ KAFKA
1883–1924

ALMOST any reader of this story will say, or perhaps cry out in distraction, "What can it mean? What can this strange narrative be trying to communicate to me?" He will find himself baffled at virtually every point—he cannot tell where the story takes place, or when, or by what logic one of its events follows another. Indeed, his first desperate question might well be, "What is this story trying *to do to me?*" For, by unsettling his sense of the actual, it will have made him uneasy and apprehensive.

And yet, for all its defiance of our reason, we cannot doubt that Kafka's story does intend to say something to us. We know, even on a first puzzled reading, what *kind* of thing it is saying: something of large import, having to do with the human spirit and its fate. We recognize the sort of story it is; we identify it as a myth, a tale which explains some circumstance of human life in terms of supernatural happenings. Myths are conceived by a people in a relatively early stage of cultural development, but even when the authority of this method of explanation has been destroyed by reason and science, the interest in myth and the mythical mode of thought is strongly maintained in literature.

Some of the elements of Kafka's story remind us—perhaps by the author's intention—of certain well-known ancient myths. The dead hunter recalls Adonis, who was killed in a hunting accident. The "death ship" was surely suggested by the burial ritual of the Egyptians, who equipped their tombs with elaborate miniature ships because they believed that the departed soul traveled by water to another world. The fate of the hunter Gracchus in his "wooden case" is similar to that of the Egyptian hero-king Osiris, who was said to have been shut up in a coffer which was sealed and thrown into the Nile.

But there are striking differences between Kafka's modern myth and the ancient ones. In the story of Adonis, the beautiful young man was loved by both Aphrodite, the goddess of love, and Persephone, the goddess of death, and it was eventually his fate to spend half the year with each of the two divinities. Among the ancient peoples of Greece and Asia Minor, Adonis was the object of intense worship; in the performance of his rites, his death was wildly mourned for one day and his resurrection joyously celebrated the next. His death symbolized winter, his resurrection the rebirth of spring. The Osiris myth also tells of resurrection. Osiris, who was often identified with Adonis (in some versions of his myth he is said to have been killed by a wild boar, as Adonis was), was restored to life through the devotion of his wife Isis, and became for the Egyptians the god of both death and resurrection. But in Kafka's myth there are neither goddesses nor love, nor is there wifely devotion, and there is no resurrection. If Adonis and Osiris embody man's hope, the hunter Gracchus embodies man's despair. He can never return to the earthly region in which he delighted, and when the Burgomaster asks him, "And have you no part in the other world?" his reply is conclusive—no, he can never reach it, try as he may.

Students of the history of religion regard Adonis and Osiris as prefigurations of Jesus, who, like them, died and was resurrected. And the dead hunter of Kafka's story can be thought of as a despairing Jesus who was not resurrected and who is never to be "received," either by his Father in "the other world" or by mankind in this one. In the hunter's saddest expression of his hopelessness, the whole earth is spoken of as becoming "an inn for the night," and we can scarcely fail to think of the Holy Family being turned away from the inn on its flight into Egypt. The same speech seems to propose the idea that the teachings of Jesus are to be forever rejected by the world. "Nobody will read what I say here, no one will come to help me; even if all the people were commanded to help me, every door and window would remain shut, everybody would take to bed and draw the bedclothes over his head, the whole earth would become an inn for the night. And there is sense in that, for nobody knows of me, and if anyone knew he would not know where I could be found, he would not know how to deal with me, he would not know how to help me. The thought of helping me is an illness that has to be cured by taking to one's bed."

The identification of the hunter with Jesus is neither complete nor final. It is suggested quite clearly, but it is not insisted on, nor enforced. We are free to think that the hunter is perhaps Jesus, or perhaps mankind itself, that it is the despairing voice of humanity which speaks in the hunter's awful words which close the story: "I am here, more than that I do not know, further than that I cannot go. My ship has no rudder, and it is driven by the wind that blows in the undermost regions of death." And we are by no means debarred from also supposing that in the hunter Gracchus the author is representing his sense of his own personal fate. Indeed, this becomes something more than an arbitrary—if natural—supposition when we consider the hunter's name, Gracchus. We can discern no connection between anything in the story and the two most famous bearers of the Roman name, the brothers known as the Gracchi, who defended the rights of the poor against the encroachments of the rich. But the Latin word *graculus* means jackdaw: from it comes the English word *grackle,* which is used to denote any kind of blackbird smaller than the crow, including the jackdaw. In Czech, the word for jackdaw is *kavka,* and the sign over Kafka's father's shop in Prague, the trademark of the business, was a picture of the bird. And Kafka often referred to himself as a jackdaw.*

Nothing in the story is more terrible than the reason for the plight of the hunter, "My death ship lost its way; a wrong turn of the wheel, a moment's absence of mind on the pilot's part. . . ." It was a "mishap." To the Burgomaster's question "And you bear no blame for it?" the hunter answers decisively "None."

In the Judaeo-Christian tradition, one way of explaining the pain of human existence while preserving belief in a beneficent God is to say that man's suffering is the direct consequence of his sinfulness. But the hunter, when the Burgomaster questions him about his fate, says that it has no relation to anything he has done. The death ship missed its way only through the fault of the boatman. There is of course no reason why we must believe what the hunter says. Yet we do believe it.

The hunter says nothing, and the story implies nothing, that negates the existence of divinity. Quite to the contrary, the hunter speaks of his labors as being "blessed." He refers to "the other world" with its "infinitely wide and spacious stair" and its shining gate, and this would seem to be the divine abode. The candle at the hunter's head is a "sacramental" candle, and the life of the people of the town is organized for the performance of a strictly enforced ceremonial. But if the world that Kafka describes lives under the aspect of divinity, it is not such a divinity as any known religion worships, and there would seem to be only a very tenuous connection between the divine and the human.

Certainly the belief in divinity kindles no hope or aspiration in human hearts. The life of the little port, although it encompasses the recognizable activities of mankind, seems to have been stricken by a terrible vacancy.† The actions of the people described in the first

---

* It should be mentioned that, throughout Kafka's youth, Czechoslovakia was part of the Austrian Empire; and that Prague was a bilingual city, part of the population speaking German, part Czech. Kafka had a good command of Czech, but his mother tongue was German, he attended German schools, and he thought of himself as a German writer.

† Riva is an actual Italian town; it is not, however, a seaport but is situated at the head of Lake Garda in the north of Italy, bordering on Switzerland. Kafka's trans-

paragraph are curiously somnambulistic. The boys playing dice, the man reading a newspaper, the girl filling her bucket at the fountain, the men drinking in the café, all seem to participate in the lifelessness of the statue on the monument. When the death ship arrives, everything about the ritual of receiving it is carried out with precision; even the doves know their part, and somehow "fifty little boys" understand that they must gather to form two rows between which the Burgomaster is to walk. Yet no one attaches any emotion to the ceremony, except for the one little boy "who opened a window just in time to see the party vanishing into the house, then hastily shut the window again." The people of the town, we feel, are scarcely more alive than the passenger of the death ship. He is more distressed than they, for once he had been a famous hunter and had known delight, and now he lies in a filthy winding sheet, unshaven and unshorn; it is a curiously revolting detail of his condition that he is covered with a "great flower-patterned woman's shawl with long fringes." Yet his condition is different in degree but not in kind from that of the townsmen.

The happenings of Kafka's story are bizarre and out of the course of nature, yet we do not for that reason incline to call it a fantasy—that word suggests to us something wild and free, a liberation of the mind from the bonds of logic and actuality, whereas this story has the effect of making us feel helplessly imprisoned in the prosaic and the intractable. But if ever we have experienced the sense that life is empty and meaningless, if ever we have suffered from the feeling that our behavior is compelled, that our will is not our own, or that it has ceased to function, we can scarcely withstand the power of Kafka's terrible imagination of man's existence.

---

lators, Willa and Edwin Muir, have been most faithful to the original text and notably sensitive in their rendering of it. But in allowing us to think of the town as a seaport they have made one error of some importance. The German word *See* is used for both *lake* and *sea;* when it means *lake* it is a masculine noun and when it means *sea* it is feminine. In the German text of the story the word is used in both genders—the death ship sails all waters, great and small. But as we see it coming to Riva, it is sailing only a rather small lake. Our awareness of this might well intensify the sense of confinement and constriction that the story generates.

Tickets, Please

D. H. LAWRENCE
1885–1930

F ROM the tone of its opening paragraphs it would be impossible to predict the kind of story that "Tickets, Please" turns out to be. Lawrence is unblushing in the quaint whimsicality with which he personifies the little tramcar, telling us that it seems "to pause and purr with curious satisfaction," that it is "abashed by the great crimson and cream-coloured city cars, but still perky, jaunty, somewhat dare-devil. . . ." He refers to it with the coy, manipulating "we" that is deplorably used with children ("We don't spit at our little sister, do we?") or hospital patients ("We are going to have our injection now"). And with the same pronoun he contrives a companionable trio of tramcar, author, and reader, in which we are presumed to connive at the enthusiasm of his "Hurray!" and be reassured by his ". . . but what matter!" When he tells us, "Therefore, there is a certain wild romance aboard these cars—and in the sturdy bosom of Annie herself," it is as if he were cozily putting his arm around Annie's shoulder to introduce her as a really nice girl who is bound to prove a satisfactory heroine.

In short, the beginning of the story commits itself to a manner which is all too consciously "literary," all too aware of its airs and graces of style, and all too pleased with itself and its jolly intimacy with the reader. Prose of this kind, with its avowed intention of charming the reader and making him warm and comfortable, was common enough in the fiction of the Victorian period, but it has long since gone out of fashion. And it is at the furthest possible remove from the startling episode which makes the substance of the story and from the quick, spare language in which its violence is set forth: "He went forward, rather vaguely. She had taken off her belt, and swinging it, she fetched him a sharp blow over the head with the buckle end. He sprang and seized her. But immediately the other girls rushed upon him, pulling and tearing and beating him." Prose—not to say action—as direct as this puts all whimsy, coziness, and jollity to rout.

Whether or not Lawrence consciously intended a particular effect by his use of these two widely divergent styles we do not know. But once we become aware of the contrast between them, we can scarcely fail to look for meaning in it. And the meaning we are most likely to discover is social—the startling discrepancy between the way the story opens and the way it develops may be said to represent the difference between an old and a new conception of women. At the beginning of the story Annie seems ready to be the satisfactory heroine of a Victorian novel; with her sturdiness go a modesty and reserve which would once have been praised as "womanly." She disappoints this first judgment in a sufficiently remarkable way. Her conduct exemplifies the drastic revision of the notion of womanliness that was made after the First World War.

All through the nineteenth century, in the United States and in certain countries of Europe, there had been an ever-growing awareness that the status of women could no longer remain what it had traditionally been. The First World War, if only because it required many women to come out of the home and do the work of men, effected a change in the relation of the sexes which had long been in preparation and which was perhaps the most radical that history can show. Its importance was not underestimated by the fiction and drama of the time. The relations between men and women came to be thought of as a "problem" which writers undertook to "solve" or at least to state as clearly and honestly as they could. And of all writers none responded to the new sexual situation quite so intensely as D. H. Lawrence, with so much sensitivity and awareness, and with so passionate a commitment of both feeling and intelligence.

Lawrence was certainly not the first modern writer to propose the idea that between men and women there exists an intense antagonism. Nor is that idea only a modern one. Chaucer celebrated the fidelity and docility of women but he also took full notice of their desire to resist male dominance and even to gain what he called "the mastery." And the imagination of the Greeks, as their drama and legends abundantly testify, was haunted by the thought of the hostility which women might bear toward men. But the idea of the antagonism of the sexes as propounded by modern authors—Ibsen, Nietzsche, Strindberg, and Shaw may be mentioned as Lawrence's predecessors in the treatment of the subject—came to the modern consciousness as a novelty and a shock. Especially for Lawrence, it was on the sexual battlefield that the fiercest conflicts of civilization announced themselves.

But Lawrence was no less engaged by the mutual dependence of the sexes. And it is his equal recognition of both the antagonism and the reciprocal need, and of the interplay between the two, that gives his writing about love its unique air of discovery and truth. "Tickets, Please" is one of Lawrence's early stories, but it constitutes a summary statement of the emotional situation with which Lawrence was to deal throughout his career as a writer.

In their dress, in their manner of life and in their deportment, these girl-conductors of the tramline strikingly describe this century's revolution in the life of women. They are spoken of as "fearless young hussies"—they have learned to live on terms of equality, or apparent equality, with men, and to accept the manners of a rough male society. They had never, it is true, pretended to the standards of behavior that prevailed for the women of the British upper classes, which had shaped the prevailing ideal of womanliness as it was celebrated in novels. These girl-conductors had not been brought up to be *ladies*. But most of them had certainly been brought up to be "respectable." They leave respectability a long way behind when they undertake to deal with Coddy Raynor.

The maenad-like behavior of these working-class girls did have, it is worth noting, a degree of upper-class sanction. It had been validated by the conduct of many women of the very gentlest breeding, for the suffragettes, as the women who agitated for the right to vote were called, come largely from the upper classes yet did not shrink from violent means to enforce their claim to political equality with men, pouring acid into letter-boxes, destroying the putting-greens of golf courses, beating cabinet ministers over the head with umbrellas, and fighting strenuously when the police took them into custody. But the suffragettes acted out of outraged pride at the implication that women were not worthy to vote. The girls who make up the fierce little vigilance party of "Tickets, Please" are no less moved by an outrage done to their pride, but what they resent is not the political and social superiority that men insist on but the male sexual advantage.

These women need Coddy more than he needs them, and all the more because the war has created a shortage of men. They are now independent economically, but they can fulfil themselves only in marriage, while for Coddy marriage represents nothing but a surrender of freedom, a submission to whatever woman he marries, a yielding of *his* pride. From the point of view of equity, the situation is infamous and not to be borne. And yet no sooner have the girls succeeded in redressing the balance against him, at least symbolically and for the moment, than they are appalled by what they have done. They undertook to destroy this arrogant male, to humiliate him and make him ridiculous; their success makes them feel lost and miserable. For it is exactly what they resent in Coddy Raynor—his masculine pride and arrogance, his lordly independence—that constitutes his attraction as a man and draws them to him. The rough justice that the girls deal out may have its rough rationality, but the situation they confront is not to be solved by rationality. Their desires and their needs transcend justice and reason.

And here Lawrence leaves the problem. He does not try to adjudicate between the sexes but only to set forth the actuality of the relationship—and to find pleasure in it. The pleasure is quite unmistakable. As between John Thomas Raynor and Annie Stone and her embattled comrades, Lawrence does not take sides. He delights in both parties to the sexual conflict. The actual physical embroilment is grim enough, and any reader—at least any male reader—is sure to share John Thomas's fear of the enraged women he has exploited and deceived. Yet Lawrence, without at all masking the grimness, treats it as only one element of a story that is curiously tender and predominantly humorous.

The essence of both the tenderness and the humor lies in the fact that the behavior of the girls, which is so extravagantly unwomanly, reveals them, especially Annie, in the full of their female nature—and reveals them so not only to us but to themselves. The conduct that "unsexes" them, as a Victorian moralist would have put it, makes plain the intensity of their female sexuality.

The Road from Colonus

E. M. FORSTER
1879-1970

I N pagan days it was the custom to place on certain shrines the
representation of a once-afflicted part of the body which had
presumably been healed by the divinity. The practice continued
in many Christian communities and it is still kept up in Greece. To
Mr. Lucas in his native England the custom would no doubt have
seemed the crudest of superstitions. But as he stands in the tree-
shrine and sees the "tiny arms and legs and eyes in tin, grotesque
models of the brain or the heart—all tokens of some recovery of
strength or wisdom or love," he not only comprehends the impulse
behind these votive displays but thinks that he would himself like to
make just such an offering, "a little model of an entire man."

It is a long time, we gather, since Mr. Lucas has felt like an entire
man. Or perhaps he has never felt so, and if he now has a sense of
wholeness, it is because he has had a unique and crucial experience.
Its beginning, we are told, was a sensation of peace so great that he
had been almost unconscious; then he had been aroused by a shock
which was "the shock of an arrival perhaps, for when he opened his
eyes, something unimagined, indefinable, had passed over all things,
and made them seem intelligible and good." The goodness is probably indispensable to the nature of Mr. Lucas's experience, but the
crucial word here is *intelligible* and its purport is emphasized in the
passage that follows. "There was meaning in the stoop of the old

woman over her work, and in the quick motions of the little pig, and in her diminishing globe of wool. . . . The sun made no accidental patterns upon the spreading roots of the tree, and there was intention in the nodding clumps of asphodel, and in the music of the water."

The intelligibility of things that Mr. Lucas suddenly perceives can never yield a statement. There is no way to formulate the "meaning" of the stoop of the old woman and the motions of the little pig, or to say to what end the "intention" of the asphodels and the music of the water is directed. The sense—or, more accurately, the sensation—of a world happily available to understanding is an experience which, although it often has a quasi-mystical aspect, is not uncommon; it arises from a condition of inner harmony or peace such as Mr. Lucas has known. This sudden access of peace had not come to Mr. Lucas because of the beauty of the little hamlet, although this surely had made it the more possible. It had come to him out of his realization and acceptance of death. Although he does not explicitly think about death, death is in his mind: it is here in this hamlet that he has had "the feeling of the swimmer, who, after long struggling with chopping seas, finds that after all the tide will sweep him to his goal." It is in this place that he wishes to end his days. The place is none other than Colonus.

Of course it is not Colonus in literal actuality. The real town, in ancient times, had been a suburb of Athens. It long ago lost its identity, having been absorbed by the city, of which it is now only an indistinguishable district, rather shabbier than others. But it had once been known for its beauty and had been loved by the great poet whose birthplace it was—Sophocles in his extreme old age made it the scene of the last play of his long career and in a lovely choral ode celebrated the holy peace of the town and its flowers, streams, and trees. In *Oedipus at Colonus* the aged hero of *Oedipus Rex* comes to the town on the last day of his life. Blinded by his own hand in retribution for his terrible sin of having killed his father and married his mother, although all unknowingly, and exiled by his own decree, he has wandered the earth attended only by his daughter Antigone.

Sin and suffering have not subdued his spirit; the former king still reveals the pride and quick anger that had marked him in the days of his glory. What for many readers is most memorable in the play is the contrast between certain aspects of the character of Oedipus and the manner of his departure from life. His pride and anger often announce themselves in bitterness and querulousness but all these manifestations which we think unworthy of a hero are forgotten in his response to the knowledge that the hour of his death has come and in his going alone into the sacred grove to meet it. By his death Oedipus is raised to a dignity greater than he has ever had in life.

Mr. Lucas has nothing of the tragic grandeur of Oedipus, and the death that might have come to him in the hamlet could scarcely have had the high significance of the hero's passing, which was less a death than an apotheosis. Yet the moment of transcendence that comes to Mr. Lucas when he realizes and accepts his death raises him, we feel, to a dignity that makes possible the comparison of this commonplace man with Oedipus, and we respond without irony to the defeat that is summed up in one word of the story's title, the sad preposition *from*. "Death destroys a man," says Mr. Foster in his novel *Howards End*, "but the idea of death saves him"; and when Mr. Lucas is led down the road from his Colonus, we know that he has been deprived of his salvation. Had he stayed he would have died that night—"What a deliverance," says his daughter Ethel when she reads of the fall of the great tree in the storm and realizes the narrowness of her father's escape. But we, seeing Mr. Lucas in his suburban safety, given over to senile petulance about the noise of children and running water, are as little inclined to agree with this false Antigone as we are with Gretta Conroy when in Joyce's "The Dead" she says of Michael Furey, "Isn't it a terrible thing to die so young as that?"

Disorder and Early Sorrow

THOMAS MANN
1875–1955

DISORDER AND EARLY SORROW" is written in what grammarians call the "historical present," that is to say, the present tense used to represent happenings of the past. As a literary device this has the obvious effect of making events seem immediate to our understanding and sympathy. But the historical present is usually employed with great circumspection and for a particular limited purpose, in order to make some part of a narrative more vivid than the rest. To use it for the whole of a story of considerable length is generally regarded as questionable practice. The device wears out; the reader comes to think of it as a naive trick, and whatever sympathy with the persons of the story it may at first induce is likely to deteriorate into mere condescension. But Thomas Mann is a writer who is especially sensitive to all the traditional devices of prose; he cannot be charged with committing a stylistic blunder: the historical present is entirely suited to his literary purpose.

For the story is about history itself, about the impulse of the human mind to hold the fleeting moment, to make permanent what is transient. A tense which pretends that the past is still the present is ideally appropriate to such a subject. And if Mann's extended use of the historical present does eventually give the narrative a tone of naiveté and leads us to regard the characters, especially the chief one,

Professor Cornelius, with a degree of condescension, this effect is appropriate too. It suggests the hopelessness—we might almost say the childishness—of the Professor's desire to hold back the onward movement of time.

I say that "Disorder and Early Sorrow" is "about history itself" and to some readers this will perhaps seem an all too abstract description. They will protest that it makes too much of the fact that Professor Cornelius is a historian and that it gives excessive weight to the single paragraph, brilliant and moving as it is, in which he thinks about the "something not quite right" in his feeling for his little daughter, that flaw in his love which, he believes, derives from "his essence and quality as a professor of history." The story, these readers will object, is about the love of a father for his child and the pain he feels when he realizes that the love she bears toward him will one day be withdrawn to be given to some other man.

Against this objection I make no defence—or none beyond saying that the breaking, or attenuation, of the bond between parent and child is the very stuff of history. What the historian coolly investigates as happening in nations and over relatively long periods of time is but the aggregate of what is painfully experienced in every family. The unit of historical time is not the century but the generation. "One generation passeth away and another generation cometh"—this is history.

But if this is history, then I have been using the word in two separate meanings, having previously spoken of history as the expression of the impulse of the human mind to make permanent that which is transient. For this contradiction I am not responsible: it lies in the nature of the word itself, which means two quite distinct things. According to one sense of the word, history is the sum of things that happen, or at least the sum of the notable things that happen, and the emphasis is on the *happening*. In this sense, history is a flux, a ceaseless stream, although perhaps the image of a stream represents something too defined—it is rather (to use a phrase of William James's) "a blooming, buzzing confusion." According to the other sense of the word, history is the *record* of happenings, not merely the objective record (if there can be such a thing) but one that imposes order upon events and finds significance in them.

The relationship between the two meanings is in part antagonistic, just as the relation between art and life is in some measure antagonistic. The historian, like the artist, imposes order upon the chaotic flux of life and says that through his efforts life may be understood. Yet in his heart he sometimes feels that he betrays life by what he does, that when he imposes upon it a form or an idea, he negates its living actuality. As Professor Cornelius puts it, the past that the historians conceive is coherent and disciplined, which is what they mean by "historical." But life in the present is not coherent and disciplined: it becomes so only when it ceases to be life in the present, when it becomes the past and is seen as history. "The past is immortalized; that is to say, it is dead," Professor Cornelius says. And he goes on: ". . . and death is the root of all godliness and all abiding significance," by which he means that all piety, law, and morality depend upon our sense of the past, upon our reference to experiences which are no longer immediate and actual, no longer alive.

Certainly the period in which the story takes place presents the greatest possible contrast of "disorder" to the "orderliness" of the past. After the defeat of Germany in the First World War, the political system of the nation had collapsed. Germany ceased to be a monarchy and became, most uneasily, a democracy. The national economy was radically dislocated; commodities were scarce, money was progressively devalued, prices were astronomically inflated, and it was literally true that people had to carry paper currency in satchels. Both the modest savings of the prudent and the fortunes of the rich were wiped out. The devaluation of the old social modes, of traditional ideas and ideal, kept pace with the devaluation of money. Young Bert Cornelius is a typical figure of the time, with his lack of any ambition for a respectable life such as his father had lived, with his manners and admirations that are quite alien to his father's comprehension.

Yet no description of the period would be accurate that did not take into account the heady sense of possibility that it brought to many young people. Exactly because they were cut off from security and respectability, they valued whatever in life was new and adventurous. The "conservative instinct," which Professor Cornelius acknowledges as his own, was held in very low esteem. If life was chaotic, it seemed to many people to be for that very reason the more intense. Because the past could assert so little authority over life, life seemed more truly alive than ever before.

And even Professor Cornelius is aware of this new sense of excitement in his society. Or at least he is not inclined to condemn the new disorder, however much he dislikes it, for his field of historical research must inevitably suggest to him the dangers of such a judgment. Professor Cornelius is a specialist in the period of the so-called Counter-Reformation, that great expression of the conservative instinct by which sixteenth-century Catholic Europe tried to hold back the rising tide of Protestantism. He has a particular interest in a leader of this resistance to the new tendencies, Philip II of Spain, who carried on what the Professor characterizes as a "practically hopeless struggle . . . against the whole trend of history: against the new, the kingdom-disrupting power of the Germanic ideal of freedom and individual liberty." Mann could count on his German readers to have a pretty vivid idea of this monarch and his desperate resistance to the new, for Philip's struggle is the subject of one of the classics of the German stage, Schiller's *Don Carlos*. It will be recalled that a new production of this play is discussed at the party given by Professor Cornelius' older children; one of the guests, the young actor, is to have the part of Don Carlos, the crown prince who becomes his father's antagonist by making himself the champion of the oppressed people of the conquered Netherlands. We might put it that Dr. Cornelius, historian of the Counter-Reformation, has no wish in his own life to emulate the grim, unloved, tragic king who tried to impose traditional principle and authority upon the new chaotic energies burgeoning about him.

And yet he cannot participate in these energies or give them his full assent—the "conservative instinct" of the historian, which is also the conservative instinct of the father of a family, is strong in him. He is aware of his "hostility against the history of today, which is still in the making and thus not history at all, in behalf of the genuine history that has already happened." And this stubborn preference for the past as against the present is, he perceives, the root of the "something not perfectly right and good" in his love of his little daughter. For his "devotion to this priceless little morsel of life and new growth has something to do with death, it clings to death as against life; and that is neither right nor beautiful." The accusation that Professor Cornelius directs against himself does not go as far as it might—he cannot bring himself to say what we know to be the truth, that what is not "right and beautiful" in his love of the child is the hidden wish that she never change from what she now is; that she always be beautiful in the way that she now is and in no other way; that the experience of life, with the pain and the loss of innocence it entails, shall not be hers. Ellie's sudden, uncontrollable, precocious passion for Herr Hergesell, in his dull complacency so unworthy an object of her devotion, makes it bitterly plain to her father that his wish is beyond any hope of realization, and, bitter though his feelings are, he can only be glad that this is so.

It is this ambivalence of the father, his wanting and his yet not wanting his daughter to have the experience of life, that makes the strong and complex emotion of the story. And it is the irony of the chaotic forces of life being embodied in this delicate, only momentarily awakened little girl, that makes the story's bitter charm.

Di Grasso:
A Tale of Odessa

ISAAC BABEL
1894-1939

O NE OF the conventional ways of praising art is to associate it with the peaceful and "constructive" virtues and to put it at the furthest possible remove from violence. But artists themselves are not misled by this pious view of their enterprise. They know how often the act of creation is bound up with the aggressive impulses. And perhaps no one has made this knowledge quite so salient in his conception of art as Isaac Babel.

Babel was one of the very few writers of genius to develop under Soviet rule. For a short period after his work began to appear in the 1920's, his remarkable gifts were recognized and he enjoyed a measure of fame, but then he fell into disfavor with the regime and was accused of political crimes. Although never brought to trial, he was sent to a prison camp, where he died in 1939 or 1940.

The great—the crucial—experience of Babel's life was his service with a regiment of Cossacks in 1920 during a campaign of the terrible civil war that followed the Russian Revolution. To understand the meaning of this experience, we must know that Babel was a Jew and that no two peoples could be more completely and significantly antithetical to each other than the Jews of Eastern Europe and the Cossacks. The Jews conceived their ideal character to be intellectual, humane, and peaceable. The Cossacks were physical and violent, men of the body, the sword, and the horse. The relation between the two groups had long been extremely hostile. Each held the other in contempt, and the hatred between them was the more intense because the Czarist government of Russia had used Cossack troops in its systematic persecution of the Jews. Nothing, then, could have been more anomalous than that a Jew—and an intellectual and rather weakly Jew at that, a man "with spectacles on his nose and autumn in his heart," as Babel described himself—should ride and fight by the side of the Cossacks. It is clear from his superb stories about this experience—they were collected in a volume called *Red Cavalry*—that Babel wanted to eradicate from his temperament the quietism that had been instilled into it by his Jewish upbringing, and that it was for this reason that he undertook to share the Cossack life of physicality and violence, even of cruelty.

Babel's wish to model his behavior on that of his Cossack comrades was not easily attained. He found, as he said, that to face death was not so very hard, but that it was hard indeed to acquire what he called "the simplest of proficiencies—the ability to kill [one's] fellowmen." Much as he admired the grace and force of the Cossacks and the fierce directness with which they expressed their feelings, he could not rid himself of the pacific ideals of his Jewish heritage. But although the way of peace and the way of violence were always in conflict in his mind, it is plain that his interest was more engaged by the way of violence. It seemed to promise him a kind of liberation of spirit and his fulfilment as a man.

No less did it promise him liberation and fulfilment as a writer. Babel was intensely conscious of the problems of style, and whenever he talked about style he resorted to metaphors of physical violence. He spoke of prose as a series of military maneuvers executed by the "army of words, the army in which all kinds of weapons may be brought into play." He remarked that "there is no iron that can enter the human heart with such stupefying effect as a period placed at just the right moment." He thought that the essence of art was unexpectedness, a surprise attack upon the reader's habitual assumptions.

This conception of art as disciplined violence is the theme of what was to be the last story that Babel wrote. "Di Grasso" is composed in the intimate, colloquial, seemingly casual manner that Babel had made his own, and on first reading it may seem to be a very simple story, not much more than an anecdote. But Babel was anything but a simple man, and this story has all the subtlety and complexity that we might expect to find in a highly developed writer's apologia for his art, which in effect "Di Grasso" is.

An Italian theatrical company has come for a repertory season to Odessa, Russia's great Black Sea port, a city famous for its cosmopolitan interest in the arts of performance. The troupe's first performance begins in a most unpromising way, for the play is a dull provincial piece, the acting is ridden by cliché and convention. But then one moment brings to an end, and redeems, all the boredom—when the actor Di Grasso "gave a smile, soared into the air, sailed across the stage, plunged down on [the villain's] shoulders, and having bitten through the latter's throat, began, growling and squinting, to suck blood from the wound." Di Grasso is to go through a long repertory, and in all his performances he will "with every word and every gesture" confirm the idea that "there is more justice in outbursts of noble passion than in all the joyless rules that run the world." But although he plays Othello and King Lear, the nature of his genius is most forcibly suggested to the young protagonist of the story—whom we take to be a representation of Babel himself —not by his performance of these great rôles but by the absurd incident of physical violence in an inferior play.

What was it in that moment of melodramatic nonsense that enchanted the audience and became so memorable to the author? Certainly the sheer virtuosity of the leap is a decisive element—the actor's extraordinary ability to "soar into the air," to "sail across the stage," to do, or seem to do, what presumably cannot be done. Although the word *virtuosity* may indeed be used in praise, it may also be used with a contemptuous intention, to suggest mere technical skill, with, by implication, a paucity of spiritual or intellectual energy. Yet mere technical skill can delight us, as in the performance of jugglers, trapeze artists, and stage magicians. And an unusual degree of technical skill has the effect of enhancing or confirming the other qualities an artist may possess. Everyone who saw Nijinski perform believed him to be the greatest dancer of all time, and almost every account of his art makes reference to one extraordinary achievement —his power of levitation, his ability, like Di Grasso's, to soar into the air and sail across the stage. Those who saw him do this seem to have had an intimation of the possibility of freedom from the bondage of our human condition. It is no small idea for a leap to propose!

The naked ferocity that Di Grasso displays has an effect related to that of his astonishing leap—it, too, suggests the idea of a liberation. This, however, is a liberation not from the general human condition but from the constraints of society, from the dullness, the passivity, the acquiescence in which we live most of our lives.

But the intention of Babel's story goes beyond its celebration of the great murderous leap and its assertion that intensity, or "noble passion," is the very soul of art. Babel is concerned with the moral effect which may result from the kind of aesthetic experience he has described.

The wife of the ticket speculator would seem to be the least likely person in the world to exemplify the moral power that art can have. She is gross in manner, grotesque in appearance, and therefore she ought not, by conventional notions, be susceptible to the noble passions; and we may easily suppose that what susceptibility she does have will not last very long. Yet, if only for the moment, the great leap of Di Grasso and his display of ferocity bring to her mind ideas of love, tenderness, and generosity, and she turns upon her cadging husband in rage at his lack of all large-minded emotions. What is more, she recalls a particular instance of her husband's meanness that she will no longer put up with. Decency has become suddenly, if fleetingly, important to her—she knows that her husband has been keeping illicitly a watch that belongs to his young assistant's father; she insists that it be returned at once and she is not to be withstood.

The story might well have come to its end with this episode, but the final paragraph carries it to a further development of great charm and profundity. The young Babel—for at this point we can no longer doubt that the narrator is the author writing about himself in his youth—is freed from the anguish and fear caused by his being unable to regain possession of his father's watch, and now, all at once, he perceives the street in which he stands with "a distinctness such as [he] had never before experienced." Now, "for the first time," he sees the things around him "as they really were: frozen in silence and ineffably beautiful." His sudden unexpected relief from anxiety and wretchedness has brought about this almost mystical perception. An aesthetic experience has produced an act of moral decency; the act of moral decency becomes the cause of a transcendent experience. We can scarcely suppose that Babel was unaware of the irony implicit in the fact that the pure and peaceful contemplation described in the last paragraph of "Di Grasso" owed its existence to the violence of the actor's leap.

The Sailor-Boy's Tale

ISAK DINESEN
1885–1962

I SAK DINESEN* always called her stories "tales." The use of this word served notice that she intended to tell a story of a particular kind. What is a tale? Perhaps it is best defined as a narrative which counts upon a certain simplicity of acceptance from the reader or hearer, an acquiescence in the possibility of strange and unlikely events, especially marvelous ones.

In cultures which have not developed a high degree of rational thought, the marvelous is taken for granted as virtually the essence of the literary experience. This is true also of children, who have always been supposed to have a natural affinity with marvels and an appetite for them. Even the modern theory, which has established itself in some quarters, that children ought not to be told fairy tales but only stories about "real life," has not been able to overcome this supposition. It has merely replaced fairy godmothers and pumpkin-coaches with infant locomotives that think, feel, and talk, and perform heroic deeds.

We cannot suppose that the child, or the adult whose culture sets less store by rational thought than ours does, accepts the marvelous in exactly the same way that he accepts the actual occurrences of daily life. Were he to do so, he would take no pleasure in the stories

---

* The pseudonym of the Baroness Karen Blixen. Her mother tongue was Danish, but she wrote in English.

in which the marvelous has a part. He merely accepts it more immediately and naively than a mature person reared in a culture in which rational thought is highly valued. And even such a person by no means rejects the marvelous. He has his own way of accepting it, for although he does not "believe" it, yet with no great effort he is able to make what Coleridge, in his famous phrase, called "a willing suspension of disbelief." For the purposes of literature, this does quite well enough. If anyone were to interrupt our reading of a story about ghosts, or walking corpses, or monsters from outer space in order to ask whether we believed in their actual existence, we should unhesitatingly reply that we did not, that such creatures were impossible. Yet it is likely that we should be giving this answer in circumstances which indicated just the opposite—our pulse rate would probably have gone up, our palms would be damp, and we would be experiencing some uneasiness about being alone in the house at night. We would have been interested, even absorbed, in the impossible story, to the point of resenting the interruption. We permit ourselves, that is, to respond to the unlikely beings in such a story *as if* we believed in them. The fact that we do not really believe in them but have only suspended our disbelief does not prevent their having their effect upon us.

In a culture like ours, which gives so much weight to rationality, the marvelous has a rather special place in the reading experience. In general, our literature is committed to fact and to the representation of reality. We tend to praise a literary work in the degree that we think it communicates the truth of actuality. But for that very reason, the marvelous, when it does appear, has a special value for the modern reader. Coleridge suggested what this value might be when, in connection with his great poem of the marvelous, *The Rime of the Ancient Mariner,* he quoted the seventeenth-century Bishop Burnet, who said that a belief in demons—he stipulated a *judicious* belief—preserved the mind from "mean thoughts," from small and merely mundane views of life. It is often said that modern science, so far from being what science used to be called, "organized common sense," has developed only through its willingness to defy common sense and the evidence of the senses—that it is based upon an acceptance, if not of the marvelous, then at least of the unlikely, and upon conceptions which do not apply to the occurrences of daily life and which require a suspension of disbelief. Certainly for the modern reader, the element of the marvelous in literature has important moral implications: it suggests that life is not to be understood in terms only of our daily practical knowledge of it, that it is also a mystery, evoking our wonder no less than our fortitude.

"The Sailor-Boy's Tale" has in common with several other stories in this book—"Di Grasso," "The Secret Sharer," "My Kinsman, Major Molineux"—the theme of initiation, of a young man's moving forward into a new stage of growth. The attraction of this theme for writers as diverse as Babel, Conrad, Hawthorne, and Isak Dinesen indicates something of the universality of its appeal. We first encounter it in the folktales we read in early childhood, which tell about the youngest son of the woodcutter or the miller, who is thought to be a fool by his family but who sets out alone to make his fortune, and succeeds, showing himself to be no mere undeveloped boy but a man. As the youth goes on his journey, he encounters circumstances that try his capacities: not uncommonly he is tested for his kindness of heart. Because he is willing to milk the cow that hasn't been milked for seven long years, or because he is courteous to the old crone whom no one will regard, some unexpected and unpredictable good befalls him. The cow and the old woman are not what they seem, they turn out to have some helpful secret to impart or some magical assistance to offer. So in "The Sailor-Boy's Tale," the peregrine hawk that young Simon frees from the rigging is a Lapland witch—the people of Lapland have always been known as the most accomplished of witches and wizards—who, when Simon is in danger, repays in kind the help he had given her.

This is the kind of marvelous event we are all familiar with from the tales of our childhood, and much of the charm of Isak Dinesen's story lies in its use of the matter of a children's tale in a story not meant for children. But all the stories of initiation included in this book, not Isak Dinesen's alone, contain an element of the marvelous.

Di Grasso's leap is beyond the powers of ordinary mortals; it is virtually the action of a divine being, and it appears to have a magical effect upon those who witness it. The young captain in "The Secret Sharer" is endangered but also aided by his double, who is essentially the *Doppelgänger* of folktale, the supernatural duplication of himself that it was once thought a man might encounter, and the experience of young Robin in "My Kinsman, Major Molineux" is compounded of supernatural episodes, or so at least they seem to the young hero. Inevitably we are led to wonder if the experience of initiation is not one we naturally incline to connect with happenings of a marvelous kind. And, indeed, is it not felt to be exactly a marvel by the young person who experiences it—does he not know that, in passing from boyhood to manhood, he has been *transformed?*

Hills Like White Elephants

ERNEST HEMINGWAY
1898–1961

ERNEST HEMINGWAY recalls that when he first began to write and his stories were being steadily refused by the magazines, they were returned "with notes of rejection that would never call them stories but always anecdotes [or] sketches." One of these early stories was "Hills Like White Elephants," and it is interesting to speculate why the magazine editors of the 1920's thought it was not really a story.

One reason may be that they thought of a story as primarily something that is *told* whereas "Hills Like White Elephants" is scarcely told at all. The author makes every effort to keep himself anonymous and out of sight; he seems to refuse to have any connection either with the reader or with the people in the episode he is presenting. The scene is set in an opening paragraph which is as brief as it can be and severely impersonal in tone; and thereafter almost everything is left to the dialogue between the man and the girl, with the author intervening only to inform us that the drinks have been served, that the man carries the bags to the other side of the station, and, on two occasions, to tell us what the girl sees when she looks at the landscape. In fact, the author is so little related to what goes on in the story that he does not even take advantage of the traditional device of describing the tone of voice in which the characters speak. He does not tell us that the girl makes a remark "bitterly" or "ironically" or that the man replies "sulkily" or "placatingly." He does not presume to know anything at all about the couple, not even their names —it is by mere accident, as it were, that we learn the girl's nickname, Jig.

Nor does he undertake to tell us anything that could be learned even from direct observation of the girl and the man. Because she is always referred to as "the girl" and he as "the man," we feel free to conclude that she is younger than he and quite young—but is she twenty or twenty-three or twenty-five? Most readers will suppose her to be attractive, partly because she seems to speak and act as if she were, but the author says not a word about her appearance. There is ground for believing that the man and the girl are married, for it is still a question between them whether or not she is to bear the child with which she is pregnant. But it may also be that they are unmarried lovers and that the question of whether or not they will have the child involves the question of their getting married.

This stubborn reticence, this refusal by Hemingway to relate himself to the characters and to say anything *about* them, must surely have led the editors to feel that "Hills Like White Elephants" lacked the degree of meaning a story is expected to have as compared to an anecdote or sketch. My use of the word *meaning* must not tempt us into an elaborate theoretical discussion of what it is that we imply when we speak of a story's having, or lacking, meaning. It will be enough to say that the meaning of a story is the *sensation* of understanding which it creates in us. It may be—it usually is—scarcely possible to say what we have understood when we laugh at a joke. A story, like a joke, is successful if it sets up in us the sensation of our having understood it.

No doubt the magazine editors who first read "Hills Like White Elephants" felt that the remoteness of the author, his refusal to comment explicitly on what he presented, implied that he was not making the expected effort to give his readers this sensation. He put before his readers a human situation of considerable potential significance, without telling them how the situation was to be resolved, or what emotions and partisanships he wanted to evoke—he seemed to be indifferent as to what meaning his story might be found to have, or whether it would be found to have any meaning at all.

Today, of course, our response to Hemingway's story is very different from that of the magazine editors of the 1920's. We are not bound by their technical preconceptions; we have become habituated to literary devices which once seemed odd and impermissible. For us there is no question but that "Hills Like White Elephants" does have point, that it really is a story. Yet we shall have responded to it in a quite appropriate way if we make this judgment only slowly, if we are at first a little baffled by it and come to see its point only after some delay, if we even believe for a while that what we have read is merely an anecdote or sketch.

Should we need a clue to where the point of the story lies, we can find it in a single word in the last of the few brief passages of narration, the paragraph which tells us that the man carries the bags to the other side of the station. "Coming back, he walked through the barroom, where people waiting for the train were drinking. He drank an Anis at the bar and looked at the people. They were all waiting reasonably for the train." Waiting *reasonably*—it is a strange adverb for the man's mind to have lighted on. (We might note that by his use of this word, Hemingway does, for an instant, betray a knowledge of the man's internal life.) Why not *quietly,* or *apathetically,* or *stolidly?* Why should he choose to remark upon the people's reasonableness, taking note of it with approval, and as if it made a bond of community between him and them? It is because he, a reasonable man, has been having a rough time reasoning with an unreasonable woman.

The quality of reasonableness is central to "Hills Like White Elephants." In his conversation with the girl, the man—once he has got over, or suppressed, his anxious irritability—takes the line of detached reasonableness. He achieves, of course, nothing better than plausibility. Hemingway has no need to supply the descriptions of his tone of voice as he urges the girl to consent to the abortion—the rhythm of his sentences, the kind of words he uses, makes plain what his tone is. You cannot say "really" and "just" (in the sense of *merely*) as often as he does without sounding insincere.

Nor do we need the girl's tones of voice labelled for us. We understand that she is referring to a desire which she does not know how to defend in words and that therefore she speaks in bitterness and irony. She wants to have the child. There is no possible way to formulate a *reason* for wanting a child. It is a gratuitous desire, quite beyond reason. This is especially true if one lives the life to which this couple has devoted itself—a life, as the girl describes it in her moment of revulsion from it, of looking at things and trying new drinks. In the terms that this life sets, it is entirely *un*reasonable to want a child. But the girl has, we may say, proclaimed her emancipation from reason when she makes her remark about the hills looking like white elephants. The hills do not really look like white elephants, as the reasonable man is quick to say. They look like white elephants only if you choose to think they do, only if you think gratuitously, and with the imagination.

It is decisive in the story that the girl's simile is what it is. Some readers will have in mind the proverbial meaning of a white elephant. In certain parts of the East, this is a sacred beast; it may not be put to work but must be kept in state at great cost. Hence we call a white elephant anything that is apparently of great value and prestige but actually a drain upon our resources of which we wish we could be rid. Quite unconsciously, the girl may be making just this judgment on the life that she and her companion have chosen. But the chief effect of the simile is to focus our attention on the landscape she observes. It has two aspects, different to the point of being contradictory. This is the first: "The girl was looking off at the line of hills. They were white in the sun and the country was brown and dry." This is the second: "The girl stood up and walked to the end of the station. Across, on the other side, were fields of grain and trees along the banks of the Ebro. Far away, beyond the river, were mountains. The shadow of a cloud moved across the field of grain and she saw the river through the trees." When she looks in one direction, she sees the landscape of sterility; when she looks in the other direction, she sees the landscape of peace and fecundity. She is aware of the symbolic meaning that the two scenes have for her, for after her second view she says, "And we could have all this. . . . And we could have everything and every day we make it more impossible." It is the sudden explicitness of her desire for peace and fullness of life that makes the man's reasonable voice ring false and hollow in her ears and that leads her to her climax of desperation, her frantic request, with its seven-times repeated "please," that the man "stop talking."

It is interesting, I think, to compare the passage in the story that begins " 'We want two Anis del Toro' " with the "A Game of Chess" dialogue in T. S. Eliot's "The Waste Land." Incommensurate as they are in artistic and moral intention and achievement, the story and the poem have much in common—the theme of sterility; the representation of the boredom and vacuity and desperateness of life; the sense of lost happiness not to be regained; the awareness of the failure of love; the parched, sun-dried, stony land used as a symbol of emotional desiccation, the water used as the symbol of refreshment and salvation. Like "The Waste Land," "Hills Like White Elephants" is to be read as a comment—impassioned and by no means detached—on the human condition in the modern Western world.

Barn Burning

WILLIAM FAULKNER
1897–1962

ASALIENT characteristic of William Faulkner's imagination is its preoccupation with conduct that is in the highest degree principled and magnanimous. Faulkner seems to take a special pleasure in representing men incapable of acting merely for their own advantage. Such men are Major de Spain of this story, and Colonel Sartoris, after whom the little boy Sarty has been named. They appear again and again in Faulkner's novels and stories as representatives of the ideal of personal honor. Their mode of life is established and affluent; their bearing is dignified and benign; their military titles suggest a heroic past and a continuing devotion to the lost cause of the Confederacy; and their sonorous and "romantic" surnames imply their patrician connection with still further reaches of the past. The past, indeed, is more their natural habitat than the present: perhaps honor is always to be regarded as an archaic virtue.

But Faulkner's imagination is no less captivated by the opposite of large-mindedness and honor, by whatever we are to call the state of moral being that characterizes the ever-proliferating family of the Snopeses. Their very name suggests—rather too obviously, some will think—both their inferior social situation and their meanness of spirit. (It makes a nice subject for speculation why so many English words beginning with *sn* have unpleasant connotations, for example, *snake, snarl, sneak, sneer, snipe, snide, snivel, snob, snore, snout, snub.* Perhaps the only pleasant *sn* words are *snow, snood, snug,* and *snuggle!*) Of lowly origin, disadvantaged in every social and economic way, the Snopeses are determined to rise by any means at hand. They find an especial satisfaction in succeeding at the expense of others, for they are consumed by resentment of those who are better off than they, and they cherish their malice and ruthlessness as Major de Spain and Colonel Sartoris cherish their honor. In Faulkner's understanding of society and social history, the two gentlemen represent the old South with its respect for the patrician values of dignity and responsibility; the Snopes clan represents the plebeian modern spirit that asserts itself in the South of the present time, a calculating, unfeeling spirit which is not checked in its self-seeking by the sanctions of tradition. As time passes in the canon of Faulkner's work, certain members of the Snopes family acquire more and more power and prestige, and at the expense of the men of honor and magnanimity.

By every ethical, social, and personal standard Faulkner condemns and despises the Snopeses, but it is plain that they fascinate him. They appear in his novels and stories with increasing frequency, and we must suppose that he creates them and the situations in which they exercise their malice and shrewdness because he takes pleasure in doing so—as a matter of fact, he seems to take as much pleasure in their contemptibleness as in the admirable traits of Major de Spain and Colonel Sartoris. This impression, derived from the works themselves, is confirmed in an interesting way by an anecdote about the author. The occasion was a large party in New York at which Faulkner was a guest; he stood surrounded by a group of admirers and discoursed about rats (the report of the event does not make plain how the subject was introduced), speaking eloquently and at length of his respect for them, praising their indomitable power of survival, their way of taking every possible advantage, their cool intelligence in making use of mankind. Some of those who listened were distressed by this avowal of sympathy with a repellent and despised animal and undertook to defend the conventional view that rats are—rats. Others tried to make out that Faulkner was being ironic. But he gravely held his ground with the air of a man who had thought long about his subject and has all his arguments in order. It can scarcely be doubted that he was talking about the Snopeses.

He was saying pretty much what Keats said in a famous letter, making his point by reference to another rodent of unpleasant reputation, the stoat. Keats is writing about the ruthlessness and cruelty displayed in what he calls "wild nature"; as he thinks about this from the moral point of view, he is horrified, but then he is suddenly caught by a sense of how brilliant are the energies that come into play in the bitter struggle for existence. "This is what makes the Amusement of Life—to a speculative Mind. I go among the Fields and catch a glimpse of a Stoat or a field-mouse peeping out of the withered grass—the creature hath a purpose and its eyes are bright with it. I go among the buildings of a city and I see a Man hurrying along—to what? The creature hath a purpose and his eyes are bright with it." He goes on to speak of morality and love and concern for others and of how little they establish themselves in life, and then it occurs to him to wonder if life may not be justified by its sheer energy, quite without reference to morality. "May there not be superior beings [he means gods of some kind, not human beings] amused by any graceful though instinctive attitude my mind may fall into, as I am entertained by the alertness of a Stoat or the anxiety of a Deer? Though a quarrel in the Streets is a thing to be hated, the energies displayed in it are fine; the commonest Man shows a grace in his quarrel. . . ."

But Keats cannot rest in this conclusion. Energy, he says, is "the very thing in which consists poetry," and then he goes on to say that if this is so, "poetry is not so fine a thing as philosophy,—For the same reason that an eagle is not so fine a thing as a truth." Energy of itself is not enough, poetry of itself is not enough—this is a great and daring thing for a poet to say. Yet if we are speaking not about life but only about poetry, then energy is paramount: "energy is the very thing in which consists poetry." The mind of the poet is defined by what Keats calls its "gusto" rather than by its moral discriminations. "As to the poetical character itself . . . it is not itself —it has no self—it is every thing and nothing—It has no character— it enjoys light and shade; it lives in gusto be it foul or fair, high or low, rich or poor, mean or elevated—It· has as much delight in conceiving an Iago as an Imogen. What shocks the virtuous philosopher, delights the Camelion Poet."

As much delight in conceiving an Iago as an Imogen: as much delight in conceiving a Snopes as a de Spain or a Sartoris. *The commonest man shows a grace in his quarrel:* the quarrel of the Snopeses with their fellow men is unending, and Faulkner does not fail to see its "grace," even though it is of a perverse kind. Again and again in "Barn Burning" he speaks of Abner Snopes's actuality of existence, the curious definiteness of his outline. It need not be thought a pleasing definiteness, "cut from tin" as it is, but it is strikingly *there*. In communicating his sense of Abner Snopes's *thereness,* Faulkner does not withhold his moral judgment, but his emphasis falls on what we might call the aesthetic aspect of the man's existence—he speaks of "that impervious quality of something cut ruthlessly from tin, depthless, as though, sidewise to the sun, it would cast no shadow." He describes Snopes's body as it confronts the traditional graciousness of Major de Spain's house as not being "dwarfed . . . , as though it had attained to a sort of vicious and ravening minimum not to be dwarfed by anything." And this harsh, metallic, impervious existence has even a kind of moral meaning and gives a kind of moral satisfaction. Like the rattlesnake on the flag of the insurgent American colonies, Abner Snopes says with his whole being, "Don't tread on me," a statement of great moral force. Faulkner is quite explicit about this curious moral power of Snopes: "There was something about his wolflike independence and even courage when the advantage was at least neutral which impressed strangers, as if they got from his latent ravening ferocity not so much a sense of dependability as a feeling that his ferocious conviction in the rightness of his own actions would be of advantage to all whose interest lay with his."

It is this quality of his father that makes the dilemma of little

Sarty's life. The boy is deeply drawn to the very things that his father hates and opposes—community, justice, truth, the peace and order that are symbolized by Major de Spain's fine house. Yet apart from the habit of family loyalty and dependence, which a ten-year-old cannot easily break, there is his father's harsh power to claim his allegiance. And the reader cannot but share Sarty's division of mind. Much as he may dislike Abner Snopes, if only for his ugly trick of whipping up the mules and at the same time reining them in, he yet must feel that, as compared with Major de Spain, Snopes has much more at stake, that he is the more morally serious of the two. In this story, indeed, the magnanimous Major de Spain does not show to the best advantage. His rage over the rug that Snopes had maliciously and contemptuously soiled is of course wholly justified, yet it sinks to a kind of childishness before Abner Snopes's passion for independence, even though that is virtually an insanity. Nor can the reader escape the uncomfortable sense that Snopes has a kind of ultimate justice on his side when he says of Major de Spain's house that its whiteness is the sweat of the men, black and white, who have worked the Major's land. Harsh and unfeeling this father certainly is, yet he has the integration and definiteness which in a better man would make a paternal virtue and which in him make a paternal force.

For many readers Sarty's conflict with his father will bring to mind the filial troubles of another Southern boy, Huck Finn. For all Huck's fear of the efforts of respectable people to "sivilize" him, he likes and admires at least as much of civilization as is to be found in the amenity of a handsome and comfortable house, and he is instinctively attracted to goodness, instinctively repelled by meanness and violence; in these respects Sarty is much like him. As for Huck's father, although he has none of the metallic integration of Abner Snopes, being a ruin of a man, yet he does share Snopes's bitter hostility to society and his sense of outraged social status, and of course his brutality.

But if the situations of the two boys are similar, there is a wide difference in the way they are presented. In *Huckleberry Finn,* Mark

Twain uses the established device of having his young hero tell his story in his own words and thus achieves a prose of beautiful simplicity. There is nothing that puzzles Huck's comprehension; he understands everything that he sees and endures, and he communicates it directly and lucidly. Faulkner tells Sarty's story in the third person, and the complexity of the rhetoric expresses the complexity of the boy's perceptions. Sarty, unlike Huck, sees nothing in a clear and distinct way. The world of his perception is still inchoate, not wholly formed; seen in its parts, it is puzzling. It is also a little threatening, as well it might be for a ten-year-old boy who is moving toward a decision that must seem so far beyond his years and powers, the breaking of his tie with his father and all his family, at the behest of his idea of order and beauty.

Summer's Day

JOHN O'HARA
1905–1970

"SUMMER'S DAY" is compounded of minute social observations and preoccupied with the feelings that arise from differences in social position. Such feelings are universally judged to be petty and even contemptible. It is nevertheless O'Hara's ultimate intention in this story to represent a situation of an elemental kind, far removed from the trifling considerations of social prestige.

The story turns on a point of actual snobbery, on Mr. Attrell's sense of social superiority to Mr. O'Donnell, on Mr. O'Donnell's sense of social inferiority to Mr. Attrell. The summer community on the New England coast to which they both belong is, as people say, "exclusive." Mr. Attrell belongs to it by natural right. Mr. O'Donnell, although he has made his way into it, has not been really, or fully, accepted; at best he is tolerated.

It is a mark of Mr. Attrell's social standing that, although he is well-to-do, even rich, he drives a car that must be near its superannuation. Mr. Attrell belongs, that is, to a social group so secure that it takes pride in refusing to exhibit the usual signs of establishment; his position does not depend upon mere wealth. The gentleness and the quiet uncombativeness—even the dullness—of his temperament lead us to suppose that in all his life Mr. Attrell has never had to fight for anything. Everything has come to him by inheritance.

Mr. O'Donnell's situation is the opposite of Mr. Attrell's. An Irish Catholic, he has had to make his social way against the resistance that has been offered to his ethnic-religious group by the old, established New England families. He has gone to Yale and this means much to him—it means too much: the author, whose origins are the same as Mr. O'Donnell's, intends us to be amused by the fact that one of Mr. O'Donnell's sons has been named Arthur Twining Hadley O'Donnell, after the man who was president of Yale in his father's time. Of the four O'Donnell boys who come to the beach with their father, three bear given names derived from families eminent in the New England Protestant tradition.

At Yale, Mr. O'Donnell had failed to achieve the social success he had hoped for. His disappointment has not diminished over the years: he still takes note of Mr. Attrell's hatband, "that of a Yale society, which Mr. O'Donnell had nothing against, although he had not made it or any other." From the fact that he is a member of the summer colony and of its beach club, we understand that Mr. O'Donnell has been financially successful, but no achievement of his mature life can overcome the uneasy memory of his college defeat. In a single telling phrase, the author suggests the extent of Mr. O'Donnell's lack of ease: "Mr. O'Donnell began his big grin for the Attrells"—aware of his charm, he uses it with conscious contrivance. And of course Mr. O'Donnell is right to be guarded in his approach to the Attrells, who clearly think of him as a stranger and regard him with firm, if gentle, condescension.

But although social behavior and social feelings, of a kind not very creditable to anyone concerned, take up a great deal of room in "Summer's Day," we come to know that they are not being presented only for what importance they may have in themselves. A large part of their interest comes from their incongruity with the intense emotional experience that Mr. Attrell is going through. It is an experience which has nothing to do with the society to which

Mr. Attrell belongs and in which he has a place so much envied by Mr. O'Donnell; it might have come to him had he been a peasant or a tribesman, a Biblical Jew or an ancient Greek. It relates to his essential humanity, to his being a man.

The terrible emotion that Mr. Attrell feels is never named in the story. We know that he and his wife have suffered a great bereavement; their daughter, their only child, has died, and, as we later learn, by her own hand. But Mr. Attrell feels something more than grief; he feels defeat and humiliation, and soon we discover what it is that gives the sore wound to his pride—his childlessness. He is ashamed because he is childless at an age when he can no longer expect to beget children in his marriage.

Summer is the children's season, the beach is the place of childhood and youth, and every incident of Mr. Attrell's short stay at the beach reminds him of his humiliation. He watches the little grandson of his friend Cartwright. He is engaged in conversation by Cartwright's courteous and attractive son. His gaze is drawn to the "vastly pregnant and pretty young woman" who passes. And by way of climax, he is greeted by Mr. O'Donnell walking among his four sons. (Mr. O'Donnell is in fact the father of seven sons: one of them is the baby whose birth has so surprised the community, for everyone had been quite sure Mrs. O'Donnell was too old for childbearing.) We have been told of Mr. Attrell that he seats himself on the bench beside his wife in such a way that he has only to raise his hand to be able to touch her on the shoulder, and that from time to time he does this, and our first impulse has been to suppose that his touch is meant to give comfort and reassurance to his wife. But this impression is at last corrected: the gesture is an effort to receive rather than give comfort and reassurance. Mr. Attrell is confronting the knowledge of his confirmed childlessness and his old age. The knowledge, only half-conscious through most of the story, is finally made explicit to him by the brutal remark of one of the gossiping adolescents he overhears in the bathhouse: "And what makes you think *he* isn't dead, he and the old biddy?"

There is, then, an extreme incongruity in "Summer's Day"—

on the one hand, the preoccupation with the feelings about social status; on the other hand, Mr. Attrell's experience of the end of his procreative life. If we wonder what reason the author could have had for contriving this incongruity, this bringing together of the trifling and artificial with the grim and elemental, the answer is, of course, that the juxtaposition constitutes the drama of the story. It is that much the more bitter for Mr. Attrell that Mr. O'Donnell, whom he regards as socially his inferior, should be so well provided with sons. But there is more than this to be said about the conjunction of social triviality with elemental despair in O'Hara's story. Mr. O'Donnell's frustrated social aspiration, although it is an experience of a quite different order from Mr. Attrell's biological defeat, is not beyond comparison with it. Both men are wounded in their pride, and each of them is the measure of the other's failure. Each can make the other feel inferior and ashamed. If Mr. O'Donnell has the effect upon Mr. Attrell of making him feel less a man, Mr. Attrell has the effect upon Mr. O'Donnell of making him feel less a person.

But of course the wound to Mr. Attrell's pride is a mortal one, and it is the more terrible because it is suffered amid the conventionalities and artificialities of the social life. One of the functions of society is to induce us to have a diminished realization of the grimmer actualities of our biological lives. And these actualities break all the more drastically upon our consciousness when they are made manifest in the very circumstances that are meant to obscure them.

Of This Time, of That Place

LIONEL TRILLING
1905–1975

I T IS not unheard of for an editor to include an example of his own work in an anthology he is making, but it is sufficiently unusual to call for a word of explanation. My thrusting upon the reader a story of my own will perhaps seem less immodest if I say that the idea of doing so originated not with me but with my publisher* and that the argument he advanced for its propriety seemed to me to be cogent—he said that something was to be gained for the understanding of literature by a writer's setting down his thoughts about his own work, especially if he gave an account of the process by which a particular work had come into being.

One possibly instructive thing that such an account can do is to suggest the relation that exists between the actual facts of a writer's experience and the process of his imagination, particularly in the creation of character. Not all writers of fiction are concerned to create characters that seem to be "true to life." (In the present volume, for example, Hawthorne and Kafka have no such concern.) But whenever the nature of the story does call for verisimilitude of character, it can usually be assumed—at least in modern literature—that the author's creation began with reference to an actual person.

An awareness of the relation between an actual person and a cre-

---

* Holt, Rinehart and Winston, publishers of *The Experience of Literature*.

ated character can have no part in our assessment of a work of fiction. Yet it is interesting in itself and it is useful in helping us understand the interplay between actuality and imagination. In the case of this story, I am conscious of how much I have relied on actuality in my representation of the two students. They were both in classes of mine in my early years of teaching at Columbia College, and I recall them as being very much as they appear in the story—so much so that if I were now to say what part my imagination played in the creation of the characters which derive from them, I should incline to claim for it nothing more than its having brought them together in the same story, for in actuality they had no connection with each other. But does this not do an injustice to my imagination, for surely it was at work in my acquaintance with the two actual students, in my observation of the details of their behavior, in the emotions and opinions I had about them?

The story had its origin, as may easily be supposed, in my feelings about the student who is represented under the name of Tertan. (I do not remember how I got this name for him, nor do I know if it is actually an Hungarian name or one that I made up, thinking it would pass for Hungarian. I have always pronounced it with the accent on the last syllable: Ter*tan*.) The moment at which the impulse came to me to write a story about him is not easily forgotten. Some time in the winter after he had been a member of one of my composition classes, I stood next to that unfortunate boy at the loan desk of the College Library; we were both waiting to charge out some books. I greeted him and he responded with a blank and haughty stare. I did not know whether I was being deliberately snubbed or whether his not recognizing me was the sign of some confusion of his mental processes. It seemed to me that both alternatives were possible. For some time I had known that he was suffering from a deep disturbance of the mind. How very deep it was and how much worse it had become since I had last seen him was made plain by his air of majestic self-reference. But also he had good reason to refuse to recognize me, for, by the end of the course he had taken with me, I had refused to recognize him—I had, that is, not consented to know him as he believed he deserved to be known, as he demanded to be known. Like his teacher in the story, I had at first been struck by his intellectual powers. But then, with the passage of time, it had become clear to me that no effort of instruction could possibly overcome the extravagant incoherence of his expression, both in speech and in writing, which I eventually had to understand as a symptom of an extreme mental pathology. He had discovered that I wrote for certain magazines he admired and this had led him to entertain an exaggerated respect for me. Very likely this flattered me into giving him a good deal of attention, which inevitably I diminished when I realized that he was beyond the help of teaching. He did not give me the affection that Tertan in the story gives Dr. Howe, and the respect he did show me was of a most abstract, impersonal kind, yet I had felt a bond with him. When I gave up my special efforts to improve his writing and when at last I communicated to the Dean of the College my opinion of his deranged condition, I felt, against all reason, that I had committed a great disloyalty.

Yet as I saw him standing at the loan desk I could not doubt that he was on the verge of actual insanity, that he was on the way to being beyond the reach of ordinary human feelings. The conflict between my knowledge of this fact and my unreasoning remorse at my "disloyalty" made an emotion which demanded a story. The story, as I at once conceived it, would present the sad irony of a passionate devotion to the intellectual life maintained by a person of deranged mind.

This was what the story was to present, but what was the story to *be?* I remember deciding that some other element was needed in addition to the student's plight and his teacher's emotions. To limit myself to these two elements would make a story that was merely static and linear—and merely pathetic. I did not want a pathetic story for Tertan. I thought he deserved something sterner than that. From the first, I conceived him to be an impressive figure, in some sense heroic, and he therefore made the demand on me that I come as close as I could to tragedy. For this a sense of emotional and physical space was needed, and the possibility of action and decision. I had no idea at all of how to go about getting what I wanted. Then, quite without my bidding, the image of the student who was the original of Blackburn popped up before me.

He had been in a class of mine two or three years earlier, and, as I say, his traits were quite precisely those that I have attributed to Blackburn. He had the same pompous busyness, the same impulse to manipulate his teachers, the same flaunting stupidity, the same sly malevolence together with the same readiness to collapse if strongly resisted or counterattacked. We got on very badly. He once really did threaten to use against me the influence he claimed to have with the Dean. The conference over his bad examination is more or less literally remembered, and in the course of that meeting he did, in a moment of intense supplication, offer to go down on his knees to me, although he did not actually do so. The thought occurred to me that this conduct was "insane," but the word presented itself more as a way of speaking than as a serious idea.

His sudden appearance in my mind to stand beside Tertan delighted me. It immediately helped me in several ways. Blackburn's malevolence rescued the teacher from being merely a sensitive, sympathetic, observing consciousness. By putting Howe in some danger, it made him that much more of a person; it made him someone with a fate and required that he should not only feel but act. And of course it gave added stature to Tertan by suggesting that, if Blackburn were to try to harm his teacher, Tertan must help or at least comfort him. Upon Howe I bestowed the insecurities I had felt as a new instructor, but I sought to give them greater point and justification by making Howe a poet, and a "difficult" and "controversial" poet at that. For the same reason I set the scene in a country college where the smallness and tightness of the community would make a newcomer more conscious of the judgments that were being passed on him.

But if the appearance of Blackburn delighted me, it also filled me with apprehension. There was, I thought, something beautifully appropriate in the juxtaposition of the two students—something all too appropriate! For it occurred to me that the juxtaposition might seem to express an idea which could be very easily formulated: that there are kinds of insanity that society does not accept and kinds of insanity that society does accept. This was an idea to which I could readily assent, and the story does of course lend support to its truth. But it was not what I wanted my story primarily to express. Not only would my feelings and the intention that arose from them be belied, but I felt that it would be an aesthetic misfortune if readers were able to make the formulation thus easily, for a story that can be "summed up" in such a way must prove lacking in power. If the reader can so readily make the point of a story explicit, he comes too quickly to terms with it and is able to put it out of his mind as a thing settled and done with.

But then it occurred to me that if my readers did understand the juxtaposition of the two students in this way, it would prove a great advantage. For the story would seem to them to say one thing when actually it was saying another. I thought it likely that my readers would wish to reverse the judgment that society makes, that they would say that Blackburn's insanity (if that is what it is) should not be accepted by society, and that Tertan's insanity should be accepted. And it seemed to me that they might go one step further and conclude that Tertan, although apparently insane, was not really so. All the authority of certain moral ideas, quite generous ones, would urge them to this conclusion. For was not Tertan terribly alone, and in a socially disadvantaged position, and benevolent, and dedicated, and was he not by way of being a genius, and are not geniuses often said to be mad, although mistakenly?

I seem to have been right in my expectation. When the story was published, many readers wrote to me—and some telephoned—to say that they had been moved by it but disappointed because I had not made it sufficiently clear that Tertan was not really insane.

The truth is, I think, that they knew he was insane and did not want him to be. If the story has any power at all, it surely lies in its ability to generate resistance to the certitude that Tertan is deranged. The impulse to resist the undeniable fact comes, I suppose, from the common apprehension, conscious or unconscious, that the fabric of our reason is very delicate and always in danger. This impulse is reinforced by our modern anxiety at confronting a painful fate which cannot be accounted for in moral terms and which cannot be said to result from some fault of society.

And if I may speak further of the source of what power the story may have, I ought to mention the challenge it offers the reader to reconcile two dissimilar modes of judgment with each other. One is the judgment of morality, the other of science. Judged by morality, Tertan's behavior is sane and good, Blackburn's mad and bad. But no psychiatrist would adjudge Blackburn insane, and no psychiatrist would fail to say that Tertan must soon go to a mental hospital.

It perhaps does not need to be remarked that the story encourages the reader to take an adverse view of the judgment of science. In the classroom discussion of Ibsen's *Ghosts,* DeWitt's expressed belief that science can solve all moral problems is arrogant and shallow, forgivable only because DeWitt is so young. When I began the story with the little scene of Hilda and her camera, I did not have in mind the concluding scene in which Hilda prepares to take a picture with such scientific accuracy; but having begun the story with Hilda taking the picture, the use I might make of her and her camera was suggested to me by the little conversation about photographic distortion in the Dean's office: it gave me the opportunity to allow Tertan to resist the judgment that had been passed on him, to murmur his scornful phrase, "Instruments of precision." And in other details the story seems to take the traditional hostile attitude of literary humanism toward science. But this must not be accepted at its face value. Nothing, I fear, can reverse the diagnosis of Tertan's illness.

Perhaps I should mention that in writing the description of Tertan on Commencement Day, I had consciously in mind Coleridge's description of the daemonic poet at the end of "Kubla Khan" and stole a few phrases from it.

The Guest

ALBERT CAMUS
1913–1960

A COMPARISON of the English version of this story with its French original makes it plain that the translator has done his work with accuracy and sensitivity. He has, however, failed in an important detail—he has not translated the title of the story in a way that conveys the whole of the meaning it has in French. For this he can scarcely be blamed since there is no English word that can render the curious ambiguity of *L'Hôte*, which does indeed mean "the guest" but which also means "the host."*

That the one word stands for both the giver and the receiver of hospitality does not usually create uncertainty about the sense in which it is being used. If there is any possibility of confusion, the French speaker or writer will employ another word for "guest," *l'invité*, although generally the context indicates plainly enough which of the two meanings of *hôte* is intended. But as the French reader encounters the word standing alone as the title of Camus' story, he has no way of telling which of its two significations he is supposed to accept. And even when he has finished the story he will not be entirely sure whether its title refers to the host, the French

---

* The double meaning of the French word is not so odd as it first appears. The English words *guest* and *host* both derive ultimately from an Indo-Iranian root, *ghosti-*, and at one time *host*, like its French cognate, had the two meanings.

schoolteacher, or to the guest, the Arab peasant who is put into the schoolteacher's custody.

The author intended this ambiguity and was sorry that the necessities of translation abolished it.* His regret is not hard to understand, for the single word in its doubleness of meaning proposes the whole import of the story. The teacher and the Arab murderer are poles apart in consciousness and culture, and when Daru is forced to accept the Arab as his prisoner, they stand in the relation to each other of enemies. But the behavior of Daru radically changes this situation. Since he is required to have the man in his charge, he must in common decency feed and bed him, and his simple acts of hospitality give rise in him to feelings of solicitude, even of concern. The Arab, for his part, begins to regard Daru as his protector. Different and separated as these men are, the same word may be used for each of them in his relation to the other: each is the other's *hôte*.

For two men to "break bread" together in the home of one of them is regarded among many peoples as making a connection between them which entails reciprocal obligations of a quite compelling kind, and among the Arab peoples the bond between host and guest has legendarily had peculiar strength. It is not, however, any conscious feeling for the traditional sanctity of the relationship that has power over Daru. Rather, it is the emotions that arise directly out of the situation in which he finds himself, his sense of the irreducible humanity he shares with his guest as they perform together the necessary acts of existence: eating, sleeping, excreting, washing. Communication between the two men must always be minimal, but the communion that develops between them is not small. Indeed, it is quite large enough, as Daru feels it, to induce him to make a considerable sacrifice. He gives the Arab the means of escape and this can scarcely fail to have serious consequences in Daru's own life, perhaps punitive transfer from his present post which he cherishes, perhaps dismissal from the colonial civil service and the loss of his livelihood.

* Camus expressed himself to this effect in a letter to his translator, Justin O'Brien.

The sacrificial act which expresses Daru's sense of the communion of hospitality is of no avail. The Arab guest, for all that he has been arrested for a crime of violence, is a poor-spirited creature, and when Daru gives him the chance to find refuge with the nomad tribes of the South, beyond the reach of French law, he is unwilling to take it. He has no confidence in the nomadic tradition of hospitality of which Daru reminds him; the French authorities, who are bound to punish him, seem less alien to him than the Arab tribes of an unknown place, and he submissively sets out to give himself up to the police.

The ambiguity of the word *hôte* is not exhausted by the meanings of "host" and "guest." In its complicated history there figures the Latin word *hostis,* which means "stranger" and also "enemy." This word developed another form, *hospes,* and another meaning, that of the stranger who is not hostile but who gives the kindness of hospitality. When Daru returns to his classroom, the message written on the blackboard by the Arab's kinsmen tells him that he who had in fact been the beneficent stranger is taken to be the hostile stranger, the enemy. This French Algerian, born to the country and loving it, had lived in at least a kind of amity among the Arabs even though they were on the verge of the revolt that eventually, after a long, cruel war, was to drive the French out of the land they had conquered and colonized. In the general hostility that is coming to prevail, Daru's act of individual humanity is misunderstood and resented, and he who had rejected the claims of his own government at the behest of natural human impulse, finds himself proscribed on all sides, wholly isolated.

Isolation of a certain kind was a condition of existence that Daru had sought and attained. We are led to infer that his experience of the Second World War has disenchanted him with life in society and with much—yet not with all—of human nature. Indeed, "disenchanted" is too mild a word for what he feels. He speaks of himself as "disgusted" with the Arab for his crime and for sharing with "all men . . . their rotten spite, their tireless hates, their bloodlust." He is no less "disgusted" by the idea of being himself co-opted by the social agency that undertakes to control the "rotten spite." And this emotion is validated by the policeman, Balducci, who speaks of himself as being "ashamed" of his work. Daru cannot be thought of as a programmatic idealist. He seems to have no principled opposition to French imperialism and can even say that, in the event of an Arab uprising, he would be willing to fight on the French side. He feels of the land that it is as much his as the Arabs', and no doubt the more because the particular region which he inhabits makes possible the isolate moral condition he desires, the separation from all in people and society that can move him to disgust and shame. The sterility of the great plateau has for him a harsh nobility and beauty: and he loves the exigent, bitter terrain because it permits him the isolateness he has come to need. The bleakly moving ironies of the story are inescapable. Daru has learned that an instinctive impulse of compassion for a fellow-being will lead to his expulsion from the austere Eden of his solitude. A single involvement of feeling will implicate him in a future of human involvements.

The Magic Barrel

BERNARD MALAMUD
1914-

MUCH of the curious power and charm of "The Magic Barrel" is surely to be accounted for by the extraordinary visual intensity of a single paragraph, the last but one, which describes the rendezvous of Leo Finkle and Stella Salzman. The glare of the street lamp under which Stella stands, her white dress and red shoes, and also the red dress and white shoes that Leo had expected her to wear (for this too is envisioned), the bouquet of violets and rosebuds that Leo carries as he runs toward her—these elements of light and color make a scene which is pictorial rather than (in the literal sense of the word) dramatic. Nothing is *said* by the lovers, the whole meaning of the moment lies in what is *seen*. Indeed, had a single word been uttered, the effect of the strange and touching tableau would have been much diminished. In their silence, the lovers exist only in the instant of their first sight of each other, without past or future, unhampered by those inner conditions which we call personality. They transcend personality; they exist in their essence as lovers, as images of loving. And our sense of their transcendence is strengthened by those "violins and lit candles" that revolve in the sky, as if the rendezvous were taking place not in the ordinary world but in a world of emblems, of metaphors made actual.

This concluding scene is striking not only in itself but in the retroactive effect that it has upon the whole story. The anterior episodes take on new meaning when we perceive that they have issued in this moment, with its dignity of pictorial silence, its dreamlike massiveness of significance. The absurd transaction between Salzman and Leo Finkle, Salzman's elaboration of deceit, the dismal comedy of Leo's walk on Riverside Drive with Lily Hirschorn, the odd speech, habits, and manners of the characters—all these sordid or funny actualities of life are transmuted by the rapturous intensity and the almost mystical abstractness of the climactic rendezvous.

The intense pictorial quality of this last scene is of course a reminiscence of the iconography of a particular painter. Whoever knows the work of Marc Chagall will recognize in "the violins and lit candles [that] revolved in the sky" a reference to the pictures of this modern master, in which fantasy suspends the laws that govern the behavior of solid bodies, giving to familiar objects—violins and candles are among his favorites—a magical and emblematic life of their own. Married love is one of Chagall's subjects; many of his paintings represent bride and bridegroom or husband and wife in a moment of confrontation at once rapturous and fearful. Even the kind of bouquet that Leo carries is characteristic of Chagall— James Johnson Sweeney, in his book about the artist, tells us that "flowers, especially mixed bouquets of tiny blossoms," held for Chagall a peculiar interest at one period of his life; they charmed him visually and also by the sentiments they implied.

The knowledge of Malamud's direct reference to Chagall is helpful in understanding the story. For Chagall is the great cele-brator of the religious culture of the Jews of Eastern Europe. It is this culture, now virtually gone, having been systematically destroyed by the Germans and Russians, that poor Salzman represents in a sad, attenuated, transplanted form, and that has put its mark on Leo, who regards it with ambivalence, and on Stella, who has rejected it. It was a culture based upon a devotion to strict religious observance, of which the highest expression was the study of God's Law contained in the Bible and in the vast body of commentary that had accumulated through the ages. Assiduity in study and distinction in learning made the ground not only of piety but of prestige—to rear a learned son or to acquire a learned son-in-law was the ambition of every family concerned with its social standing.

The American reader can comprehend something of the quality of this life by bringing to mind what he knows of the towns of Puritan New England in the seventeenth century. The two theocratic cultures were alike in the intensity of their faith, in the omnipresence of religion in daily life, in the pre-eminence given to intellectual activity both as an evidence of faith and as the source of authority and status—if one recalls the veneration given to Mr. Dimmesdale, the learned young minister of Hawthorne's *The Scarlet Letter,* one has a fair notion of how the rabbi of an orthodox Jewish community was regarded. The two societies are also alike in the harsh and difficult view they took of life, in their belief that life is to be lived under the control of the sterner virtues. Neither can properly be called ascetic, for both—and perhaps especially the Jewish—held marriage in high esteem. But in both societies devotion to the Word of God implied a considerable denigration of the charms and graces of life and a strict limitation upon the passions.

The artist who portrays a culture of this kind will in all probability be concerned with the elements of feeling that it represses or denies; his partisanship will be with the graces of life and the passions of human desire. *The Scarlet Letter* is a case in point—Hawthorne directs all our sympathy to the doomed love of Arthur Dimmesdale and Hester Prynne rather than to the Puritan godliness that chastises it. Chagall depicts with affectionate reverence the religious life he knew in his childhood in the little Russian city of Vitebsk, but his representation of love is marked not only by the joy that is natural to it but also by the joy of its liberation from the piety that had held it in check.

It is a great advantage to art to be able to assert its partisanship with passion as against piety and godliness; in the exercise of this preference the artist is necessarily dealing with a situation charged with high feelings. The passions of human desire probably gain in intensity, and they certainly gain in interest, when they meet with adversity. The love that proclaims itself in the face of strict prohibition has more significance for us than a love that is permitted and encouraged. And of the several kinds of illicitness in love, that which is prohibited by religion and called sin is likely to seem the most intense and interesting of all—it borrows something of the grandeur and absoluteness of the power that forbids it. The rapture of Leo's rendezvous with Stella is not merely that of a young man's erotic urgency. It has something of the ecstasy of religious crisis—Leo is experiencing the hope of what he calls his "redemption." His crisis is the more portentous because he believes that his redemption will come to him through sin.

For that Stella is sinful, that she is sin itself, is the judgment passed upon her by her father's tradition. Her father curses her, although he loves her, and he mourns her as dead because she is unchaste. He speaks of her as "wild," "without shame," "like an animal," even "like a dog." And the young man, bred to the old tradition, is no less ready to recognize her sinfulness, although his image of sin is not repellent but attractive: he eagerly anticipates Stella's appearance in a red dress, red being the color of an open and shameless avowal of sexuality. Red may be the color of sin in general, as when the prophet Isaiah says, "Though your sins be scarlet, they shall be white as snow," but more commonly it represents sexual sin in particular—one of the synonyms the dictionary gives for *scarlet* is *whorish.*

The reader, of course, is not under the necessity of believing that Stella is what her father makes her out to be—possibly her sexual life is marked merely by a freedom of the kind that now morality scarcely reproves. Her dress is in fact not red but white, the virginal color; only her shoes are red. And in her eyes, we are told, there is a "desperate innocence." We see her not as Sin but as what William Blake called Experience, by which he meant the moral state of those who have known the passions and have been marked, and beautified, by the pain which that knowledge inflicts. This is the condition to which Leo Finkle aspires and which he calls his redemption. His meeting is with life itself, and the moment of the encounter achieves an ultimate rapture because of the awareness it brings him, like an illumination, that the joy and pain he had longed to embrace, and had been willing to embrace as sin, need not be condemned.

3 · POETRY

Edward

ANONYMOUS
15th century

IT IS obvious that the extraordinary force of this poem depends largely on its element of surprise. There are two occasions of surprise, both intense, but the one that comes midway in the poem is less shocking than the one at the end because in some measure we have been led to anticipate it. We know that we can expect the disclosure of an especially terrible deed when, to the mother's question about the blood on his sword and the look on his face, the son returns the first of his two prevaricating answers, saying that he has killed his hawk. The substance of this lie is dismaying enough—in the days when hawking was a common sport of the nobility, there was felt to be a close communion between the falcon and the falconer. For a man to kill his horse, as Edward then says he did, perhaps goes even further against natural feeling. And if Edward had in fact killed neither the hawk nor the horse, if the blood on his sword and the look on his face are to be explained by some other killing, we expect it to be yet more horrifying, and of course it is—Edward has killed his father. Shocking as this revelation is, we have been at least a little prepared for it. But we are wholly unprepared for the second revelation, that he has killed his father at the behest of his mother.

In the face of the enormity it sets forth, "Edward" maintains an entire imperturbability. *We* are taken aback, but the poem is not even startled. The violence of its subject does not disorder the strict formality of its pattern; its composure is never ruffled. And this decorum transfers itself to the two characters: the mother's first question, which is asked in a tone that is not especially agitated, is answered in kind by the son, and once the question-and-answer mode of dialogue is established, it is sustained up to the end of the poem, when all the accumulated restraint releases itself in the explosion of the son's last terrible answer. The son is certainly not without emotion from the beginning—he is "sad," he speaks of his father as "deir" to him and bewails the murder, and his reply to his mother's question about his life in the future is bitter. Yet his emotions can scarcely be considered sufficient to his deed, and they do not become so until his last utterance. Up to that point he has submitted to his mother's questioning with a kind of grim courtesy; when at last the curse is torn from him, it is that much the more terrible because it has been so long held back. Yet even when he does utter the curse, which reveals his mother's part in the murder, his utterance is in the strict form the poem has established. What I have called the imperturbability of the poem creates the quiet out of which the terrible surprise leaps at us.

Of a piece with the poem's manner is its objectivity of view, which is uncompromising. Just as "Edward" refuses to make any emotional response to its subject, it refuses to make any moral comment on it—it is wholly detached from what it represents. By employing the dialogue form without a single narrative phrase, it refuses to assume even such involvement as is implied by *telling* what has happened; it undertakes to do nothing more than record what two persons said to each other. We are left free to judge the persons of the dialogue as we will, or must, while the poem itself is silent.

Nor does it say anything by way of explaining the dire happening that it reports. It does not consent to tell us the "whole story." This would consist of many episodes, of which the confrontation of the mother and the son would be only the last. If the events that took place before the dialogue have a claim upon our interest, it is a claim the poem does not recognize. We shall never know what sort of man the dead husband and father was, nor why his wife wanted him dead, nor by what means she induced her son to serve her purpose.

This frustration of our curiosity is strangely pleasurable. We do not find ourselves at a loss because the antecedent events of the poem have not been given us; we willingly consent to the high-handed way in which the poem denies the past. Its actually represented time is a brief moment of the immediate present. Of the five questions and seven answers that occupy this moment of the present, four questions and their answers have to do with the future. But to the past there is no reference at all until the last line, when the past is loosed in all its retributive ferocity. It has, of course, been lying in wait all through the poem. Doubtless the force of that last line is in large part achieved by its effect upon our moral sense: the intensity of our surprise does indeed relate to our horror at the mother's wickedness. Yet it is not only, and perhaps not even chiefly, the moral enormity that so satisfyingly disturbs us: it is rather the sudden, inexorable—we might almost say vengeful—return of the past, which the poem had seemed determined to exclude from its purview.

It has been said of "Edward" that it is "one of the best of all ballads," and it may enhance our sense of the poem to be reminded that its characteristics are not unique but are shared by many poems in the same tradition.

Ballads divide, roughly, into two categories, literary and traditional, the latter sometimes called "popular" or "folk" ballads. In the eighteenth century there developed a considerable interest in the traditional ballads—the genre, in England and Scotland, took its rise in the fifteenth century—and many poets began to write in imitation of them or under their inspiration. But none of the traditional ballads can be assigned to any known author. This is not to say that they were not first composed by individual poets—no credence is now given to the theory, so attractive to many scholars in the nineteenth century, that the ballads were communal creations, that "the people" or "the folk" made them up by some process of composition the nature of which was never explained. The ballads are "popular" in the sense that they were made for and loved by the people, that is to say, by those members of a society who do not belong to the nobility: the literature of the people is distinguished from the literature of the court. But though each ballad was composed by an individual poet, his name was not attached to it and it did not long remain peculiarly his, nor did it necessarily circulate in its original form. For the ballads were not composed in writing nor were they meant to be read. They were intended to be sung and they had their existence in the memories of the people who sang them. The tune of a ballad was more likely to stay constant than its words, which might be altered by the whim of the singer, or by his failure to recall accurately what he had learned, or by his inability to understand one or another detail, such as a custom or an idiom no longer familiar to him. As a consequence, most of the traditional ballads exist in a number of versions.*

What may be thought of as the hallmark of the traditional ballads, the trait common to all examples of the genre, is their way of telling a story. Usually the story concerns an act of violence; it consists of a single situation which is presented at its point of climax, as near as possible to its conclusion. The method of presentation is dramatic rather than narrative, in the sense that it proceeds largely by dialogue; descriptions of scene and the use of what might be called stage-directions are kept to a minimum and are always very simple (in "Edward" there are none). Although the action is violent, the manner in which it is recounted is restrained. No effort is made to achieve originality of diction—the ballad-maker uses simple language and relies upon phrases that are traditional, or even clichés of the tradition. Explanation of motives and comment on morality are rigorously suppressed, and the attitude is one of detachment. It will readily be seen that many of these characteristics derive from the fact that the ballads were sung.

---

* The taking down of the words of ballads from the lips of the singer began in the eighteenth century and still goes on.

In "Edward" two traditional devices of the ballad play a decisive part in the poem's dramatic effectiveness. One of these is called by scholars "incremental repetition," a parallelism of phrase and idea that is strictly maintained, often in the form of question and answer; in "Edward" the natural effectiveness of this device is pointed up by the reiteration of courteous vocatives: "Edward, Edward" and "Mither, mither." Incremental repetition often takes the form of the so-called "nuncupative testament"—*nuncupative* means oral, as distinguished from written, and the phrase refers to a series of questions and answers in which a person in an extreme and usually fatal situation is asked what, upon his death or exile, he will bequeath to each of his relatives. Characteristically the answers are bitter and ironic, and the answer to the last question is usually climactic in its fierceness.

Many of the traditional ballads came over to America and some of them are still sung in part of the country. "Edward" is one of these, but the American version has none of the tragic import of the Scottish. The son explains the stain on his "shirt sleeve" first as the blood of his "little yellow dog," then as the blood of his "little yellow horse"; it is his brother, not his father, he has killed; the cause of the quarrel is fully explained; his mother is not implicated in the murder; he speaks of his departure not as exile but as escape, and he plans to take "Katie dear" with him "to bear [him] company."

They Flee from Me

SIR THOMAS WYATT
1503-1542

O NE OF the things that are bound to strike us early in our acquaintance with this poem is the shift from the "they" of the first stanza to the "she" of the rest of the poem. In the first lines the poet seems to be recalling the high favor in which he stood with many women, or women in general. In the second stanza he recalls one erotic occasion "in special," with a woman who is strongly particularized. And the emotions that follow upon this encounter occupy his bitter and bewildered thought in the third stanza.

Some interpretations of the poem tell us that we must not take the "they" literally, that from the beginning the poet is really talking about "she." There is an advantage in this view—if we accept it, we can suppose that the happening the poet remembers "in special" is not the first love-encounter with one mistress out of many, but one peculiarly memorable encounter out of many with the same woman; of the two possibilities, the latter is the more interesting. But if "they" is really "she," it is by no means clear why the poet pluralized and generalized his mistress. In any case, the visual effect that "they" makes in the first stanza cannot be easily obliterated—one has the de- lighted impression that all the women the poet may ever have made love to are present at the same time in his chamber, all "stalking" together, a little multitude of glimpsed presences, rather like a flock or herd. The adjectives used of them evoke the image of delicate and charming animals: the "naked foot" evokes their lightness of step; their graceful stealth is suggested by their "stalking." This word has more than one meaning—it can refer to the action of a hunter trying to approach an animal without being seen, heard, or scented; or it can describe a way of walking, of humans or animals, with stiff, high, measured steps, like a long-legged bird—but Wyatt probably intended the now obsolete use of the word, which means the soft, cautious tread of an animal. No doubt he wished to create the image of a little herd of light-stepping deer which, in the park of some great manor house, become tame enough to take food from human hands.

But in the conclusion of the stanza three words occur which, for Wyatt's contemporary audience, would tend to modify, even to dispel, the enchanting picture of the preceding lines. Hunting was the chief sport of the gentlemen and ladies of the sixteenth century and they were conversant with its elaborate technical vocabulary. "Range," "seek," and "change" are hunting terms, all referring to the behavior of dogs. "Range" was the word used to describe the action of dogs who rove and stray in search of game. "Seek!" (or "Seek out!") was the command to a dog to begin the search, and "a seek" was a series of notes upon the hunting horn calling the hounds to begin a chase. A "change" was an animal which the hounds meet by chance and then hunt instead of the quarry. These technical meanings are certainly not exclusive of others, and of course they contradict the idea that the pleasing animals, once "gentle, tame, and meek," have become "wild"—hunting dogs and hounds, even when fierce, are not wild. Yet it is probably not an accident that Wyatt uses three words associated with the hunt. The vocabulary of the field suggests that "they" who might once have been hunted have taken on the character of hunters.

"They" were perhaps never without their predatory aspect, and certainly "she" was not. The charm of the remembered erotic scene of the second stanza lies in the mistress's boldness in seduction, her overt display of her erotic power over her lover. Her ever-remembered utterance on the occasion makes this plain, and to Wyatt's audience her way of addressing her lover, "Dear heart," would have brought the idea of a deer, a hart, the pun being then a common one, the easier to make because there was no established difference in the spelling of the two words.

The "specialness" of the episode is superbly conveyed by the first line of the last stanza, "It was no dream; I lay broad waking," of which the very sound suggests the lover's incredulity over the delight of the event at the same time that he insists on its actuality.

Wyatt's poem makes a particular appeal to modern taste because of the directness and colloquial simplicity of its diction: it avoids, as modern poetry characteristically does, any reliance on "poetical" language. Another claim upon modern admiration is the way it handles its metre. The basic pattern of the verse is iambic pentameter, a line of five feet, the foot being typically of two syllables with the stress on the second; for example, the first line of the poem, "They flée from mé that sómetime díd me séek," conforms to this pattern. But many of the succeeding lines—"Busily seeking with a continual change"; "And she me caught in her arms long and small"; "It was no dream; I lay broad waking"—clearly violate this metrical scheme. The prevailing modern supposition is that Wyatt knew exactly what he was doing, that he broke the pattern to achieve the effects he desired. But according to older opinion, Wyatt wrote as he did out of ignorance or incompetence; he was thought to have a bad ear and no control over metrics.

This opinion was established, at least by implication, within a few years after Wyatt's death, in 1557, when Tottel's famous miscellany, *Songs and Sonnets,* was published. Although Wyatt would seem to have had a considerable reputation as a poet, his poems had never been printed in his lifetime, and the *Miscellany* was his first significant publication. To judge by the large space he gave to Wyatt's poems, the editor of the volume had a general admiration of the poet. But he took a rather dim view of Wyatt's skill as a metrist, revising the poems extensively to make them suit the taste of a period which esteemed verse that was "musical" in a mellif-

luous way. The text of the poem that I use in this book is that of
Wyatt's manuscript, except that the spelling has been modernized.
Here is the revised and "corrected" version as it appeared in the
Miscellany, with the spelling modernized:

> They flee from me, that sometime did me seek
> With naked foot stalking within my chamber.
> Once have I seen them gentle, tame, and meek,
> That now are wild, and do not once remember
> That sometime they have put themselves in danger,
> To take bread at my hand; and now they range,
> Busily seeking in continual change.
> 　　Thanked be fortune, it hath been otherwise
> Twenty times better; but once especial,
> In thin array, after a pleasant guise,
> When her loose gown did from her shoulders fall,
> And she me caught in her arms long and small,
> And therewithal so sweetly did me kiss,
> And softly said, "Dear heart, how like you this?"
> 　　It was no dream, for I lay broad awaking.
> But all is turned now, through my gentleness,
> Into a bitter fashion of forsaking;
> And I have leave to go, of her goodness,
> And she also to use newfangleness.
> But since that I unkindly so am served,
> How like you this? what hath she now deserved?

The emendations make a poem that is no doubt prettier than the
original but, by that token, a poem less masculine and strong. They
dispose of any questions about stress that the original version might
present to us, but in doing this deprive the poem of a considerable
part of its interest. When, for example, the two syllables are added to
the line we have had occasion to notice and we read it as regular
iambic pentameter, "It wás no dreám, for Í lay bróad awáking,"* it
comes very smoothly off the tongue, but how much firmer, bolder,
and more dramatic is the line as Wyatt actually wrote it. When we
speak the original line aloud, our emphasis falls very decisively:

---

* The concluding extra syllable does not make it irregular. Even a strict adherence
to rule does not require only a series of five iambics to a line.

once we are aware that it is not conforming to the pattern, we say, "It was nó dream," or perhaps, "It was no dréam," for either stress is possible and our freedom to choose between the two makes the phrase the more engaging. Then as we go on to the second half of the line, "I lay broad waking," our stress falls weightily on "broad" and we naturally tend to sustain the sound for a perceptible instant in order to accomplish the somewhat difficult transition to the stressed syllable that immediately follows, for in the line as Wyatt wrote it we naturally stress "waking" equally with "broad." The emended line, compared to the original, is light, easy, and relatively characterless, and the same judgment can be made on all the other editorial changes in the poem.

But aware as we may be of Wyatt's bold colloquialism and his roughness of metre, we must not leave out of account in our response to the poem the part played in it by formal strictness. The stanza that Wyatt uses is the so-called Rhyme Royal, which has a tradition going back to Chaucer and the Scottish poets; Shakespeare was later to use it for his *Rape of Lucrece*. The stanza moves with an energy that is at once vivacious and grave, and its inherent elegance makes a happy frame for the colloquial directness of the lines themselves.

There is one point at which we may regard the Tottel version with some degree of sympathy, in its revision of the last two lines of the poem. The editor's repetition of "How like you this?" would seem to express his sense that the stanza should be brought into a firmer relation with the rest of the poem, that it dissipates rather than discharges the energy that the first two stanzas have built up. Certainly the lover's plaint creates the effect of diffuseness, even of anticlimax. In fact, for many readers the meaning of these lines proves far too elusive, or, if discovered, inadequate to the earlier stanzas of the poem. It is not difficult to understand that the lover's "gentleness" should have been the cause of his mistress's indifference and infidelity. But why is the "fashion of forsaking" a "strange" one? (Although one would rather have it a "strange" than a "bitter" fashion, as in the revised version.) That the lover should have been given "leave to go" by the mistress's "goodness" is an irony which is either obscure or too simple, and it is certainly not clear why she has need of her own "goodness" to give her leave to "use newfangleness." Even if we have in mind the old meaning of "kindly"—that is, "naturally"—the irony of "But since that I so kindely am served!" seems querulous (perhaps this is one reason why Tottel changes it to "unkindly") and the question about what the mistress "hath deserved" has the aspect of mere petulance.

Yet so great is the authority of what has gone before in the poem that many readers are not disposed to be severe upon the faults they find in the conclusion. Their love of the whole leads them to decide that the troubling part is not so much a failure as a puzzle.

A Valediction: Forbidding Mourning

JOHN DONNE
1573-1631

I N 1912 the Oxford University Press published Professor H. J. C. Grierson's edition of the poems of John Donne, two handsomely printed volumes bound in the familiar Oxford dark-blue cloth. The first volume contained the poems, many of which had never before been printed; the second volume was devoted to notes which dealt with problems of the text and explicated the often obscure philosophical, scientific, and historical allusions. Perhaps no other work of English literary scholarship in our century is so famous or has had so much influence.

It would not be true to say that Donne had been unknown or unvalued in the nineteenth century and the first years of the twentieth. Edmund Gosse's biography in 1899 and three editions of the poetical works between 1872 and 1896 attest to a continuing awareness of the poet. But he was likely to be considered a minor figure, interesting chiefly for the vivacious idiosyncrasies of his style and for the discrepancy between the bold cynicism of his early poems and the passionate religious intensity of his later years when, after taking holy orders, he became one of the notable figures of the Church of England. Historians of literature were not disposed to study his work in any particularity and the criticism of the day scarcely took him into account. After Grierson's edition, however, Donne came to be seen as a pre-eminent figure not only of the seventeenth century but of the whole of English literature. The scholarly and critical studies of his work proliferated rapidly and are by now innumerable.

Yet Donne in his own time had been greatly admired; he had fallen into disesteem only in the eighteenth century. The reasons for the decline were formulated in Dr. Samuel Johnson's essay on Cowley in *The Lives of the English Poets*. In a passage that has become a *locus classicus* of English criticism, Johnson dealt with the group of seventeenth-century poets whom he called "metaphysical." He used the word, in the fashion of his time, with the intention of reproach, to characterize a kind of poetry that he considered so abstruse, fine-drawn, and far-fetched as to be quite out of accord with good sense and even nature itself. Johnson's name for the group established itself and is still in use, although without any of its former pejorative meaning.*

The first characteristic of the metaphysical poets remarked on by Johnson was their learning and their desire to exhibit it. They took pleasure in deriving the elements of their poems from esoteric knowledge of all kinds and, in what to Johnson seemed an extravagant desire to be original and striking, they brought together facts and ideas which he thought incongruous and therefore unnatural; they filled their poems, he said, with "enormous and disgusting hyperboles," their figures of speech were often "grossly absurd" and sometimes "indelicate." They gave precedence to ingenuity over emotion, with the result that "their courtship was void of fondness and their lamentations of sorrow. Their wish was only to say what they hoped had never been said before."

By their excessive concern with minute particularities they transgressed against a chief tenet of eighteenth-century poetic theory, which held that poetry's most impressive effects were to be gained through spacious generalizations. "Great thoughts," said Johnson, "are always general, and consist in positions not limited by exceptions, and in descriptions not descending to minuteness." Dryden, while belittling Donne as a poet, had conceded that he was to be

---

* Although Dryden had earlier said that "Donne affects the metaphysics," it was Johnson who gave currency to the adjective as a way of characterizing a mode of writing.

praised for his wit, but Johnson, defining wit "as a kind of *discordia concors,* a combination of dissimilar images or discovery of occult resemblances in things apparently unlike," concluded that "of wit thus defined" Donne and his fellows "have more than enough." The versification of the metaphysical poets won as little approval from Johnson as their diction and imagery—he judged it to be wholly contrived and inept. He does not deny these poets a measure of respect, but the praise it yields is small indeed: "Yet great labor, directed by great abilities is never wholly lost: if they frequently threw away their wit upon false conceits, they likewise sometimes struck out unexpected truth; if their conceits were far-fetched, they were often worth the carriage. To write on their plan, it was at least necessary to read and think."

But early in the nineteenth century the pendulum of taste began its swing to a more favorable view of the metaphysical school, especially Donne. Coleridge anticipated modern opinion when he spoke of Donne's "force" and observed that his "most fantastic out of the way thoughts" were expressed in "the most pure and genuine mother English." Still, that a sense of Donne as odd and eccentric and not in the line of succession of the great English poets qualified Coleridge's admiration is made clear in his much-quoted lines describing Donne's poetical mode:

> With Donne, whose muse on dromedary trots,
> Wreathe iron pokers into true-love knots;
> Rhyme's sturdy cripple, fancy's maze and clue,
> Wit's forge and fire-blast, meaning's press and screw.

Later in the century, two other poets, Browning and Hopkins, both of them antagonistic to the prevailing belief that English verse was at its best when it was harmonious and "smooth," found an affinity with Donne and his dromedary-mounted muse, and Rossetti and Swinburne held him in esteem especially for his love-poetry. But no poet of the nineteenth century could speak of him with Yeats's intensity of praise, an intensity that actually comes close to nonsense —writing to thank Professor Grierson for the gift of his edition, Yeats says of Donne that "he who is but a man like us all has seen God."

The new enthusiasm for Donne is explained, of course, by the confirmation he gave to an important tendency of modern poetry. A celebrated statement of what the new poets found in him was made by T. S. Eliot in his review of an anthology of the metaphysical poets that Grierson published in 1921. For Eliot the characteristic virtue of the seventeenth-century poets was their ability to "feel their thought," to experience it as if it were a sensation, "as immediately as the odor of a rose." At some point later in the century, Eliot goes on to say, there occurred a "dissociation of sensibility," and thought and feeling in poetry became separated from each other. Eliot does not refer explicitly to Johnson's objection that metaphysical poetry was excessively intellectual at the cost of feeling, but when he says of Donne that to him "a thought was an experience, it modified his sensibility," it is obviously Johnson's view which he has in mind and means to contradict. Yeats had said much the same thing in his letter to Grierson: "Your notes tell me exactly what I want to know. Poems that I could not understand or could but understand are now clear and I notice that the more precise and learned the thought the greater the beauty, the passion; the intricacies and subtleties of his imagination are the length and depths of the furrows made by his passion."

It was not only Donne's power of conjoining thought and emotion that seemed so important to the modern poets but also his taking it for granted that any of the seemingly disparate elements of experience might be brought together with interesting and significant effect. The conjunction of things and ideas not usually believed to consort with each other had seemed to Dr. Johnson to be a poetical vice, a departure from nature. The modern poets, and after them the modern critics, held it to be a poetical virtue, and exactly because it was natural, at least for poets. "When a poet's mind is perfectly equipped for its work," Eliot said, "it is constantly amalgamating disparate experience; the ordinary man's experience is chaotic, irregular, fragmentary. The latter falls in love or reads Spinoza, and these two experiences can have nothing to do with each other, or with the noise of the typewriter or the smell of cooking; in the mind of the poet these experiences are always forming wholes."

This well-known passage exemplifies the tendency of modern writers to reject the belief that there are orders of experience, distinct in themselves and separate from each other, of which some are appropriate to art, others inappropriate.

Donne's versification was no less important to the new poets than the quality of his thought and feeling. What Dr. Johnson and most eighteenth-century readers heard as "rugged" verse and therefore unpleasing, what Coleridge heard as powerful but ungraceful, the trot of the dromedary, the limp of the sturdy cripple, was heard by the poets of the twentieth century as the authoritative accent of actuality. They understood—as had the readers of the seventeenth century—that Donne did not fail in an attempt to conform to the demands of a metrical system but that he wrote a kind of verse in which the rhythms of the natural speaking voice assert themselves against, and modify, the strict pattern of the metre. It is worth noting that Yeats received the gift of Grierson's edition at the point in his development when, under the influence of Ezra Pound, his verse was moving steadily away from the relatively soft and "poetic" mode of his early work to the harder, more downright and forceful versification (and diction) of his great period.

In reading "A Valediction: Forbidding Mourning" it is the voice of the poem that first engages our attention. The opening line is audacious in its avoidance of the metre that is to be established in the following lines of the stanza and maintained through the rest of the poem, although not in a strict or mechanical way; no matter how we read it, we cannot scan that opening line, and its bold freedom leads us to feel that it is saying something "actual" rather than "poetic." The succeeding lines, although controlled by metre, sustain this feeling; they sound in the ear as the utterance of a present speaker. It is in the ambience of the speaker's voice that the metaphysical elements of the poem are presented to us. The comparison between the significance of earthquakes and the "trepidation of the spheres" and the brief simile of the beaten gold, the elaborated simile of the pair of compasses, are the less likely to seem merely ingenious, or studied, or out of the way, because they are suffused with the tones of the voice that proposes them, its directness and masculine vigor, its gravity and its serious humor.

Dr. Johnson took particular notice of the compass simile, introducing his quotation of the three stanzas in which it is developed with this sentence: "To the following comparison of a man that travels and his wife that stays at home, with a pair of compasses, it may be doubted whether absurdity or ingenuity has a better claim." For Johnson the absurdity lay in the fact that compasses seemed to him to be incongruous with the emotional circumstances they were meant to represent. A pair of compasses suggests what is mechanical and unfeeling: it is metallic and stiff, and an instrument of precision employed in, and emblematic of, the sternly rational and abstract discipline of geometry; it therefore stands at the furthest remove from the emotion of love. The simile of the compasses substantiated Johnson's opinion that metaphysical poetry cannot express emotion and is "void of fondness."

Although we will perceive as readily as Dr. Johnson that there is some measure of unlikelihood in the comparison, this will not prevent our having pleasure in it. On the contrary, we will tend to be pleased exactly because we are taken aback. For us, the figure's suggestion of cold rationality and abstractness is modified by the humor with which it is developed, a humor which does not in the least diminish the direct sincerity of the utterance. Isaac Walton, in his brief life of his friend, tells us that Donne composed the poem in 1611 while he was on a diplomatic mission to France and that it was addressed to his wife Anne. The marriage was a famous one in its day, both because of the tempestuous courtship that preceded it and the unbroken tender devotion of the husband and wife. Walton mentions the circumstance in which the poem was written and the person to whom it was addressed out of his sense that the poem, for all the ingenuity of its "conceits," is a direct, personal, and fully felt communication, wholly appropriate to its occasion. With this judgment the modern reader would find it hard to disagree.

Lycidas

JOHN MILTON
1608–1674

I T IS often said by critics and teachers of literature that "Lycidas" is the greatest lyric poem in the English language, and very likely it is. But the word "greatest" applied to a work of art is not always serviceable; the superlative judgment can immobilize a reader's response to a work, or arouse his skeptical resistance. It may be that we are given a more enlightening introduction to the poem by a critic who held it in low esteem—so far from thinking that "Lycidas" was superlatively great, Samuel Johnson thought it a very bad poem. Without doubt Dr. Johnson was wrong in this judgment and the grounds on which he bases it are quite mistaken. But his erroneous views, stated in his characteristically bold and unequivocal fashion, make plain how the poem ought to be regarded.

The sum of Dr. Johnson's objections is that "Lycidas" is insincere. It purports to be a poem of mourning; the poet is expressing grief over the death of a friend. But can we possibly believe in the truth of his emotion? Grief, Dr. Johnson says in effect, inclines to be silent or at least to be simple in its utterance. It does not express itself so elaborately, with as much artifice as Milton uses or with such a refinement of fancy and such a proliferation of reference to ancient legend and lore. "Passion plucks no berries from myrtle or ivy," Dr. Johnson said, "nor calls upon Arethuse and Mincius, nor tells of rough *satyrs* or *fauns with cloven heels*. Where there is leisure for fiction, there is little grief."

Of the poem's elaborateness of artifice, even of artificiality, there can be no question. The poet does not speak in his own person but in the guise of a "shepherd" or "swain." That is to say, he expresses his grief, such as it is, through the literary convention known as the pastoral, so called because all the persons represented in it are shepherds (the Latin word for shepherd is *pastor*). This convention of poetry has a long history. It goes back to the Greek poet Theocritus (c. 310–250 B.C.), who, in certain of his poems, pretended that he and his poet-friends were shepherds of his native Sicily. Far removed from the sophistication and corruption of cities, the fancied shepherds of Theocritus devoted themselves to the care of their flocks and to two innocent pursuits—song and the cultivation of love and friendship. Their only ambition was to be accomplished in song; their only source of unhappiness was a lost love or the death of a friend, the latter being rather more grievous than the former and making the occasion for an *elegy,* a poem of lament. Virgil brought the pastoral convention into Roman literature with his *Eclogues,* and it was largely through his influence that it became enormously popular in the Renaissance. This popularity continued through the eighteenth century, but the mechanical way in which it came to be used in much of the verse of that period justifies Dr. Johnson in speaking of the pastoral mode as "easy, vulgar, and therefore disgusting." In the nineteenth century the convention lost its vogue, but even then it was used for two great elegies, Shelley's "Adonais" and Matthew Arnold's "Thyrsis." For the poets of our time it seems to have no interest.

The fictional nature of the pastoral was never in doubt. Nobody was supposed to believe and nobody did believe that the high-minded poetic herdsmen were real, in charge of actual flocks. Yet the fiction engaged men's imaginations for so long a time because it fulfilled so real a desire of mankind—it speaks of simplicity and innocence, youth and beauty, love and art. And although the poets were far from claiming actuality for their pastoral fancies, they often used the convention to criticize actual conditions of life, either explicitly as Milton does in the passage on the English clergy (lines 108–131) or by implication.

The traditional and avowedly artificial nature of the pastoral was exactly suited to the occasion which produced "Lycidas." Milton could scarcely have felt at Edward King's death the "passion" that Dr. Johnson blames him for not expressing, for King, although a college mate, had not been a close friend. He composed "Lycidas" not on spontaneous impulse but at the invitation of a group of Cambridge men who were bringing out a volume of poems to commemorate King. For Milton to have pretended to an acute sense of personal loss would have been truly an insincerity. Yet he could not fail to respond to what we might call the general pathos of a former comrade's dying "ere his prime," and by means of the pastoral elegy he was able to do what was beautifully appropriate to the situation—he associated King's death with a long tradition in which the deaths of young men had been lamented. Ever since the dawn of literature the death of a young man has been felt to have an especial pathos—how often it is evoked in the *Iliad;* and few things in the Bible are more affecting than David's mourning for his young friend Jonathan and his young son Absalom. It is this traditional pathos that Milton evokes from the death of Edward King. Had he tried to achieve a more personal expression of feeling, we should have responded not more but less. What engages us is exactly the universality of the emotion.

The pastoral convention is also appropriate to King's commemoration in two other respects. One is the extent to which the pastoral elegy was known and cultivated by young men in the English universities of Milton's time, if only because in their study of the ancient languages they were assigned the task of composing verses in this genre. Milton's own earliest-known poems are such college exercises, and all the poets who are mentioned or referred to in "Lycidas"— Theocritus, Virgil, Ovid—were subjects of university study. And in Milton's age as in ours, the college days of a young man were thought to have something like a pastoral quality—from mature life men look back to that time as being more carefree, and to their relationships then as having been more generous, disinterested, and comradely than now: why else do college alumni return each spring to their old campuses? Our very word *alumnus* expresses what Milton means when he says that he and King were "nurs'd upon the self-same hill," for an *alumnus* is a foster child, a nursling of *alma mater,* the fostering mother.

Dr. Johnson did not make it an item in his charge of insincerity that Milton, mourning a young man dead, is so preoccupied with a young man alive—himself. But we cannot fail to see that this is the case. Milton begins his poem with an unabashed self-reference, to his feeling about himself as a young poet who has not yet reached the point in his development when he is ready to appear before the public. One reason he gives for overcoming his reluctance and undertaking the poem in memory of King is his hope that this will make it the more likely that someone will write to commemorate him when he dies. When he speaks about the poetic career and about poetic fame in relation to death, it is manifestly his own career and fame and his own death that he has in mind—the thought arouses him to a proud avowal of his sense of his high calling. And as the poem concludes, it is again to himself that he refers. Having discharged his duty of mourning, he turns from death and sorrow back to life and his own purposes:

> At last he rose, and twitch'd his mantle blue:
> To-morrow to fresh woods, and pastures new.

These passages have led many readers to conclude that "Lycidas" is not about Edward King at all but about John Milton. They are quite content that this should be so. They take the view that though the poem may fail in its avowed intention, it succeeds in an intention that it does not avow—they point to the fact that the most memorable and affecting parts of the poem are those in which Milton is his own subject. But in weighing this opinion we might ask whether it is ever possible to grieve for a person to whom we feel akin without grieving for ourselves, and, too, whether the intensity with which we are led to imagine our own inevitable death is not a measure of the kinship we feel with the person who has already died. Certainly nothing in "Lycidas" more strongly enforces upon us the pathos of untimely death than that it puts the poet in mind of his own death—for what he says of himself we are bound to feel of ourselves. And how better represent the sadness of death than to put it beside the poet's imagination of the fulness of life?

It must also be observed that Milton speaks of the death of Edward King and of his own imagined death and actual life in a context that does not permit our mere ordinary sense of the personal to prevail. He brings them into conjunction not only with the traditional pathos of young men dead ere their prime but also with the traditional evocations of the death of young gods, and their resurrection. No religious ceremonies of the ancient peoples were more fervently performed than those in which the death of a young male deity—Osiris, Adonis, Atys, Thammuz—was mourned and his resurrection rejoiced in. The myths of these gods and the celebration of their death and rebirth represented the cycles of the vital forces; the dying and reborn god symbolized the sun in its annual course, the processes of vegetation, the sexual and procreative energy, and sometimes, as in the case of Orpheus, poetic genius. Once we are aware of this, Milton's concern with himself takes on a larger significance. It is not himself-the-person that Milton is meditating upon but himself-the-poet: that is, he is thinking about himself in the service not of his own interests but of the interests of the "divine" power that he bears within him.

In this service Milton is properly associated with Edward King, who was also a poet—it does not matter that King was not distinguished in his art. But there was yet another aspect of the service of divine power in the fact that King was a clergyman, a priest of the Church of England, which licenses the inclusion in the elegy of St. Peter's explosion of wrath against the negligent and corrupt clergy of the time. This famous passage constitutes only a small part of the poem, but the importance that Milton gave it is made plain by his extended reference to it in the "argument." Some readers will find a bitter condemnation of clerical corruption inappropriate to an elegy, and will be jarred and dismayed by the sudden introduction of Christian personages and considerations into a poem that has been, up to this point, consistently pagan. That Milton is himself quite aware that the passage will seem incongruous to the pastoral form is indicated in the lines in which he invokes the "return" of the "Sicilian Muse," who has been scared away by St. Peter's "dread voice." But in Milton's thought ancient pagan literature and mythology and the Judaeo-Christian religion were never really at odds with each other. It is a salient characteristic of his great and enormously learned mind that Milton gave allegiance to both, and used for Christian ideas the literary forms of paganism. In the pastoral convention he found a natural conjunction of the two: we can readily see that the poetic convention has affinity with the feelings attached to the pastoral life by Biblical Judaism and, more elaborately, by Christianity. The peaceable Abel was a shepherd and so was Abraham. So was David, and a poet-shepherd at that, one of whose psalms begins, "The Lord is my Shepherd, I shall not want." It was shepherds who saw the Star of Bethlehem rise; Jesus is both the Lamb of God and the Good Shepherd. *Pastor* is the name for the priest of a parish, the congregation being his flock, and the form of a bishop's crozier is the shepherd's crook.*

As the poem moves toward its conclusion the mingling of pagan and Christian elements is taken wholly for granted. This conjunction of the two traditions exemplifies yet another characteristic

---

* The affinity between the pagan and the Christian idealizations of the pastoral life was no doubt affirmed by the common belief that Virgil's fourth *Eclogue* was a prophecy of the birth of Christ. The Christian acceptance of the pagan convention imposed one small condition which it is amusing to note: although I have referred throughout my comment to shepherds, the herdsmen of the Greek bucolic poets herded either sheep or goats, and, indeed, Milton took the name Lycidas from a character in a poem by Theocritus who was not a shepherd but a goatherd. But Christianity separates the sheep from the goats, regarding the latter with suspicion and even aversion—in fact, it assigns the physical attributes of the goat to the Devil himself—and does not permit their presence in pastoral poetry. When Spenser in *The Shepheardes Calender* mentions a "Goteheard," his anonymous contemporary who annotated the poems explains: "By Gotes in scrypture he represented the wicked and reprobate, whose pastour also must needes be such."

of the poem, its inclusiveness. "Lycidas" gathers up all the world, things the most disparate in space and time and kind, and concentrates them in one place and moment, brings them to bear upon one event, the death of the poet-priest. The poem's action is, as it were, summarized in the lines about "the great Vision" of St. Michael the Angel who, from Land's End, the southernmost tip of England, looks afar to Spain but is adjured to "look homeward." So the poem looks afar to the ancient world and also turns its gaze upon contemporary England. From "the bottom of the monstrous world" it turns to heaven, and from all the waters of the world to all the flowers of all the seasons of the Earth, and from the isolation of Lycidas in death to the "sweet societies" of his resurrection and everlasting life through the agency of Christ. It plays literary games with the most solemn subjects, and juxtaposes the gravest ideas with the smallest blossoms, using their most delicate or homely names (culminating in the daffadillies, which sound like the very essence of irresponsible frivolity). And then, when it has brought all the world together, and life out of death and faith out of despair, it has its "uncouth swain," the shepherd-poet, with the jauntiness of a task fully discharged, announce that the mourning is now at an end. Life calls the poet to other work and he must answer the call.

To His Coy Mistress

ANDREW MARVELL
1621–1678

IN HIS essay on Andrew Marvell, T. S. Eliot remarks that Marvell's best poems, which are few in number, "must be well known from the *Golden Treasury* and the *Oxford Book of English Verse*." Eliot regards "To His Coy Mistress" as one of the best of Marvell's poems and certainly it is quite the best known, occupying a special place not only in the awareness but in the affection of the readers of our time. And it is, to be sure, found in the *Oxford Book of English Verse*. But it does not appear, as Eliot supposed, in the *Golden Treasury*, the famous anthology of English lyrical poems which has been in print ever since it was first published in 1861. The editor of the *Golden Treasury*, F. T. Palgrave, was a man of excellent literary judgment. From among Marvell's poems he chose three very good ones for his volume. But he did not choose "To His Coy Mistress"—which tells us much about the Victorian age and the nature of taste and how it changes.

Its omission is particularly interesting in the light of what Palgrave tells us of the high esteem in which it was held by his close friend Tennyson, an esteem that Palgrave himself clearly shared. When the *Golden Treasury* was in the making, Palgrave often discussed the selections with Tennyson; in his account of their conversations, the only one of the poet's opinions that he records in detail is the one about "To His Coy Mistress," which, Palgrave says,

Tennyson delighted to read aloud, "dwelling more than once on the magnificent hyperbole, the powerful union of pathos and humor." Yet despite the great authority his friend's judgment had for Palgrave, it did not induce him to include the poem in his collection.

It would seem that a poem for which two Victorian gentlemen might express great admiration in private conversation could, because of its unsuitable moral and emotional tone, be thought inappropriate for the general public. The erotic content of the poem is of a quite explicit kind, and the intentions of the lover are not what the Victorian audience would have called "honorable," for it is not marriage that his urgency proposes to the lady. He speaks openly of his "lust" and slightingly of the lady's ideas of honor and virginity. Despite his preoccupation with time and mortality, he does not promise the lady that his love, after its consummation, will endure at least until death: he is concerned only with *now*, and in the last of the three movements of the poem the word occurs three times. Victorian morality put a great value upon chastity; it did not sanction the directly erotic impulse outside of marriage nor did it permit the literary representation of the erotic even in the married state. It could only have been offended by Marvell's frank naturalism, which takes no account of moral considerations and even suggests that they are set at naught by the inexorability of time and the inevitability of death.

The "powerful union of pathos and humor" to which Tennyson responded so warmly is undoubtedly the element of the poem that chiefly engages the present-day reader. But Palgrave had reason to suppose that the Victorian audience would be made uncomfortable by this very thing. The Victorian reader was certainly not unused to a union of pathos and humor, but he—perhaps more especially she—was not likely to be at ease with an instance of the union that issued in an irony at once gay and bitter, especially when the irony touched the subject of love. The double-mindedness of irony is alien to the tradition of Victorian love poetry, which cherished a direct singleness of emotion.

The humor of the poem begins, of course, in the "magnificent hyperbole" and it is directed both to the lady herself and to the conventions of courtly love, according to which the lover dedicates himself to the beloved, who accepts his adoration but holds out no hope that his wooing will ever be successful. The lover says that the lady deserves to be wooed according to this convention, virtually *ad infinitum,* and he goes into precise detail to explain how much time might properly be given to the contemplation and praise of each of her charms, were the couple to have, as we say, all the time in the world. In this gay absurdity we hear a note of solemnity, even of fear—the reference to *so much* time, to the long procession of centuries and ages which is to culminate in "the last age" that brings the world to an end, cannot fail to be awesome. Yet the awe is only lightly suggested; as yet it yields no more than a faint undertone to the humor with which the lover teases his lady.

The teasing breaks off, however, with dramatic suddenness when the lover brusquely evokes "Time's winged chariot" and the death it is bringing. The huge leisure of the first movement is instantly dispelled. The world has been seen as a Garden of Eden through which the couple, its Adam and Eve, wander at will; now, at the sound of the hurrying chariot of Time, the garden, fertilized by its rivers, the distant exotic Ganges and the homely Humber, is transformed into the "deserts of vast eternity," which are not to be traversed and which do not accommodate the unceasing growth of a "vegetable love." Now the tone of the lover's urging becomes brutally explicit in its reference to death, for it is not death in the abstract that the lady is asked to think about but the physical decay which makes a mockery of the scruples that keep her from putting her body to what her lover thinks is its right and natural use. But his bitter, desperate evocation of death modulates to the magnificent whimsicality with which the second movement concludes:

> The grave's a fine and private place,
> But none, I think, do there embrace.

It is as if the lover, having done all he could to frighten the lady into an awareness of the human situation, would now wish to lighten the imposed weight of reality by a humor that is at least as tender as it is grim.

The poem, we readily perceive, is an argument in quite strict logical form. Each of the three movements is a step in a syllogism: 1. If we had all time at our disposal. . . . 2. But we do not. . . . 3. Therefore. . . . What the "therefore" proposes is, of course, love upon the instant. The metaphors in which the proposal is made are curious and of great intensity. In the second movement Time had been given something of a divine character, for the "winged chariot" brings to mind the sun-god, Phoebus Apollo, who, in ancient Greek myth, was represented as a charioteer coursing through the heavens. But now Time, in a vague yet powerful image, is represented as a carnivorous beast, the more dreadful because it is not swift and fierce; and the lover speaks of himself and the lady as no less predatory than their foe—they are to be "amorous birds of prey," capable of devouring Time itself by the ferocity of their love. The image of the lovers as birds of prey, which inverts the old conventional image of the amorous dove, was intended to be startling. To the modern reader the phrase "birds of prey" will perhaps have unpleasant connotations, but to Marvell's contemporaries it would have brought to mind the falcon, which, in a day when hunting with the falcon was still a sport of the aristocracy, was thought to be a particularly noble and beautiful animal.

The conjunction of "strength" and "sweetness," in itself one of the striking details of the poem, naturally proceeds from the representation of Time as a carnivorous beast. When the young Samson killed a lion, he left the carcass in a thicket and a swarm of bees hived in it; returning to the spot, Samson ate some of the honey and this made the substance of the famous riddle he put to the Philistines: "Out of the eater came forth meat, and out of the strong came forth sweetness." The Philistines, unable to puzzle out the riddle by themselves, prevailed upon Samson's wife to find out the answer and were able to say, "What is sweeter than honey? and what is stronger than a lion?"*

* See the Book of Judges, Chapter 14.

The lover's suggestion that he and the lady should "roll" all their strength and all their sweetness "into one ball" is curious, even bizarre. The figure may possibly have its source in the scarab or beetle by which the Egyptians symbolized Horus, their god of the sun. It is characteristic of the scarab that it makes a ball of dung in which it lays its eggs; this ball appears in the innumerable representations of the scarab that the Egyptians made. It was thought of as the sun that the god propelled before him.

The "iron gates of life" through which the pleasures of the lovers are to be "torn" are difficult to visualize and to explain. Tennyson thought that the iron gates might better have been iron *grates,* as suggesting more directly the difficulty of tearing the pleasures through them, but this change would have destroyed the awesomeness of the great vague trope which, for Marvell's contemporary readers, would probably have brought to mind the two gates of Hades in Virgil's *Aeneid,* one of ivory through which the false dreams come, the other of horn through which come the true dreams. That the iron gates cannot easily be visualized in relation to the pleasures will suggest that the force of a metaphor does not depend on its visual explicitness.

Certain words of the poem should perhaps be glossed to ensure that they are understood in the sense that Marvell intended. *Coy* means reluctant and hesitant, with implications of a certain self-consciousness or insincerity, but it does not have the overtone it later acquired, of vapidity or cuteness. In our modern usage, a man's *mistress* is a woman with whom he has an established sexual relationship, but in Marvell's day the word denotes the woman to whom a man has pledged his love. The *vegetable* quality of the love that the poet imagines if the lovers had all time at their disposal does not have the pejorative meaning we might now find in it, of being wholly dull, without sentience; it refers to the power of growth and implies the vitality or livingness of the growing thing. *Quaint* did not have its modern sense of something pleasantly old-fashioned but rather of something elegantly fanciful, with a touch of what we should call affectation.

An Essay on Man:
Epistle I

ALEXANDER POPE
1688–1744

MODERN critics, even those who take the greatness of Pope for granted, are likely to use a tone of advocacy when they write about him. They are aware that the taste of most of their readers does not readily respond to the poet whose genius was universally acclaimed in his own time. Pope is the chief English poet of the eighteenth century and it is he who bore the brunt of the Romanticists' repudiation of the poetic standards of that age. To Wordsworth and Coleridge, he stood for everything in poetry that they contemned. They saw him as virtually an anti-poet, the corrupter of poetry's true essence. Only Byron among the Romanticists found it possible to admire him, and Byron's enthusiastic praise was thought by many to be a mere perversity. The nineteenth century's antagonism to Pope was brought to a climax and codified by Matthew Arnold in his famous essay, "The Study of Poetry." Speaking of the importance that poetry would have in the modern world and calling the roll of those English poets who were likely to be of the greatest spiritual value, Arnold explicitly excluded Pope and his great predecessor Dryden from the illustrious roster on the ground that they were really not poets at all. "Though they may write in verse," he said, "though they may in a certain sense be masters of the art of versification, Dryden and Pope are not classics of our poetry, they are classics of our prose."

In the early decades of the twentieth century the reputation of the two poets took a decided upward turn among serious students of literature: now no informed person would think it possible to say of either of them that he is not a classic of our poetry. The counter-revolution against nineteenth-century opinion as summed up by Arnold found its most notable agitator in T. S. Eliot, who, in his essays on Dryden, repelled "the reproach of the prosaic" that had so often been made and went on to question in a radical and telling way the whole nineteenth-century view of what was and what was not poetic.

Yet despite the thorough-going change in the estimate of Pope that has taken place among critics and scholars, it is still probably true that the great majority of readers who come to him for the first time and without critical indoctrination tend to resist him and to echo Arnold's judgment that he is not really a poet at all, that such virtues as are most salient in his work, those that Arnold identified as "regularity, uniformity, precision, and balance," are prose virtues; and perhaps they will go so far as to say that, of these virtues, not all pertain to the kind of prose that interests them most.

What probably makes the root of the difficulty is the verse form with which the genius of Pope is identified, the heroic couplet. It is likely to strike the unhabituated modern ear as limited, repetitive, and all too committed to syntax, justifying Keats's vehement charge that it was nothing but mechanical. The disaffected reader should know, however, that the better acquainted Keats became with the form, the more he admired it and admitted its influence upon his own verse.

Nothing could be simpler than the defining characteristics of the heroic couplet: two rhymed lines, each of five iambic feet, that is, feet of two syllables, the accent falling on the second. But as it came into wide use in the late seventeenth century and especially in the hands of Dryden, the simple form developed toward complexity and ever stricter demands were made upon it. It became the rule (which might, however, be broken now and then for the sake of variety) that each couplet be self-contained, its meaning complete. This tended to make for a sententious and even epigrammatic quality of utterance, which was much esteemed. Considerable attention was given to the caesura, a discernible pause in the progress of a line which is dictated not by the metre but by the natural rhythm of the language; variations in the placing of the caesura had the effect of helping the heroic couplet avoid its greatest danger, monotony. Rhetorical devices, such as parallelism and antithesis, were favored by the nature of the verse and came to be highly valued.

The chief advantage that Dryden ascribed to the heroic couplet will make it plain why the Romantic poets disliked the form and why many modern readers find it uncongenial. "That benefit which I consider most in it," Dryden said, "is . . . that it bounds and circumscribes the fancy." And he goes on: "For imagination in a poet is a faculty so wild and lawless that, like an highranging spaniel, it must have clogs tied to it, lest it outrun the judgment. The great easiness of blank verse renders the poet too luxuriant; he is tempted to say many things which might better be omitted, or at least shut up in fewer words; but when the difficulty of artful rhyming is interposed, where the poet commonly confines his sense to his couplet, and must contrive that sense into such words that the rhyme shall naturally follow them, not they the rhyme; the fancy then gives leisure to the judgment to come in. . . . That which most regulates the fancy, and gives the judgment its busiest employment, is like to bring forth the richest and clearest thoughts."

Nothing could be further from the nineteenth-century sense of how the poet should go about his work, of what poetry should be and do. And although modern poetry has in some measure responded to the influence of Dryden and Pope, there are few contemporary practitioners or theorists of poetry who would give their approval to a conception of poetry that was directed chiefly to bringing forth *thoughts,* no matter how rich and clear.

By Pope's time the advantages of the heroic couplet no longer seemed to be in need of reasoned defense; it was the accepted form for most poetic undertakings of importance.* If Pope ever thought of the limitations of the form, it was only as a challenge to his virtuosity. To him it was beyond doubt that the couplet in skilled hands—in hands made skillful as much by study and practice as by native endowment—was an instrument capable of producing the widest and most delightful range of effects. In an often-quoted passage of "An Essay on Criticism" he brilliantly demonstrated how various the "music" of the couplet may be and how precisely it could be related to the meaning that is being expressed. This correspondence of sense and sound, he says, is something to which the poet must give close attention—

> 'Tis not enough no harshness gives offence,
> The sound must seem an Echo to the sense.

He illustrates the precept by a couplet in which the sound of the verse is consonant with the "softness" of the action being referred to:

> Soft is the strain when Zephyr gently blows,
> And the smooth stream in smoother numbers flows.

There follows an example of a rough action expressed in a rough-sounding verse:

> But when loud surges lash the sounding shore,
> The hoarse, rough verse should like the torrent roar.

Then an example of laborious effort:

> When Ajax strives some rock's vast weight to throw,
> The line too labours, and the words move slow.

And, in contrast to this, lightness and speed:

> Not so when swift Camilla scours the plain,
> Flies o'er the unbending corn, and skims along the main.

This famous display of virtuosity will suggest how large a part in Pope's art was played by the poet's sense that he was a performer,

---

* But the taste of no period is monolithic and the dislike of the heroic couplet that was expressed by at least one considerable poet of the eighteenth century should be noted—Matthew Prior objected to it because it "produces too frequent an identity in the sound," moves too readily toward epigram, and is tiring to the reader.

that it was his purpose to give pleasure to an audience whose right to judge his performance depended only upon a proper training of its faculty of judgment, its taste. The characteristic relation of later poets to their audiences will be very different: the idea of performance will come to be abhorrent to them and they will conceive it to be their purpose to serve not the pleasure of the reader but only the truth of their own feelings, which the reader is probably not competent to judge.

The poetry of exposition and argument, to which the heroic couplet so happily lends itself, has virtually no place in the modern tradition. In the eighteenth century the word "didactic" was used in a neutral descriptive sense when applied to poetry; early in the nineteenth century its meaning became opprobrious and has remained so. It means nothing more dreadful than "teaching," but, although we believe that much is to be learned from poetry, we now believe that it must not intend to instruct. To the poets of Pope's age, however, our adverse opinion of didactic poetry would have seemed arbitrary and pointless; they thought it nothing but natural that poetry should engage itself directly with ideas.*

But even if the modern reader should consent to give up his prejudice against didactic poetry in general, he is pretty sure to find that another barrier stands in the way of his coming to terms with "An Essay on Man." This is the poem's purpose of demonstrating that man has no justifiable complaint to make of the conditions of his life, that, if he truly comprehends the nature of the universe, he must see that his relation to it is wholly in accord with reason and be gratified that things are as they are and not otherwise.

Such a view can scarcely win assent in our day, when it has be-

---

* But, again, the broad cultural generalization must be modified—in 1746, Joseph Warton, an important critic, protested the fashion of didactic poetry. And it should be said that in his preface to "An Essay on Man" Pope raised the question, perhaps only in a formal way, of whether he should not have treated his subject in prose, and he apologizes, again perhaps only in a formal way, for not having treated parts of his discourse "more *poetically*." It would seem to have been the abstruseness of the subject that raised doubts that had not existed in connection with the earlier "Essay on Criticism," which was no less didactic but considerably easier.

come virtually a commonplace of much of our influential literature that man's relation to the universe is so far out of accord with reason as to be absurd. Yet exactly the currency of this idea makes "An Essay on Man" of rather special interest to us, for the poem takes its impetus from the assumption that anyone who thinks about his relation to the universe will, as a first conclusion, judge it to be unreasonable to the point of absurdity. The Essay, of course, then undertakes to prove that the first conclusion is in error, but the arguments it advances in the demonstration are as desperate as they are ingenious. Where the ingenuity fails to convince us, the desperateness may yet succeed in moving us: there is something deeply affecting in the Essay's passionate defeated attempt to force the universe to be rational.

When it is said that man's relation to the universe is not in accord with reason, what is primarily meant is that there is no discernible answer to the question of why man suffers or why there is an overplus of pain as against pleasure in human existence. That the question should be asked at all implies the belief that the universe is controlled by principles that are analogous with those more or less rational principles that man has evolved for the control of his own behavior. It is expected, that is, that the answer will be given in terms of man's own reason in its various social aspects—the reason of the father in the family, of the judge in the court of law, of the king in the city or nation. And when the question about the reason of the universe is posed in the Judaeo-Christian tradition, it takes the form of asking why the perfect Father, Judge, and King, the God who is believed to be both omnipotent and wholly beneficent, should have ordained man's suffering. The terms of the question being what they are, the answer is not hard to make—it is possible to "justify the ways of God to man," as Milton expressed his intention in writing *Paradise Lost,* by telling the story of a man's fall from innocence through his disobedience to the divine command and of God's consequent anger. The pain of human life is explained as a punishment for sin, mitigated by the permitted hope of an eventual redemption. Such rationality as is thought to inhere in the human concept of morality and justice is proposed as the controlling principle of the universe.

This answer is in many ways satisfactory so long as the imagination is disposed to accept its terms and to sustain the belief in a God who is Father, Judge, and King, and who is susceptible to the emotions that are appropriate to each of his functions. But in the eighteenth century the imagination of educated men was not so disposed. "An Essay on Man" undertakes to "vindicate the ways of God to man," and the conscious echo of Milton's line informs us that Pope wanted to connect the purpose of his poem with that of *Paradise Lost*. Yet the elements out of which Pope constructed his argument were very different from those available to Milton. The God of the Essay is not personal except insofar as wisdom and beneficence may be attributed to him. Having once ordained his universe in perfection, he does not intervene in its processes. Where Milton, in the traditional way of religion, frames his explanation of man's destiny in terms of man's own thought and feeling, showing that God's ways are essentially in accord with man's ways taken at their best, Pope vindicates God's ways by demonstrating the difference—which does not, however, imply the discontinuity—between the divine and the human. The famous conclusion, "Whatever is, is right," asserts the rationality and perfection of the universe as God has created it, a rationality and perfection of which man's suffering—so runs the terrible line of reasoning!—is a necessary element.

At no point in "An Essay on Man" is the actuality of human suffering denied. Indeed, the poem is charged throughout with an awareness of pain, as well it might be, considering how much of it its author had endured. The opening lines are explicit about the unsatisfactoriness of life, which "can little more supply / Than just to look about us and to die." It is this acceptance of the fact of suffering that gives the poem its desperate tragic force, for the essence of its position is not merely that human suffering is inevitable but that without it the universe would be less rational and perfect than in fact it is. The argument is based on a conception of a universal order in which all created things stand on a scale of perfection from the lowest to the highest. On this scale there may be no gaps; the gradation from the lowest to the highest is continuous, constituting a "vast Chain of Being." From this premise of the order of Nature two conclusions follow. (1) Man has his place or "station" in this order of perfection, above the animals and below the angels, and if he did not occupy this place, there would be a link missing in the chain of being, a circumstance which, if it were thinkable, would be a diminution of the perfection of the universal order. (2) Situated where he is on the scale, or in the chain, man must be understood to have been endowed in a way that makes all his attributes appropriate to his station; both his power and his weakness are exactly right for that place. Which is to say that, in relation to the universal order, man himself is perfect.

More than once the point is made that nothing would be gained for man's well-being if his powers were greater than they are. It is said, in fact, that the contrary is so. If, for example, man were better able to foretell the future, he would have a greater apprehension of the calamities that are destined to befall him and he would therefore be the less able to bear his existence. But such considerations, adduced for what comfort they may give, are of no more than secondary importance to the argument; its primary intention is to demonstrate that the perfection of the universal order depends upon man's suffering.

It is generally said that Pope derived his general position and the particularities by which he expounded it from his friend Lord Bolingbroke, the St. John to whom all four epistles of the *Essay* are addressed, but an educated man of the time could scarcely have read any philosophy without gaining knowledge of a doctrine that was fashionable and received. Yet it was not everywhere received; Dr. Johnson, for one, would have none of it. Johnson had the highest admiration for Pope as a poet and he said of "An Essay on Man" that it "affords an egregious instance of the predominance of genius, the dazzling splendour of imagery, and the seductive powers of eloquence." But the praise he gives to the poet is the measure of his scorn of the philosopher. "Never," he goes on, "was penury of knowledge and vulgarity of sentiment so happily disguised," and he proceeds to show that the doctrine of the Essay may be reduced to a series of truisms and platitudes. "Surely," he says when the demolition is complete, "a man of no very comprehensive search may venture to say that he has heard all this before. . . ." And then, his antagonism to the philosopher having been given full vent, he is free to return to his praise of the poet: ". . . But it was never till now recommended by such a blaze of embellishments, or such sweetness of melody. The vigorous contraction of thoughts, the luxuriant amplification of others, the incidental illustrations, and sometimes the dignity, sometimes the softness of the verses, enchain philosophy, suspend criticism, and oppress judgment by overpowering pleasure." The double opinion recommends itself.

Tyger! Tyger!

WILLIAM BLAKE
1757-1827

THE reader who comes to "Tyger! Tyger!" for the first time will have no trouble understanding what a Tyger is. But he will want to know why it is spelled in this, rather than in the usual, way. In Blake's time the spelling of the word was the same as now; Dr. Johnson, in his great dictionary, which set the standard of correctness for the period, noted *tyger* as an alternative form of *tiger,* but he did not expect anyone to use it. Yet Blake's error, if such it is, is perpetuated: most modern editors, when they reprint the poem, conscientiously maintain the poet's spelling. They feel that to make the Tyger into a tiger would alter the nature of the beast and of the poem that celebrates him.

One reason for this feeling lies in the circumstances of the poem's original publication. The book in which "Tyger! Tyger!" appeared, *Songs of Experience* (1794), was not printed in the common way, from type. Blake was an engraver by trade and also an artist of considerable stature, and he made the whole book himself, designing each page as an elaborate picture in which the text of the poem was part of the design and the elements of the picture wove themselves in and out of the lines of the text. He engraved the texts and the outlines of the pictures on copper plates from which he printed the pages; he then colored by hand each page of each copy of the book. It is a tendency of modern criticism and scholarship to pay heed to every detail of a poet's work, even such "mechanical" matters as punctuation and spelling; if one of the older poets wrote *speke* where we would now write *speak,* or *sovran* where we would now write *sovereign,* many editors think that the very look of the words is an essential quality of the poem and should be preserved. How much more is this idea likely to prevail when the poet presents his poems, as Blake did, as actual visual objects, to be looked at as well as read.

And certainly the spelling has its effect, if only that of being curious and therefore of making the animal which the word denotes the more remarkable—a Tyger is surely more interesting than a tiger. It startles our habitual expectations, it jolts our settled imagination of the beast and prepares us to see it as we never saw it before, as Blake saw it. Then, too, the *y* is a stronger, as it is a larger, letter than *i;* it suggests a longer-held sound and therefore supports the idea of an animal even fiercer than the tiger. (Conversely, the little boy in A. A. Milne's stories calls one of his animal friends Tigger, and by the shortening of the *i* wipes out all possibility of the creature's being dangerous.)

The dominant, the single, emotion of the poem is amazement, and perhaps no poem has ever expressed an emotion so fully—it is as if the poem were amazement itself. The means by which it achieves this effect is in part very simple: in the course of twenty-four lines it asks fourteen astonished questions. Up through Stanza IV the tempo of the questions is in continuous acceleration, generating an intense excitement. At Stanza V the speed of the questions diminishes and the excited wonder modulates to meditative awe.

But not only does the tempo of the poem change at the fifth stanza; its point of reference, its very subject, alters. Up to Stanza V the poem has undertaken to define the nature of the Tyger by the nature of God—such is the beauty and strength and wildness of the Tyger that he must be thought to have been created by God's greatest exercise of power, a power put forth against resistance and even with some risk of failure. But at the fifth stanza the Tyger is no longer defined by the nature of God; now, in the two remaining stanzas, it is God who is defined by the nature of the Tyger. The amazement first evoked by the Tyger is now directed to God, as

God reveals himself through his wonderful and terrible creature. And what the poem finds most amazing about God is not his power but his audacity—not the fact that God *could* (as in the first stanza) but that he *dared* (as in the last stanza) create the Tyger!

To ask a question about the audacity of God is in itself an act of inordinate audacity. For to dare to do a thing implies the possibility of fearing to do it, and what can God conceivably fear? The very idea of God, since it implies omnipotence, denies the possibility of his fearing anything at all. And yet there is one thing which, at least in a formal sense, God may be imagined to fear—the violation of his own nature by himself. The import of the last question of the poem, "What immortal hand or eye / Dare frame thy fearful symmetry?" is that, in creating the Tyger, God has perhaps committed just such a violation, that he has contradicted the self-imposed laws of his own being.*

This idea is quite explicitly proposed in the fifth stanza:

> When the stars threw down their spears,
> And water'd heaven with their tears,
> Did he smile his work to see?
> Did he who made the Lamb make thee?

The scholars tell us that for Blake the stars are the symbols and agents of reason, law, and order. If this is so, we must understand that the stars threw down their spears in token of defeat and watered

---

* That Blake thought the distinction between *could* and *dare* to be of great importance is made plain by the way he revised the poem. In the early drafts of "Tyger! Tyger!" the first stanza was exactly the same as the last; in both stanzas the question read, "What immortal hand or eye / Dare frame fearful thy symmetry?" But as Blake worked over the poem and understood better what it was trying to say, he perceived the striking—we might say shocking—effect that would be achieved by changing the phrase in the first stanza to the neutral "Could frame," reserving *dare* as a startling climax in the last stanza. To be sure, this is not the only use of the word *dare* in the poem, for it occurs twice in Stanza II and once in Stanza IV. We might wish that it did not, that it occurred uniquely and therefore the more startlingly in the last line. Yet the word as it is used in Stanzas II and IV may be said to differ in meaning from the word as it is used in Stanza VI. The questions in Stanzas II and IV all have to do with the executive part of creation, with physical acts, with power. Who would venture to put his power to the text of undertaking to create the Tyger? The answer implied by the question is that God alone would take this risk; but because God is all-powerful, there really is no risk—the word *dare* therefore comes to mean no more than *could*. But in the last stanza *dare* refers to the conceptual part of creation, to the idea of the Tyger as conceived by the mind of God. And because this idea may possibly be thought a contradiction of God's nature, the word has its full dramatic force.

heaven with their tears in chagrin because they disapproved of God's having created the Tyger. It seemed to them a controversion of that very order which God himself had instituted and which he had enjoined them to enforce.

What chiefly makes it possible to think of God as being inconsistent with himself is having created the Lamb before the Tyger. Just as "Tyger! Tyger!" is the central poem of *Songs of Experience,* so the poem called "The Lamb" is central to the volume called *Songs of Innocence,* which Blake had published five years before, in 1789. In the established symbolism of Western culture, the Lamb stands for harmlessness, gentleness, and defenselessness; in Christian iconography, it stands for Jesus—for the Jesus who said, "Resist not evil," and who offered himself as a sacrifice for mankind. In "The Lamb" it is a child who asks of the Lamb the same question that the poet, speaking in his own voice as a mature man, asks of the Tyger: *Who made you?* The little questioner is in no doubt about the answer:

> Little Lamb, I'll tell thee;
> Little Lamb, I'll tell thee:
> He is callèd by thy name,
> For he calls himself a Lamb.
> He is meek, & he is mild:
> He became a little child,
> I a child, & thou a lamb,
> We are callèd by his name.

That God, who had created the Lamb and had incarnated himself in Jesus who *is* the Lamb, should also have created the Tyger as another aspect of his being—this seems to the stars, who are the agents of divine law, to be a clear contradiction by God of his own nature as he had declared it to them, and as the negation of the terms of their commission to maintain reason and order.

The poem, however, does not substantiate the view of the matter that is held by the reasonable stars. Rather, it would seem to present the opinions of these guardians of order with considerable irony, as being limited, even stupid, as failing to comprehend the wonderful complexity of God's nature. In the opinion of the poem—although this is not made fully explicit—the Tyger is not the negation or contradiction of the Lamb. He is by no means the Anti-Christ. The Jesus who is meek and mild, who speaks of turning the other cheek, and who is symbolized by the animal commonly used in ancient sacrifices, is the Jesus most frequently represented to the religious imagination, but this does not mean that he is the only Jesus. There is also the Jesus who said, "I bring not peace but a sword," who undertook to disrupt the habitual respectable lives of·men, commanding them to leave their fathers and mothers and to follow him, who questioned and denied the established Law, who—so he is represented by Dostoevski in "The Grand Inquisitor"—offered men a freedom too terrible for most to accept. This is the Jesus whom T. S. Eliot, in "Gerontion," could precisely call "Christ the tiger."

When Blake brought together his *Songs of Innocence* and his *Songs of Experience* in a single volume, he called it *Songs of Innocence and Experience, Shewing the Two Contrary States of the Human Soul,* and the title makes it sufficiently plain that in Blake's view a "state" which is "contrary" to another state is not necessarily a negation of it or antagonistic to it. The contrary of Innocence is not Wickedness or Evil but Experience, which is the condition in which a human being comes to realize and exercise his vital energies and in which he knows both the joy and the sorrow that follow upon their use. Both the state of the Lamb and the state of the Tyger are appropriate to mankind; both are sanctioned by the nature of God.

But although Blake is so nearly explicit in making the Tyger stand for one of the two aspects of Christ, or one of the two states of man, his symbolic intention is not limited to this alone. The Tyger, in its fierceness and beauty, can be regarded as that manifestation of the human mind which we call genius. (It is interesting to compare this representation of genius with that of Babel's story, "Di Grasso.") And it can be thought to stand for the ruthless ferocity of political revolution, specifically of the French Revolution, with which Blake was much preoccupied.

Resolution and Independence

WILLIAM WORDSWORTH
1770–1850

LET US suppose that someone who had never read "Resolution and Independence" were to ask us what it is about and we were to comply with his request. Would there be much likelihood of his believing that this could make the material of one of the finest poems in the English language? I use the phrase "what is it about" in the simple and quite natural sense in which we employ it when we inquire about some story or play with which we have no acquaintance, expecting to be answered with a summary account of its chief happenings. We do not of course think we have been told much when we have been told only this, yet we do feel we have been supplied some ground for estimating the interest the story or play will have for us; we assume some relation between even a scant *résumé* and the real nature of a work. And in general we are right in this assumption. But not always, and not, surely, in the instance of "Resolution and Independence."

What is the poem about? It is about the poet's meeting with a very old man and the beneficent effect that this encounter has upon him. On a fine spring morning, the poet, who is a young or youngish man, is walking on the moors. He is in a happy frame of mind, but suddenly his spirits fall, and he is overcome by an intense anxiety about his future; he thinks about the disastrous fates that have befallen other poets and that might befall him. As he walks on in his painful state of depression and fear, he comes across a solitary decrepit figure standing in a shallow pool. To the poet's questions about his way of life, the old man replies with simple dignity. He makes a bare living by gathering leeches; the work grows ever more difficult for him; he is quite alone in the world. He is so old that it seems scarcely possible that he should go on living; and he has, as we say, nothing to live for; yet he utters no complaint and shows no self-pity. The poet is moved to shame for having been so much distressed by the mere imagination of misfortune; he resolves to make the old leech-gatherer his example of fortitude.

If this is a fair statement of what happens in "Resolution and Independence," it is certainly reasonable to conclude that the content of the poem is rather trivial and dull. What is more, it has the unpleasing quality of moral didacticism; it seems to have the intention of teaching a lesson in simple morality, or even something more boring than that, a lesson in mental hygiene: "Do not allow your imagination to bedevil you with thoughts of personal disaster. Confront the chances of life with a firm and equable mind." What, then, are the elements of the poem that make for its great quality?

The first of these is the idea of greatness itself. The chief characteristic of the old man is his dignity. The simile by which he is first described compares him to a "huge stone," a massive boulder such as we sometimes see "couched on the bald top of an eminence," which raises in our minds the question of how it came there. If we do not think rationally of the glacier or flood that transported the boulder to its present unlikely place but suppose that it had moved of its own volition, its imagined movement is wonderful and awesome, and no less so is the movement of the old man. He leans on a staff because he is feeble, but his posture is majestic; his staff is an attribute of his majesty. The difficulty with which he moves appears as a sign not of weakness but of firmness, of a nature that is not easily moved by circumstance.

> Motionless as a cloud the old Man stood,
> That heareth not the loud winds when they call;
> And moveth all together, if it move at all.

In all cultures the quality of majesty is associated with weightiness and a degree of immobility, or at least slowness of movement—a king in a hurry seems a contradiction in terms. The ceremonial robes of the king express the idea that he has no need to be active. And the impression of the old man's kingliness is borne out by his "stately" speech and the imperious "flash" of his "yet vivid eyes."

In addition to this majesty, the old man has for the poet something like a supernatural authority. He seems "like one whom I had met with in a dream"—

> Or like a man from some far region sent,
> To give me human strength, by apt admonishment.

The "far region" suggests a divine region; to the poet the leech-gatherer is an agent or messenger of God, an angel is disguise. This idea is sustained as the poet speculates on how it came about that he met the old man at this particular moment, when the meeting is of such momentous significance to him. He wonders if the encounter takes place "by peculiar grace, / A leading from above, a something given." These are theological terms having reference to divine intervention in the lives of individual persons.

But if the old man, despite his actual feebleness, is a figure of majesty, so, in his way, is the poet, who speaks not merely in his own person but as the representative of all poets. For him the sorrow of poets in misfortune is the sorrow of kings in misfortune—he speaks of "mighty Poets in their misery dead." The characteristic attributes of poets are not only "joy" but "pride" and "glory." They are, indeed, even greater than kings, for their divine right is from themselves: "By our own spirits are we deified."

Yet it is by their own spirits that they are cast down—no sooner has the poet made his proud boast than he confronts the tragic fate that threatens the possessors of the poetic power. His words are shocking in their explicitness:

> We Poets in our youth begin in gladness;
> But thereof come in the end despondency and madness.

The life of poets, our poet is saying, follows the course of his own feelings of that very morning: his despondency had succeeded his high spirits as if caused by them. His joy and its evanescence have their visual counterpart in the hare he described in Stanza II:

> All things that love the sun are out of doors;
> The sky rejoices in the morning's birth;
> The grass is bright with rain-drops;—on the moors
> The hare is running races in her mirth;
> And with her feet she from the plashy earth
> Raises a mist; that, glittering in the sun,
> Runs with her all the way, wherever she doth run.

Wherever she doth run—but not for as long as she runs. For the earth will dry and the mist that enhaloes her will vanish. We know from other of his poems that Wordsworth feared the loss of his poetic gift, which he associated with his youth and which he often represented in terms of some effect of light.

The poem, we can say, is organized by an opposition between what is suggested, on the one hand, by the hare racing in its luminous mist, and, on the other hand, by the "huge stone" to which the leech-gatherer is compared—on the one hand, movement, speed, brightness, but also evanescence; on the other hand, immobility and lack of sentience, but also endurance. The poetic temperament, which is characterized by its quick responsiveness, Wordsworth associates with the quick-moving hare. To this he opposes—what? What name are we to give to the other temperament?

We are tempted to call it religious because one of the salient facts about the old leech-gatherer is that he belongs to a Scottish religious sect. And religion may indeed, and often does, play a part in what we seek to name. But it need not. And then, even apart from the fact that there have been many religious poets, religion and poetry have too much in common to permit us to set up any simple opposition between them. What stands here in contrast to the poetic temperament is the temperament that finds its fulfilment in strictness of control, in what we have come to call "character." The nature of the poet, at least in the modern view, is defined by sensitivity and free responsiveness. These traits no doubt have their connection with morality as well as creativity, yet a strict moral training will undertake to limit them in the interests of character. This is exemplified in a striking way by the statement of the famous physician Sir William Osler, who, in one of his lectures to medical students, spoke of the physician's need for the quality which he called "imperturbability." He also called it "immobility" and "impassiveness" and even went so far as to call it "callousness." He admitted that this quality might appear to patients and their friends as hardness of heart, an indifference to the suffering of others that verged upon the inhuman, but he went on to say how disconcerted the patient and his family would be if the physician lacked this quality, for upon his ability to shut off his sensitivity depend his "firmness and courage," his ability to make difficult decisions and carry them out.

The poem, then, may be said to ask this question: Must the poet, for the sake of his survival, take to himself some measure of imperturbability, of rock-like fortitude, even at the cost of surrendering some of the sensitivity and responsiveness which constitute the essence of his poetic power? The question has an intrinsic psychological interest. But what gives it its peculiar force in the poem is the circumstance in which it is posed, the aura of tragic destiny which attends this confrontation of two modes of human self-realization.

Considered from the point of view of prosodic technique, "Resolution and Independence" is a most remarkable achievement. We begin our understanding of how the poem "works" by taking note of the punctuation, the sheer amount and weight of it: in the first three stanzas almost every line has a strong stop at its end. This has the effect of making each line a decisive and dramatic statement. The energy of one line is not continuous with that of the next; each line initiates its own movement, of which we become the more conscious as it discharges its energy upon the semi-colon, colon, or period that stops it; the effect is like that of watching breaker after breaker rising up to hurl itself upon a cliff. After the first three stanzas, the punctuation becomes lighter, although it is still decisive, and now we become aware of the stanza rather than the line as the unit of energy. Each stanza is as discrete as, at the beginning of the poem, each line had been, for the lengthened last line of the stanza acts as a full stop. The poem is thus a series of initiations of energy and of resistances to it, an equal display of movement and solidity.

Many readers are disturbed, even distressed, by the concluding couplet. And with some reason, for there is no doubt that

> "God," said I, "be my help and stay secure;
> I'll think of the Leech-gatherer on the lonely moor!"

is in all ways an anticlimax. It is emotionally insufficient and its tone is downright jaunty, so that it almost seems to dismiss the great episode which it brings to an end. The casual appeal to God seems merely conventional and a negation of the powerful if vague reference to the divine "far region." To these objections an admirer of the poem offers no defence, except perhaps to say that, although cogent, they do not much matter.

Kubla Khan or A Vision in a Dream: A Fragment

SAMUEL TAYLOR COLERIDGE
1772–1834

ALTHOUGH the intrinsic qualities of "Kubla Khan" justify the admiration that has been given to it, some part of its great fame must surely be attributed to the prefatory note in which, upon its first publication in 1816, Coleridge told his readers how the poem came to be composed, some eighteen years before. The circumstances that Coleridge relates have so engaged the interest of the world that we can scarcely think of the poem without having them in mind—they have become virtually an element of the poem itself.

"In the summer of the year 1797," Coleridge writes,* "the Author, then in ill health, had retired to a lonely farm-house between Porlock and Linton. . . . In consequence of a slight indisposition, an anodyne [it was opium] had been prescribed, from the effects of which he fell asleep in his chair at the moment that he was reading the following sentence, or words of the same substance, in 'Purchas's Pilgrimage': 'Here the Khan Kubla commanded a palace to be built, and a stately garden thereunto. And thus ten miles of fertile ground were enclosed with a wall.' The Author continued for about three hours in a profound sleep, at least of the external senses, during which time he has the most vivid confidence, that he could not have

---

* But his memory played him false. All evidence points to the impossibility of his having written the poem in that year. It was probably written in 1798, but 1799 and 1800 also fall within the possible range.

composed less than from two to three hundred lines; if that indeed can be called composition in which all the images rose up before him as *things,* with a parallel production of the correspondent expressions, without any sensation or consciousness of effort. On awaking he appeared to himself to have a distinct recollection of the whole, and taking his pen, ink, and paper, instantly and eagerly wrote down the lines that are here preserved. At this moment he was unfortunately called out by a person on business from Porlock, and detained by him above an hour, and on his return to his room, found, to his no small surprise and mortification, that though he still retained some vague and dim recollection of the general purport of the vision, yet, with the exception of some eight or ten scattered lines and images, all the rest had passed way like the images on the surface of a stream into which a stone has been cast. . . ."

This account of how "Kubla Khan" was written was for a long time accepted without question. But the researches of an American scholar, Professor Elisabeth Schneider, have brought the literal truth of the story into serious question; they suggest that these circumstances of composition were as much the product of the poet's imagination as the poem itself. Yet in some sense the truthfulness of Coleridge's account does not matter—the important thing is that the poet believed that it was possible, if singular, to compose a poem in his sleep, without the aid of his conscious mind, without, as he puts it, "any sensation or consciousness of effort," and also that a particular virtue might be assigned to such a mode of composition.

We must not exaggerate the novelty of this proposition. Ever since literature has been the object of thoughtful curiosity, men have supposed that the composition of poetry may be other than a willed and conscious process. This has been commonly explained by the concept of "inspiration," the idea that a spirit—of the Muse or some other nonhuman being—enters the poet, takes possession of his mind, and speaks through him. Plato, not in order to disparage poets but to explain them, said that they were "mad," and the idea of the poet's being "possessed," out of his own control, as an insane person is, became part of the popular conception of the poetic character—

everybody in Shakespeare's audience knew what Theseus was talking about when he equated the lunatic and the poet and spoke of "the poet's eye, in a fine frenzy rolling." This notion of poetic composition persisted even into the era of rationalism; Dryden paid tribute to it in his famous couplet about the close alliance between great wit—by which he meant poetic genius—and madness.

Yet the rationalism of the late seventeenth and eighteenth centuries put its critical emphasis less upon the uncontrolled processes of composition than upon those that were conscious and reasoned, less upon the poet's inspired vision than upon his careful revision. Pope, like Dryden, admitted the primacy of inspiration, but the chief direction of both his precept and example was toward correctness, polish, and good taste. If nonrational inspiration was to be acknowledged in the composition of great poems, it was to be admired only if it submitted to the rule of good judgment, which might be defined as the codified knowledge of what will please men of good sense.

The preface to "Kubla Khan" constitutes, therefore, a radical denial of the character of the poet that had prevailed in the eighteenth century. We cannot read Pope's brilliant "Essay on Criticism" without understanding that it regards the poet as primarily a performer, and, as such, committed to pleasing an audience and submissive to the judgment of his audience's taste. This view of the poet was not supposed to diminish his dignity—his position can fairly be compared with that of a great performing musician or dancer of our own time. Pope assumes that in general the audience's taste is correct and to be relied upon in much the same way we now assume the authority of people who love music and the dance—if a performer can consistently meet the requirements of persons with a highly developed sensibility in his art, we by and large take it for granted that he is good. And as for the performer, he assumes that if he meets his own standard of what makes a good performance, he will be liked and praised; his standard of judgment and that of his audience are much the same.

But Coleridge's preface quite negates the idea of the poet as performer and of the poem as an artistic commodity offered to the audience for its approval. Indeed, "Kubla Khan" was so little a performance that it was not even finished. (Actually, of course, even though the poet calls it "a fragment," the poem is felt by most readers to be complete in the sense of being an aesthetic whole. But the preface inevitably tempts us to imagine how it would have continued if the person on business from Porlock had not paid his visit.) It is not something that the poet wrote with the intention of interesting or pleasing or edifying his audience. It came into being as if by its own necessity and by its own will—it is a fact in nature as much as in art, a psychological fact as much as a poetic fact. It would seem, that is, that the mind quite naturally makes poems, as it makes dreams, without intention, without effort, without thought, without revision or any awareness of the rules of literature.

Coleridge's preface is to be read, however, not only as a kind of manifesto on the working of the poetic mind but also as an explanation of how this particular poem is to be responded to. When it first appeared, there would still have been many readers whom it would have troubled and puzzled; they would have thought that Coleridge was not being unduly or falsely modest when he said that he was publishing it "rather as a psychological curiosity, than on the ground of any supposed *poetic* merits." Such readers were no doubt fewer than if the poem had appeared in the year of its composition, for in the intervening time other poets had begun to habituate the public to certain of its poetic qualities—its exoticism, its fantasy, its indifference to rational considerations. Yet there were still many who would have been at a loss to know what the poem was trying to "say" or "do," and for these the preface was, in effect, a guide. It suggested that "Kubla Khan" was not to be judged by the criteria which in its day were conventionally applied to poetry and that the reader was thus free to respond to it in new terms, the terms of the poem itself.

The modern reader is surely less likely to resist making this kind of response than was the reader of Coleridge's time. This is not to imply that we today are more sensitive to poetry and more intelligent about it than our forebears were, but only that the tendency of literary criticism and education has changed. In our time the poet's personal fantasy is given large license and authority. Less and less do we think it possible to ask that a poem conform to some preconception of what a poem should be; we even believe that we should have no such preconception. We tend to think that every poem suggests its own aesthetic criteria and that it should be judged by our sense of its being an authentic representation of the poet's state of feeling—so long, at least, as we have reason to suppose that this state of feeling is significant. We may even incline to the belief that the more alien from our own state of feeling a poem is, the more authentically it represents the poet's feelings and the more authority it has. For readers today it neither constitutes the failure of a poem nor a deficiency in our aesthetic perception if we are not readily able to say what the work means in all its various parts or as a whole. After all, we have never understood music in the sense of being able to explain its meaning, and nowadays we are surrounded by pictures which give us pleasure although (as the painters themselves are the first to say) we have no way to "understand" them rationally and articulately. We admit the possibility that a work of art can exist in its own right, without reference to us, like a tree, or a mountain, or an animal; it need have no relation to us except as we elect to have a relation to it, by finding interest and pleasure in it. We think of the work as a meaningful expression of its creator's mind but not, in any usual definition of the word, a communication.

"Kubla Khan" offers no literal difficulty to the reader—its statements, taken by themselves, are perfectly clear. Yet most readers, however strong their response to it, feel that they would be incapable of formulating what the poem as a whole is *really* saying. The concluding sentence of Coleridge's prefatory note may help us to become conscious of what it is that we respond to. "As a contrast to this vision," Coleridge says, "I have annexed a fragment of a very different character, describing with equal fidelity the dream of pain and disease." He is referring to his poem, "The Pains of Sleep," which describes in a very direct way the distress which opium and physical and mental ill-health introduced into his repose, the horrors of—as the poem calls them—"life-stifling fear, life-stifling shame."

What "Kubla Khan" represents is indeed a contrast; it is the very opposite of whatever might be life-stifling—the vision is of life at its most intense. Life's power is announced in the decree of the great Khan, the mere utterance of which brought the "pleasure-dome" into being, by the ejaculative force of the "mighty fountain," by the passion of the "woman wailing for her demon-lover," by—finally— the great image of the poet in the transcendent strength of his magical art. Here, surely, is nothing "life-stifling." Nor does the war prophesied by the "ancestral voices" bring any fear: for the Khan, war is the very business of life. The woman who wails for her demon-lover utters her cry without any possibility of shame, and the poet envisages his dangerous strength ("Beware! Beware!") without compunction. To be sure, the meandering course of the "sacred river" comes to its end in a "sunless sea," a "lifeless ocean"; but the river is perpetual, having its source in the mighty fountain which is "momently" forced from the earth. The "caves of ice" beneath the "sunny pleasure-dome" contradict the fertility of the gardens and the forests, yet if they, like the sunless sea and the lifeless ocean, evoke the idea of death, they suggest the idea of a holy mystery rather than a denial of life; the fear or awe they generate is consonant with the sacredness of Alph, the sacred river; and when the poet says that with the power of his music he will "build" these caves of ice, he is as enraptured by this prospect as by the thought of building "that sunny dome" itself. The poem and what it implies of the nature of poetry celebrate pleasure but even more they celebrate life in its might and in its mystery of contradictions.

Don Juan:
An Episode from Canto II

GEORGE GORDON, LORD BYRON
1788–1824

DON JUAN is one of the celebrated books of the nineteenth century, and the odds are that it is quite the gayest. It is a very long poem, consisting of sixteen cantos ranging in length from 60 to 160 stanzas. It breaks off in the middle of a lively erotic adventure which the hero has embarked upon, brought to an end not by the poet's intention but by his death, and that it should stop rather than conclude is entirely appropriate to its nature. The poem has been called formless, and in some sense this is true—at least it can be said that Byron intended it to have no more form than is supplied by a single hero whose adventures and sexual escapades the poet follows, having first contrived them. Byron said that he planned to have Juan die on the guillotine during the French Revolution. But before reaching this grim consummation, he could have carried Juan through as many adventures as it pleased him to write. He intended that the chief interest of the poem should not be in the hero's living his life and dying his death but in the poet's writing the poem. Yet it would be wrong to think of Juan as a "mere puppet" —he is too engaging a figure to be regarded so; we come to have too much affection for his innocence and sweetness and readiness; and this is not to mention Byron's affection for him, as being—although of course not literally—a representative of his own youth. Nevertheless, Juan is not meant to create the illusion of being an autonomous person, like many characters in literature. His dependent status is announced in the poem's opening stanza:

> I want a hero: an uncommon want,
>   When every year and month sends forth a new one,
> Till, after cloying the gazettes with cant,
>   The age discovers he is not the true one:
> Of such as these I should not care to vaunt,
>   I'll therefore take our ancient friend Don Juan—
> We all have seen him in the pantomime
> Sent to the devil somewhat ere his time.*

Having announced his selection of a hero, Byron goes on to tell us what his literary methods are going to be. Most epic poets, he says, start in the middle of the story—he quotes the famous phrase from Horace's *Art of Poetry*—and then, by some device, give the reader an account of what has gone before:

> Most epic poets plunge "in medias res"
>   (Horace makes this the heroic turnpike road),
> And then your hero tells, whene'er you please,
>   What went before—by way of episode,
> While seated after dinner at his ease,
>   Beside his mistress in some soft abode,
> Palace, or garden, paradise, or cavern,
> Which serves the happy couple for a tavern.

"Most epic poets"—does *Don Juan,* then, presume to think of it-self as an epic poem? It does fulfill one requirement of an epic: it is very long. But what epic poem ever spoke in a voice so colloquial and casual, so downright careless, so lacking in high seriousness? And what epic poem was ever at such pains to destroy all possibility

---

* There are two things that the reader ought to know about Byron's Don Juan. The first is that his name is not pronounced in the Spanish fashion (*hwan*), but as if it were an English name spoken phonetically: Byron rimes it with "new one" and "true one." The second is that he has only the faintest connection with the Don Juan of legend. It is true that all his adventures involve love affairs of one kind or another, but he is nothing like the universal seducer of Molière's play or Mozart's opera. Indeed, he is a rather modest and virtuous young man whose love affairs either happen to him or are forced upon him by women.

of illusion, to make sure that the reader will not give the usual credence to the story he is being told? This epic poem—if that is what it is—mocks the very idea of epic poetry.

Don Juan is, in short, what we call a burlesque. The meaning of that word has been largely lost to a kind of theatrical entertainment, which is devoted to rowdy humor, chiefly of a sexual kind, and to female nudity. But the modern burlesque show had its beginnings in actual burlesque—in, that is, the mockery of a serious play that was well known to the audience. Burlesque is a very old form of art —it was highly developed by the ancient Greeks—and many notable and even great works have been conceived in its spirit. Cervantes began *Don Quixote* as a burlesque of the elaborate prose romances of the sixteenth century. Fielding's *Joseph Andrews* is a burlesque of the moralism of Richardson's *Pamela*, and his *Tom Jones* teases the literary conventions of classical antiquity. Jane Austen's *Northanger Abbey* affectionately mocks the terror-novels of the day.

Burlesque is usually directed against a particular literary work or kind of work, with the intention of showing that it is false or foolish. But it may also be directed against the whole enterprise of literature, which it represents as an institution licensed to traduce reality. Parts of Flaubert's *Bouvard and Pécuchet* take this direction, as do parts of the great modern instance of burlesque, Joyce's *Ulysses*. And this is true also of *Don Juan*. The poet's ceaseless intrusion into his story, his avowed manipulation of it, his "asides," which must surely occupy more space than the narrative, his open references to himself, all enforce the idea that he is much too sensible a man to be taken in by the conventions of poetry, that he knows literature for what it really is, an elaborate game. He is perfectly willing to play the game, being the best-natured of men, but he will not pretend, or ask the reader to believe, that it is reality.

But although the episode of Juan struggling to maintain his high-minded sorrow against the assaults of the rising nausea of his sea-sickness is a notable example of burlesque, it quite transcends its genre. It goes beyond the mockery of a literary tradition, that of the faithful grieving lover, to raise radically subversive questions about the dignity of human nature and the autonomy of the human mind.

In any culture we are pretty sure to find two opposing views of man's nature. According to one view, man is at least potentially a being of great dignity, a spiritual being in the sense that he is not wholly or finally conditioned by material considerations. His dignity, spirituality, and freedom derive from his power, and courage. In simpler societies power and courage are thought to belong almost exclusively to socially dominant figures, to the king, the warrior, and the priest. All these personages express by their mode of dress and by their bearing and manner of speech the dignity they claim for themselves. (The comments on the "kingliness" of Wordsworth's old leech-gatherer are relevant here—one of the tendencies of the literature of the late eighteenth and early nineteenth centuries was to assert the dignity of people not of the dominant classes.) The other view concentrates upon man as an animal creature, who provokes not respect but laughter. Contrary to a common assumption, even quite primitive peoples do not take their animal functions wholly for granted; in every culture sexuality and defecation are thought to be funny—they are "accepted" as "natural" but they are thought to derogate from human dignity; they are always joked about. The same is true of the impulse to self-preservation: cowardice is thought to be "natural"—and funny.

Among the Greeks these two views of man's nature were expressed in two distinct literary forms. The view of man as a dignified, free, and spiritual being was represented by tragedy, with its persons of royal or noble birth, its grave and exalted language, its conscious suppression of all petty and sordid considerations. Comedy represented the view that man was bound by his animal nature; in the frankest possible way it took account of all the exigencies of animality, all the "low" conditions of human existence.

Aristotle said that tragedy showed men as better than they really are and that comedy showed men as worse than they really are. And of course he is right in suggesting that neither the bias of tragedy nor that of comedy tells the whole truth. But in defiance of Aristotle, as it were, comedy does claim truth for itself. If tragedy denies the comic view of man, it does so implicitly and silently; but comedy is quite often explicit in its opposition to tragedy—again and again it says straight out that the form and manner of tragedy are false and highfalutin. It claims reality for itself, insisting that reality is what is comprised by the "facts of life," by man's need and greed for food and drink, by his running away from danger, and by his copulation and defecation.

In general it can be said of the Greeks that they were able to hold the two views of man's nature in balance. They gave as much sanction to the subversive view of comedy as to the ideal view of tragedy. Yet at least one Greek, Plato, was distressed by man's double nature; his philosophy makes a strong commitment to the belief that man is most truly himself when he is free of the animal conditions of life. Christianity followed Plato in this—the essence of Christian morality lies in the wish to overcome the bondage of flesh. The way in which Christianity describes this bondage varies with the changes in the secular culture. The seventeenth century, for example, was a period of great intellectual achievement, and Christian thought at that time undertook to check intellectual pride by reminding man how conditioned by physical things his intellect was. It did this, we may say, in the manner of burlesque. The Christian poet John Donne took wry note of the fact that at a moment when his thoughts were fixed on God in prayer and meditation, a fly buzzing around his head could distract his attention from its great object and that no effort of will could restore his rapt concentration until the fly was silenced. And Pascal, one of the great mathematicians of all times as well as a profound psychologist of the religious emotions, based his whole sense of the religious life upon similar observations, upon the discrepancy between man's "greatness" and his "littleness," reminding us that, powerful as the human intellect is, a man is never in full control of the right exercise of his mind, which is always at the mercy of the most trivial material circumstances.

The early nineteenth century was an age that took pride not so much in intellectual as in emotional power; it looked upon love and passion as an indication of human freedom and dignity, and perhaps no one had done more to establish this idea than Byron himself. Whatever else Byron is burlesquing in *Don Juan* he is burlesquing his own early work, in which love and passion asserted themselves without regard to the facts of animal existence. He did indeed represent love and passion as meeting with opposition from the world and as often ensuing in pain and defeat, but this of course constitutes anything but a skeptical comment upon them—in literature the pain and defeat of a person who lives according to his belief in his spiritual nature are taken to be the affirmation of spirit itself. What Byron is now saying, however, is reductive enough; he is proposing that it is not by the great catastrophes that the life of spirit is brought into question but by the small ones. Man's sense of his autonomy and dignity is not limited by his tragic sufferings but by those that are traditionally thought to be comic—the cold in the head and the passing afflictions of the stomach.

Ode to the West Wind

PERCY BYSSHE SHELLEY
1792-1822

THIS is a strangely primitive poem to have been written in the nineteenth century. Not that its language and form are primitive—they are anything but that. The primitive quality of the poem is found in certain of its modes of thought. To a very considerable extent the "Ode to the West Wind" deals with the world as men of early pagan cultures dealt with it.

The poet represents himself as experiencing a crisis of the spirit; he is at the point of despair, and in his extremity he invokes the aid of the autumn wind, asking that it give him its wild energy— "Be thou, Spirit fierce, / My spirit!" We know, certainly, that a wind cannot in actual fact do for a man what Shelley asks it to do for him. Nothing is more likely than that the poet's asking help of the wind should seem to be a mere conceit, a play of poetical fancy, and that we should satisfy our sense of actuality by explaining to ourselves that the wind "is of course only a symbol." Yet in fact we do not think of the West Wind as functioning in the poem in a merely symbolic way. We find ourselves believing that it really is the spiritual and moral force Shelley represents it as being, that, indeed, it is just what he calls it, a spirit, and that it might perfectly well enter a man and restore the power he has lost. We believe this because the poem believes it—the Ode is based on the primitive identification of spirit and wind, for the word *spirit* comes from the Latin *spiritus,* meaning breath, which in turn comes from *spirare* meaning "to blow." Shelley is entirely literal in making such an identification. Dispirited, he asks to be again inspirited, to have the breath of life blown into him.

And he goes about getting what he wants in primitive fashion. The people of an earlier time believed that words had power over things and over the unseen forces of the universe; poetry and magic were once closely allied, virtually interchangeable. The Ode assumes this old connection; Shelley would seem to have been conscious of his magician's rôle, for he speaks of "the incantation of this verse." *Incantation,* although derived from the Latin word which means simply to sing or chant, always means the singing or chanting of magic spells. Another form of the word is, of course, enchantment.

Shelley's method of incantation or enchantment is in the orthodox tradition of magic. Each of the first three stanzas is an invocation —literally, a "calling" in the sense of "summoning"—of the spirit. All the three invocations follow the same form: each opens with an address to the Spirit; each ends with the plea—or is it a command? —"Oh, hear!"; in each the Spirit is characterized by his powers, and each characterization has two parts, the second beginning with the reiteration of the pronoun "Thou." The repetitiveness of this form is quite in keeping with the lore of magic, which gives great importance to the precise repetition of a fixed form of words. The order of the words is as important as the words themselves. A spell has to be exactly right or it will not work. (In this connection, it is interesting to note that our word *glamour,* in its sense of "enchantment," comes from *grammar*—the modest art of using words correctly, according to rule, comes to be thought of as a magical power.)

The device by which the Spirit is summoned is also quite in accord with established magical practice. Primitive people believe that there is an integral connection between a person and a representation of him, and that by means of the representation it is possible to control him. One can, for instance, injure or destroy a human enemy by making a figure of him and mistreating it in appropriate ways; the spirit of a god is supposed to enter an image of him set up before his shrine. It is an analogous belief that the name of a person or god is integral with him and that, like an image, it can be used to control him. For that reason, in some societies, people keep their real names secret, and in the ancient Jewish ritual the name of God was permitted to be uttered only once a year, by the High Priest, and in great solemnity and fear. In the light of these primitive beliefs, we can see what the first three stanzas of the Ode are doing—they are making a verbal image of the Spirit; they are naming him as completely as possible by detailed description of his attributes, his power over the earth, over the sky, and over the sea. To define him is to circumscribe him. To know him is to have the power to influence his behavior.

The process of control by representation extends to the very structure of the verse in which the West Wind is described. *Terza rima* is a form which has an unusually urgent forward movement—such is the arrangement of the rimes (a b a, b c b, c d c, etc.) that scarcely have we begun one tercet than the rime-sound of the next is announced. In the three invocation stanzas this forward impulse is given the greatest possible freedom, for the sense of the line does not require the voice to pause at the end, but, on the contrary, carries it rapidly over to the next line. (In this respect the verse is at an opposite extreme from the opening of Wordsworth's "Resolution and Independence.") And the syntax is as open and unchecked, as onward moving, as the verse.

In the first stanza the Spirit is addressed in a striking epithet—he is called "destroyer and preserver." This has led some readers to believe that the West Wind represents the continuing spirit of the French Revolution, for revolution, ideally conceived, may be said to destroy in order to preserve; it destroys the old and outworn elements of society in order to allow the new to develop. The interpretation is entirely consonant with what we know of Shelley's temperament and political beliefs and it does seem to be sustained by details of the poem. Thus, the line "Wild Spirit, which art moving everywhere" suggests that the Spirit moves not only over earth, sky, and sea, but also in the hearts, councils, and cities of men. And the identification might seem to be made virtually explicit in such phrases as "quicken a new birth," "my words among mankind," "the trumpet of a prophecy," which all point to the poet's hope of a great social and political redemption.

We do well to have this possible meaning of the West Wind in mind. But we must be careful not to allow it to make the concluding part of the poem simpler, or more simply optimistic, than in fact it is. It may be the poet has been led beyond his personal despair by the thought that the autumnal destruction of what is bad in society will bring a springtime of happiness to mankind and that in this renovation his own ideas and suffering will have had some part. And this may permit him to feel that his autumnal despair, the devastation of his own life, is but a state in the process of life in general, and that he may hope for a personal renewal; he draws this hope from the analogy of the cycle of the seasons, for the death of the year is the augury of its rebirth—

> O, Wind,
> If Winter comes, can Spring be far behind?

So the poem ends. The terms of the poem, however, do not really allow us to assume that the concluding line expresses, though with pathetic interrogation, the emergence of the poet from despair to some degree of optimism. Actually they do not permit Shelley to rest in hope, for if his vision of the human fate, and of his own fate, must be in accord with everything to be inferred from the cycle of the seasons, it requires little skepticism, and no cynicism at all, to understand that if spring follows winter, so too does winter follow spring. Renovation may indeed come to society and to individual man but if we derive this hopeful thought from contemplation of the cycle of the seasons, we must recognize that the coming of spring portends the eventual autumnal decay. Perhaps it is the poet's repressed consciousness of this sad irony that accounts for the memorable poignancy of the triumphant cry at the end of the poem, in which there is almost as much despair as there is comfort.

Almost, but not quite. The cycle of the seasons must always have its import of despair, but its import of hope seems to be more insistent. Men have always celebrated the shortest day of the year as the time when the year turns and the days begin to grow longer, and we hang the baubles on our Christmas trees in token of our happy expectation of the blossoms of spring and the fruits of summer.

Ode to a Nightingale

JOHN KEATS
1795–1821

THE nightingale, which is a species of thrush known in Europe and Asia although not in America, has haunted the imagination of poets for centuries because of the beauty of its song and the strangeness of its nocturnal habit, for the nightingale sings only in darkness. Actually it is the male bird that sings, and medieval poetry conformed to this fact. But ancient Greek legend makes the singing bird female. Keats, in the first stanza of his Ode, follows the Greek mythological tradition; he addresses the nightingale as a dryad, a tree-nymph. But in the rest of the poem we can have no doubt that he means us to think of the bird as male. The song of the nightingale is of course erotic; the male bird sings only in the mating season and this knowledge was adhered to in medieval poetry. Keats's nightingale, however, does not sing of love. And when Keats speaks of the bird as "happy," as singing in "full-throated ease," he quite controverts both the Greek and the medieval view that the song is sorrowful. The Greek nightingale lamented the terrible wrongs done to her as a woman, before her metamorphosis into a bird. The medieval nightingale was believed to sing out of the pain of unfulfilled desire, although there was a charming fancy that he pressed his breast against a thorn to induce the pain that he uttered so beautifully. But it is exactly the point of Keats's poem that the nightingale sings in spontaneous and unremitting joy.

An ode has no very exact definition in the usage of English poets, but in general it may be said to be a poem on a lofty theme, of no prescribed length but long enough to allow for considerable elaborateness of development. The subject to be dealt with must be worthy of great praise, and we expect of an ode that it will reach a high point in intensity in bestowing this praise. In Greek *ode* is the word for "song"; the Greek odes were sung. The English poets did not write their odes to be set to music but they nevertheless had the ancient practice in mind and sought to approximate a musical immediacy and passionateness.

Few odes achieve this goal as fully as the Nightingale Ode. The poem does more than celebrate the song of the bird, it emulates and rivals it. Although the mode of feeling of the poem is different from that of the song it describes, for the song is said to be happy whereas the poem is sad, the poem affects the reader much as the nightingale's song does the poet—to the point, indeed, where many readers are so entranced by its lyric charm that they are content with only a limited sense of what, precisely, is being said. This is unfortunate since our delight in the Ode is bound to increase in the degree that we comprehend its complexity. The general purport of the Ode is clear enough. The poet feels the burden of mortality, not only death itself but illness and pain, the passing of youth, fatigue at the consciousness of the human condition. The nightingale's song suggests, and is, the opposite of all this; it is immortal and it is not subject to adverse circumstance. We understand, of course, that in actuality a nightingale is as surely destined for death as the poet himself. But it is not this particular bird that is the object of the poet's emotions, rather the generic nightingale, which is what it is by reason of its song—it is as if Keats were saying that the immortal and unchanging song creates new generations of actual birds to utter it.

In some degree the poem is dramatic; its action consists of the attempts which the poet makes in his imagination to achieve or approximate the existence of the nightingale. All these attempts fail. The first of them is represented in the opening stanza. The poet speaks of the painful depression of spirit—it seems to him the very threshold of death—into which he has fallen when his intense response to the nightingale's song has reached its climax. The human mind would seem not to be capable of sustaining the joy it can momentarily know; as Wordsworth says in "Resolution and Independence":

> . . . from the might
> Of joy in minds that can no further go,
> As high as we have mounted in delight
> In our dejection do we sink as low.

This cycle of feeling, from intensity or ecstasy to obliviousness or dissolution and pain, appears three more times in the course of the Ode. The second dissolution is achieved through wine. It is real wine that the poet asks for, even though the name that he gives it is not that of any known vintage but of a well-known water—the Hippocrene is the fountain of the Muses on Mount Helicon; a draft of its water was supposed to give poetic inspiration. Between the song of the nightingale and the wine which bears the name of the inspiring water there is a close association; the bird sings "of summer in full-throated ease" and the wine is said to be summer itself—the beaker that the poet longs for is to be "full of the warm South." The delight of the imagined intoxication turns out, however, to be only mediate, a step on the way to a desired extinction. This extinction, to be sure, is pleasurable, consisting as it does of fading, dissolving, forgetting, and it is meant to be redemptive, the means by which the poet frees himself from the burdens of his mortal condition. But the imagination of an ecstasy which will lead to extinction, and of an extinction which shall be an escape, ends in the vivid realization of what is being escaped—"the weariness, the fever, and the fret," all the frustrations of human existence as they are set forth in Stanza III.

In Stanza IV wine is rejected in favor of poetry as a means of escape. But the imagined flight of poetry toward the light ends in the darkness of Stanzas IV and V, which suggests the idea of liberation from the burden of life through death, as do also, perhaps, the ephemeral flowers and the short-lived May flies of the exquisite fifth stanza. It is not a new idea for the poet; he has, he says, "many a time / . . . been half in love with easeful Death" —the epithet "easeful" recalls the "full-throated ease" of the nightingale's song—and "now more than ever" he thinks of death as a "rich" experience. In some degree death is comparable to the nightingale's ecstasy: the image of Death taking "into the air my quiet breath" may not be equal in intensity to that of the nightingale "pouring [its] soul abroad" but there is a general likeness between them.

It is not uncommon for poetry to represent death as a positive and pleasurable experience. Death and dying seem naturally to associate themselves with love—the words are used to express the ultimate degree of erotic pleasure, and all great love stories end in death, as if this were the sign and validation of the lovers' passion. Even in casual speech, we express the force of a desire by the locution, "I am dying to . . ." or "I am dying for. . . ." We think only of grace and charm when we speak of music "dying away," or when we see a dancer perform "The Dying Swan." This association with agreeable things indicates something of the nature of Keats's imagination of death as it is first expressed in the poem. But if the words "die" and "death" can suggest a pleasurable and even a voluptuous experience,* the word "dead" cannot; it is a harsh, grim word, meaning all that we can conceive of insentience. Although Keats first thinks of dying as an experience of ecstasy equivalent to the nightingale's song, his awareness of reality supervenes to tell him that dying leads to *being dead*—the fancy of the "richness" of dying yields to this brute fact, best communicated in a brutal word: he speaks of himself as becoming a "sod," a mere inanimate piece of earth such as that under which we are buried.

---

* See the commentary on Whitman's "Out of the Cradle Endlessly Rocking."

But it is the seventh stanza which is for many readers the most memorable part of the poem, presenting us with a curious and deeply moving paradox. The poet speaks of the long-dead persons who have heard the voice of the nightingale; it is his purpose to contrast the joyous immortality of the song with the sad evanescence of human life. We understand this intention; yet we are not wholly willing to accept the validity of the contrast that is being proposed. The sadness of Ruth amid the alien corn, the peril of the seas, the forlornness of the faery lands, so far from being incongruous with the nightingale's song, seem to us to be at one with it in beauty and immortality, and we may even suppose that they are what the song is *about,* for it can often seem that the pain of human life is the subject of our most beautiful poetic utterances. In "The Solitary Reaper," a poem that Keats would have known, Wordsworth finds the charm of the girl's song in what she is singing about:

> . . . old, unhappy, far-off things,
> And battles long ago . . .

But although Keats, by the nature of his poetic imagination, may have been momentarily seduced into suggesting that human mortality and sorrow, seen through the veils of time and art, are more beautiful than painful, he cannot rest with this idea. His sense of reality once more enforces upon his imagination an admission of the actuality of the pain of human life.

It is with this in mind that Keats opens the eighth stanza with a repetition of the word "forlorn" which ends the seventh, pointing to it with the phrase, "the very word." And he describes its effect upon him in terms which suggest that whereas in the seventh stanza he had been speaking as one whose concern was only with beauty, now it is actuality that is his main concern—his affinity with the nightingale is at an end, now he must exist as a "sole self." In Stanza VII he had used the word "forlorn" for its charm, which derives from its lovely sound and from its possible connotation of a sadness that is distant and unreal. Now the full literal import of the word breaks upon him—it really means abandoned, lost, without hope, desperate*—and he is moved to a critical examination of himself as a poet; he speaks slightingly of one of a poet's faculties, the fancy. (We could wish he had called it almost anything but a "deceiving elf"!) Up to now the vanishing song of the nightingale had been only joyous; at this point it becomes "plaintive," as if the poet's certitude of the bird's joy were being denied. Still, at the same time it is called an "anthem," which is a song of joyful praise.

In sharp contrast with the lyricism which sustains itself through the whole poem and which is quite as apparent in the expressions of sadness or despair as in the expressions of ecstasy, the question with which the poem concludes—"Do I wake or sleep?"—shocks us with its sudden flatness and harshness of tone. That question was both explicated and answered by Shelley in "Adonais," his great elegy for Keats:

> Peace, peace! he is not dead, he doth not sleep—
> He hath awakened from the dream of life.

* It is possible that Keats knew that "the forlorn" was the old name for the call on the hunting-horn that brought back the hunters from the chase.

Dover Beach

MATTHEW ARNOLD
1822–1888

MATTHEW ARNOLD occupies a rather strange place in the community of English poets. Few people, I think, would include him among the great poets of England. The body of his work is not large, certainly not in comparison with the production of other poets of the Victorian age, and of this relatively small canon only a handful of poems are wholly successful. Yet Arnold is generally ranked as one of the three most important poets of his time, the other two being Tennyson and Browning. Indeed, despite his manifest faults, Arnold as a poet makes an appeal to the reader of today which is likely to be greater than that of either of his two imposing contemporaries.

A phrase I have just used, "Arnold as a poet," will perhaps seem odd and need explanation. We do not speak of "Tennyson *as* a poet" or of "Browning *as* a poet"—they *were* poets, we know them as nothing else. But Arnold, having begun his literary life in poetry, gave up what we might call the professional practice of the art at about the age of thirty. It was not possible for him to make an adequate living by writing alone and he therefore accepted an appointment as an inspector of elementary schools; he served in this capacity until a few years before his death. The work was fatiguing and depressing, and he could command neither the leisure nor the emotional energy that poetry requires. He did, however, find it possible to write prose, and, working in that medium, he became one of the leading intellectual figures of England. He was the most admired literary critic of his day, and, indeed, is generally accounted one of the great critics of the world. He was a very notable theorist of politics, and his writings on religion played an important part in the crisis of faith which so deeply distressed many of his contemporaries. Perhaps more than any other man of his time and nation he perceived the changes that were taking place in the conditions of life and in the minds of men to bring into being the world we now know—in certain respects he was, of all the intellectual figures of his period, the most modern.

The sensitivity to the cultural circumstances of his day which Arnold showed in his prose does much to explain his interest as a poet. Both in his early poems, which make up the larger body of his canon, and in the infrequent later poems, some of which are among his best, Arnold showed an awareness of the emotional conditions of modern life which far exceeds that of any other poet of his time. He spoke with great explicitness and directness of the alienation, isolation, and excess of consciousness leading to doubt which are, as so much of later literature testifies, the lot of modern man. And it is plain that he speaks from an unabashedly personal experience of pain, fatigue, and thwarted hope—his poetry has for us the authority of authenticity even when it lacks a high poetic grace.

"Dover Beach," however, can scarcely be said to be lacking in grace. It is one of the handful of Arnold's wholly successful poems and among these it is pre-eminent. For many readers it is the single most memorable poem of the Victorian age. In it the authenticity that is in general the characteristic note of Arnold's poetry achieves a peculiar pathos. The diction is perfect in its lightness and simplicity. The verse, moving in a delicate crescendo of lyricism from the muted beginning to the full-voiced desperate conclusion, is superbly managed. Not the least of the elements of its success is that a poem so modest in tone and in apparent scope should contain within it such magnificent vistas of space and time.

The poem is dramatic in the sense that, although there is only one speaker, there are two characters, the speaker and the woman he addresses as his love, presumably his wife. The setting of the dramatic scene is of central importance; the American reader might not recognize what an English reader would know at once, that the couple are staying at a hotel, for Dover is one of the two English ports from which one takes ship to cross the English Channel to France. The circumstance that the couple are setting out on a journey abroad makes it all the more likely that they should be inclined to think of the world as being "so various, so beautiful, so new."

The window through which the speaker is gazing and to which he invites his companion might well bring to mind the "magic casements" of the "Ode to a Nightingale." Like the window in Keats's poem, it opens "on the foam / Of perilous seas," and on forlorn lands, although not faery lands. It has the effect of framing the view and of emphasizing the sense of vista that plays so material a part in the poem. The immediate view—the great white chalk cliffs of Dover, the French coast twenty miles off, indicated by the momentary light, the moonlit waters of the Channel between— is in itself sufficiently impressive. But it opens out both in space and time to reach across Europe to the Aegean Sea and ancient Greece. It is worth noting that several of Arnold's poems depend for their most moving effects upon similar representations of great vistas both of geography and history and that in one of his early sonnets Arnold refers to Europe as "The Wide Prospect," deriving the phrase from a possible translation of the Greek name, and seeming to suggest that it was the essential quality of the European mind that it could encompass great reaches of space and time. Although in general Arnold's distances imply liberation and even joy, in "Dover Beach," when the imagination goes beyond the Aegean, it proceeds in darkness to the "vast edges drear / And naked shingles of the world."

The emptiness and despair of the vision bring the speaker back to the place from which his imagination had started, to the room from whose window he looks out, and he turns in despairing sadness to his companion, at that moment seemingly the only other person in the world, to offer her, and ask from her, loyalty in love. Perhaps literature does not know a love avowel and a love plea so sad as these—perhaps never before in literature has a lover given a *reason* for love, and a reason which, while asserting its necessity, denies its delight. It is believed by all lovers that love has the power not only of making the world various and beautiful and new, but also of maintaining it in variety, beauty, and novelty. But the lover of "Dover Beach" denies love's efficacy in this respect. Of all that love may be presumed to give, he asks only loyalty in a world that promises neither joy nor peace.

It is to this pass that the lover has been brought by his sense of modern life, which has seen the ebbing of the sea of faith. We assume that he means religious faith, and this assumption is borne out by other of Arnold's poems in which the diminution of religious faith is a reason for melancholy. But Arnold felt that the lessening of religious faith went hand in hand with the lessening of personal energy, vitality, and confidence, of that happy, unquestioning attachment to life which William James called "animal faith." When Arnold speaks of Sophocles hearing the roar of the pebbles on the beach under the receding wave and of its having brought "into his mind the turbid ebb and flow / Of human misery," he is almost certainly making reference to the opening of the third chorus of Sophocles' *Antigone*. Here is the passage in the translation of R. C. Jebb: "Blest are they whose days have not tasted of evil. For when a house hath once been shaken from heaven, there the curse fails nevermore, passing from life to life of the race [i.e., family]; even as, when the surge is driven over the darkness of the deep by the fierce breath of Thracian sea-winds, it rolls up the black sand from the depths, and there is a sullen roar from the wind-vexed headlands that front the blows of the storm." The chorus ostensibly speaks of the misery of the members of certain families living under a curse, and not of "human misery" in general. But the generalization can of course be made, and we may readily believe that Arnold had in mind the contrast between the passage from the third chorus to which he refers and the more famous second chorus of *Antigone*, which begins "Wonders are many, and none is more wonderful than man," and goes on to sing with joy of man's triumphs. It is the faith in man and his destiny so proudly expressed by the second chorus that has ebbed, leaving the world to bleakness.

The great grim simile with which the poem ends has attracted much attention, and efforts have been made to find the inspiration for it in Arnold's reading. The likeliest possibility is the account of the battle of Epipolae given by Thucydides in his *History of the Peloponnesian War* (Book VII, Chapters 43–44); this guess is encouraged by the circumstance that Arnold's father, Thomas Arnold, had published a well-known edition of the *History*. A striking quality of the simile is its unexpectedness. Up to this point the lovers have looked out on a world of wind and water, quite empty of people; now the scene is a plain filled with armies in strife. The suddenness of the shift reinforces the violence of the dark image of deteriorated existence.

Out of the Cradle Endlessly Rocking

WALT WHITMAN
1819–1892

HISTORIANS of American literature often speak of Walt Whitman and Henry James as virtually symbolic representatives of two opposed tendencies in our national culture. Whitman in his lifetime undertook to make himself a symbolic figure—he wanted, both in his person and his art, to stand for all that was "democratic" in American life, by which he meant whatever was free, impulsive, and accepting; he spoke of himself as "one of the roughs," and described his poetry as "a barbaric yawp." James had no conscious wish to put himself before the world in a symbolic light, but it was almost inevitable that he should be seen in this way. He came of a patrician family and he had as strong a feeling for elegance and decorum as Whitman had for looseness and the free-and-easy. He lived his mature years away from his native land because of his liking for the complexity of English society and his strong commitment to the artistic traditions of Europe. By reason of his style of life, he has been taken—often all too simply—to stand for conservatism, propriety, and gentility; and by reason of the nature of his art he has come to be regarded as the very spirit of consciousness, control, and precision.

The extreme differences between the two men make the dramatic point of a famous anecdote which Edith Wharton relates in her autobiography. Mrs. Wharton was a close friend and great admirer of Henry James and she tells of an evening party at her country home at which, in the course of conversation, "someone spoke of Whitman, and it was a joy to me to discover that James thought him, as I did, the greatest of American poets." James, Mrs. Wharton tells us, read poetry aloud in a very beautiful way, and now the discussion led to his being asked to read from Whitman's *Leaves of Grass,* "and all that evening we sat rapt while he wandered from 'The Song of Myself' to 'When Lilacs Last in the Door-yard Bloomed' (when he read 'Lovely and soothing Death' his voice filled the hushed room like an organ adagio), and then let himself be lured on to the mysterious music of 'Out of the Cradle' reading, or rather crooning it in a mood of subdued ecstasy till the fivefold invocation to Death tolled out like the knocks in the opening bars of [Beethoven's] Fifth Symphony."

Mrs. Wharton concludes her story by saying that James's admiration of Whitman, "his immediate response to that mighty appeal, was a new proof of the way in which, above a certain level, the most divergent intelligences walk together like gods." The generalization is not true. We can be fairly certain that Whitman would not have given James's work the same respect that James gave his. And James himself, fine critic though he was, was incapable of responding to certain "divergent intelligences" of his time, Thomas Hardy, for example, or the young D. H. Lawrence. But it is greatly to his credit that, with so much that might stand in the way of his sympathy, he did respond to Whitman. What might have intervened was the erroneous belief, which prevailed at the time and is sometimes met with even now, that Whitman wrote on mere free impulse, without the consciousness and self-criticism that normally go into poetic composition. James, whose feeling for conscious artistry was almost a religion with him, was happily not deceived into any such false notion.

Whitman himself did much to foster the misconception of his poetry when he spoke of it as a "barbaric yawp" and in general insisted on his radical difference from all preceding poets. And the mistake is likely to be confirmed by wrong ideas about the kind of verse he wrote, whose very name, "free verse," is misleading. In point of fact, Whitman was a consummate craftsman. No poems were ever more carefully composed than those which James chose to read aloud that evening at Mrs. Wharton's; we know from Whitman's manuscripts how extensively they were revised and worked over.* Whitman's verse-form, so far from being prosaic because it does not use metre and rime, is supremely musical, as James made plain by the manner in which he read it. James was a man not given to public display, yet when he read "Out of the Cradle Endlessly Rocking," he surrendered wholly to the demands it made upon him and, as Mrs. Wharton tells us, "crooned it in a mood of subdued ecstasy."

"Out of the Cradle Endlessly Rocking" is not the first poem in this volume in which the ecstatic song of a bird is involved with thoughts of death, and in which death is regarded in an ambiguous way—the similarity of this poem to Keats's "Ode to a Nightingale" will be readily apparent. In both poems the poet makes an identification between the singing bird and himself in his character of poet. In both poems, although in different ways, death is the source not only of sorrow but also of the hope of transcendence.

Yet the more we are aware of the affinity which the two poems have with each other, the more striking their differences become. Certain of these differences arise from the fact that one is an English and the other an American poem. The birds they celebrate are nationally distinct: there are no American nightingales and no English mocking-birds. And Whitman, as if to emphasize his bird's American habitat, tells us the name of its native state, Alabama. It is almost as if he had Keats's nightingale in mind—its identification with the poetic traditions of Europe, its place in Greek mythology— and as if he were saying, "*That* is the bird of the Old World, *mine* is the bird of the New."

The very names of the birds—"nightingale" with its euphonic,

---

* It is a fact worth noting that even Whitman's letters, which are marked by an extreme simplicity of style, were very fully revised and recopied before they were mailed.

remote loveliness, "mocking-bird" with its hard immediacy and
explicitness—suggest a national difference in the language of the
two poems. It was part of Whitman's conception of his poetic
mission to write in the American mode of the English tongue,
both in order to express the American temperament and to make
his poetry readily accessible to American readers. To these ends, he
used the vocabulary, syntax, and rhythms of colloquial speech, and
what literary models he did turn to were such as Americans would
know without special education, the oration and the Bible. But
we must not suppose that Whitman was unique in his use of everyday speech. It is one of the recurrent concerns of poetry to seek to
reduce the distance between the speech of the people and the special
language that any tradition of poetry tends to evolve. Dante said
that he wanted a language for his poetry that would be compre-
hensible to housewives; and Wordsworth undertook to purge poetry
of artificiality by using "the real language of real men." And a
comparison of the language of Whitman with that of Keats must
proceed with caution, for Keats too was concerned to free himself
from the linguistic conventions of poetry; his realization that he
must no longer submit to the influence of Milton's elaborate diction
made a crisis in his poetic life. To the first readers of the "Ode to
a Nightingale" the diction might very well have seemed too
relaxed and insufficiently "literary." Still, in the use of the common
speech for poetry that yet aims at a beautiful exaltation of tone,
there is no doubt that Whitman went further than Keats—further,
indeed, than anyone before him had gone. The following lines will
suggest how bold was his use of colloquialism and to what an exquisite effect:

> Oh night! do I not see my love fluttering out
> > among the breakers?
> What is that little black thing I see there in the white?

Or again:

> Whichever way I turn, O I think you could give me my
> > mate back again if you only would . . .

And quite apart from the colloquialisms of lines like these, we are aware—an English reader would be still more aware—that their rhythm and idiom are American rather than English. Keats said of Milton's majestic style, "It is magnificent but it is not English." In effect, Whitman said of all English poetry from Shakespeare down, "It is magnificent but it is not American."

In one of his essays, W. H. Auden tries to account for the differences between English and American poetry by reference to the dissimilar landscape and climate of the two countries and their influence on temperament and feeling. Certainly nothing could be less alike than the settings of "Ode to a Nightingale" and "Out of the Cradle Endlessly Rocking," especially the sense of geography which each poem conveys. The topography of Keats's Ode is comprised of glades, dells, and valleys, of enclosed, discrete places. Even the darkness encloses. Indeed, the dominant emotion of the Ode can be described as a response to limitation. The one great vista in the poem is that of time rather than of space, the view back to the "ancient days" in which the nightingale's song was heard. When the poet expresses the wish to "fade far away," the furthest destination he can imagine is "the forest dim," which seems to be quite near at hand and where he is again enclosed. And even the description of the bird's flight, which carries its song out of hearing, does not propose the idea of great distance:

> . . . thy plaintive anthem fades
> Past the near meadows, over the still stream,
> Up the hillside; and now 'tis buried deep
> In the next valley glades . . .

But the spaces of "Out of the Cradle" seem limitless—the unending stretch of Long Island beach, the dunes behind, the sea in front, the sky unobstructed. And we are mindful of the thousand miles the mocking-bird has flown to come to Long Island from Alabama. There are no demarcations of place, no dells and valleys. Nor are there any trees—lilacs somewhere, but not near the great scene, and certainly none of the luxurious blossoms that blow in the fifth stanza of the Ode, only briars and blackberries. Although it is true that no human habitation is referred to in the Ode, yet the fertile landscape permits the possibility of it, and nothing in the poem contradicts our extraneous knowledge of the fact that Keats heard the nightingale and wrote his poem in the garden of his pleasant house at Hampstead, near London. The scene of "Out of the Cradle" is far less genial, and in it there is only one sign of human life, the single stake in the water upon which the mourning bird sits, the one vertical object in the poem, the one fixed thing upon which the eye may focus:

> All night long on the prong of a moss-scallop'd stake,
> Down almost amid the slapping waves,
> Sat the lone singer wonderful causing tears.

But even more divergent are the ways in which the two poems respond to death. Although Keats is able to conceive of death as a purging of life into pure being, and although, almost against his will, he represents mortality as the source of beauty, these are only momentary fancies. They give him no real consolation in the face of his knowledge that death is insentience and extinction. The ideas that Keats rejects are intensely affirmed by Whitman. For him passion itself arises from death, and it was his having heard and understood the mocking-bird's song of sorrow that changed him from a boy into a man—and into a poet. Nor is it passion only, but life itself, that arises from death: death is "the word" which the sea, the mother of all life, "lisps" and "hisses" and "whispers" to him in response to his plea for the "clew"; and that word, the poet says, is even "more" than the mocking-bird's song: it is the word "of the sweetest song and all songs."

We can scarcely think of these differing attitudes to death as in any way national. And yet Whitman himself thought that the celebration of the beauty of death was appropriate to America and pertinent to the health of the republic. In 1871 he published a great embittered essay, *Democratic Vistas,* in which he indicts America for its failure to fulfill its true moral and political destiny and speaks of the redemption that may yet come, in part from the good effects of an appropriate national poetry. "In the future of these States," he says, "must arise poets immenser far, and make great poems of death. The poems of life are great, but there must be poems of the purports of life, not only in itself, but beyond itself." The great poem of death, he says in sum, will check the growing American vulgarity by bringing faith and large-mindedness. "Then will man indeed confront Nature, and confront time and space . . . and take his right place, prepared for fortune and misfortune. And then that which was long wanted will be supplied, and the ship that had it not before in all her voyages, will have an anchor."

Perhaps Henry James had in his own way a not dissimilar conception of death. Mrs. Wharton tells us in her autobiography that when James suffered the first of the series of strokes that were to end his life, "in the very act of falling . . . he heard in the room a voice which was distinctly, it seemed, not his own, saying: 'So here it is at last, the distinguished thing.'"

The Leaden Echo and the Golden Echo: Maidens' Song from St. Winefred's Well

GERARD MANLEY HOPKINS
1844–1889

THE poems of Gerard Manley Hopkins were first published in 1918, nearly thirty years after the poet's death, and to their early readers they seemed difficult and odd. They now stand in very high repute, but even a half century of habituation has not made them exactly easy for us. As for their oddness, this the poet himself was ready enough to concede; on one occasion he described himself as being taken aback by it. In a letter to his friend and future editor, Robert Bridges, Hopkins said that the oddness of his poems "may make them repulsive at first" and told how shocked he was when he read one of them that a friend had borrowed and sent back to him. ". . . I opened and read some lines, as one commonly reads whether prose or verse, with the eyes, so to say, only, and it struck me aghast with a kind of raw nakedness and unmitigated violence I was unprepared for. . . ." It needed a perceptible moment for Hopkins to perceive the true nature of his own poem. ". . . But take breath," he went on, "and read it with your ears, as I always wish to be read, and my verse becomes all right."

To take breath and read with the ears is what we must learn to do with any poem of Hopkins. "Read Hopkins aloud," says his latest editor, W. H. Gardner, "and you will find that his obscurity is never entirely opaque. . . ."

Hopkins was born in 1844, of a gifted family of the comfortable middle class. An excellent student, he devoted himself at Oxford to the study of Greek and Latin, in which he distinguished himself. In his Oxford days he came under the influence of John Henry Newman, later Cardinal Newman, and converted to the Roman Catholic Church in 1866; two years later he entered the Society of Jesus. The duties of that exigent order were arduous and sometimes personally uncongenial to Hopkins, but he discharged them with exemplary assiduity and still found time to speculate profoundly upon the nature of prosody, to develop his theory of English verse, and to write the poems which were to establish his posthumous fame. If the poems seemed odd in 1918, when literary experiment in England began to be the order of the day, they would have seemed far odder in the poet's lifetime, yet Hopkins might have risked publication had not the Jesuit discipline prevented it.

Many elements contribute to the radical novelty of Hopkins' style, but his chief theoretical statement, his preface to the manuscript volume of his mature poems, deals with one subject only, that of rhythm. The preface is not polemical: it says nothing adverse about the practice of other poets. But the implication of Hopkins' theory is that English verse had curtailed its strength by submitting to the rule of metre, by conforming, even though not with mechanical exactitude, to fixed line-patterns. His conception of the course that English verse should take has a considerable affinity with Wyatt's practice, although of the two poets Hopkins is much the more radical. Hopkins would have stood in opposition to the "correct" taste that had contrived the version of "They Flee from Me" which appeared in Tottel's *Miscellany* and that would have led Victorian readers to prefer this revised version to the original. He would have defended the rightness of Wyatt's departures from the pattern of the iambic pentameter line and of all the roughness and irregularities by which the poet exploited the actuality of the speaking voice. But in his preface Hopkins confined himself to explaining his own practice; he did not advance the ideas which he obviously held, that the established system of

English verse seemed to its practitioners to be the only possible one merely because of long habit. For his own prosody, he drew upon the verse systems of Welsh and Greek poetry and upon the tradition of English alliterative verse which had prevailed before the Renaissance.

He also drew upon music, of which he was an accomplished amateur, and for the better understanding of his rhythmic effects he devised a system of marks, analogous to the directive marks on a musical score, which he placed over syllables, words, and groups of words in order to show the reader how to read the poem with his ears. But on the manuscript of "The Leaden Echo and the Golden Echo" he wrote this note: "I have marked the stronger stresses, but with the degree of the stress so perpetually varying no marking is satisfactory. Do you think all had best be left to the reader?" He seems to have answered his own question affirmatively; and any reader who deals with the poem as a singer deals with a new song, "running through" it experimentally a few times to see how the voice should proceed, may reasonably feel that he is not betraying Hopkins' trust in him.

Although rhythm is Hopkins' chief aural concern, it is by no means the only one. He uses alliteration to an extent that no poet has ever ventured; and internal rime; and assonance; and subtle, planned progressions and modulations of vowel sounds. The following portion of the first line of "The Leaden Echo and the Golden Echo" illustrates all these effects: ". . . is there none such, nowhere known some, bow or brooch or braid or brace, láce, latch or catch or key to keep." The elaborate devices of Hopkins' prosody are especially in evidence throughout the poem because of its avowed vocal nature. It is not a "lyric" in the sense of being a poem to be set to music for singing and therefore kept simple and modest so that the music may have its way. It is a lyric in the sense of being the whole song itself, words and music together, the vocal line and the accompaniment, both of considerable complexity and virtuosity.

But no doubt because it is so much a song, two characteristics of Hopkins' verse are not strongly apparent in this particular poem.

One is the intense visuality that Hopkins usually sought after, the rendering of the specificity of beauty that he called "inscape," though we do have an example of it in the lines descriptive of beautiful girlhood:

> Come then, your ways and airs and looks, locks, maiden gear,
>   gallantry and gaiety and grace,
> Winning ways, airs innocent, maiden manners, sweet looks,
>   loose locks, long locks, lovelocks, gaygear, going gallant,
>   girlgrace—

The other is Hopkins' idiosyncratic rhetoric, which often, but not here, makes for difficult or delayed comprehension. In the passage

> Not within the singeing of the strong sun,
> Tall sun's tingeing, or treacherous the tainting of the earth's
>   air . . .

the last phrase offers only a momentary resistance—we quickly see that "treacherous the tainting" is to be understood as "the treacherous tainting." Nor are we much puzzled by the charming rhetorical idiosyncrasy of "it is an everlasting of, O it is an all youth!"

In common with the rest of Hopkins' poems, "The Leaden Echo and the Golden Echo" is suffused with religious feeling, which, as in many of the poems, is aroused (and colored) by the perception of beauty, frequently human beauty, and, as in this case, by the recognition of its transience. The passing of youth is of course one of poetry's oldest-established and most frequently recurrent themes; sadness or despair are the emotions which generally accompany its statement, and Hopkins, taking these to be the natural first response to transience, proposes the comfort that will be given by the resignation of youthful beauty into God's keeping. The recommendation is perhaps less a serious religious idea than a tender religious conceit; as such, it has an appealing sweetness of intention and but little power to hold grievous feelings at bay. It does, however, serve as the occasion for a peculiarly fresh and poignant celebration of the passing physical beauty for which it seeks a spiritual permanence.

"Go Tell It"–What a Message–

EMILY DICKINSON
1830–1886

O NE of the tenets of modern literary criticism is that a poem is a self-contained entity, that it must be regarded as wholly independent of all considerations that are not proposed by its own elements. For example, any knowledge of the personal life of the poet, even of the circumstances that led to the writing of the poem, is considered irrelevant—it may be interesting in itself but it cannot tell us anything we need to know in order for the poem to have its right effect upon us. There are critics who go so far as to say that an interest in the personal existence of the poet interferes with our direct response to the poem.

This idea must be granted the merit of its intention. When we read "Resolution and Independence," it is not necessary to know that Wordsworth, shortly before he wrote the poem, actually did meet an old man such as he describes, or that he was soon to be married and might therefore be expected to feel anxiety over the future. For a precise response to "Ode to a Nightingale" we do not have to know that it was written not many weeks after Keats had witnessed the death of his younger brother. And if we felt it necessary to seek out such information, the poem could of course be thought by that much the less complete in itself, for in part it would then depend for its effect upon something outside itself.

But the truth is that extrinsic information, whether we wish it or not, and whether the critics in their strictness like it or not, often does impinge upon our awareness of a particular poem and become an element in our relation to it which we cannot ignore. When we read "Lycidas," we cannot dismiss from our minds the fact that the young poet who speaks so proudly of the profession of poetry and of his noble desire for fame is to become one of the world's great poets, as famous as ever he could have wished. How different our response to "Lycidas" would be if Milton had died not long after its composition! We should then not take the poem to be, among other things, the superb prelude to a triumphant career, but a vaunt which had been made pathetic and ironic by circumstance. In this instance, the mere awareness of Milton's reputation is an extraneous knowledge that inevitably plays some part in our reading of the poem, and it would be a strict critic indeed who would say that it should not.

Another kind of information which properly has its share in our response to a poem comes from our familiarity with other poems from the same pen. Anyone acquainted with the canon of Wordsworth's work knows that the poet conceived of his creative power as being dependent upon the emotions of his childhood and early youth and that he believed that the passing years would diminish it. Whoever has read even a few of Keats's poems is aware that the poet was preoccupied with the antithesis between what is eternal and "pure" and what is transient and mundane. Such awarenesses constitute some knowledge of the poets as persons, and this knowledge cannot fail to have its effect upon our way of responding to a single one of their poems, nor does there seem to be any good reason for supposing that this effect is anything but natural. It is a positive advantage in our reading of "Resolution and Independence" to know that Wordsworth's fear of losing his creative powers is not a momentary fancy but an emotion that conditioned his whole life. It can scarcely confuse our response to "Ode to a Nightingale" to know that Keats is *again* moved to a passionate consideration of the eternal and the transitory.

And in the case of Emily Dickinson's striking little poem, there is at least one personal fact about the author which it is essential we bring to our reading—that the poet is a woman. If we were not aware of this, we might well be made uncomfortable by the poem, for its tone and diction seem appropriate to a woman but not to a man, and we would surely be ill at ease if we thought a man had been the writer.

The poem is, as it were, based upon the femininity of the poet. The word femininity is never used in a neutral sense but always with the intention of praise; it connotes charm, delicacy, tenderness. These qualities are no doubt readily seen, or heard, in the poem, but they will be the more quickly perceived by the reader who has some previous acquaintance with Emily Dickinson's work and knows the extent to which the poet represents herself in the postures of femininity, as a young woman, or girl, of high sensitivity, delicate, fastidious, quick to be apprehensive yet courageous and even daring, standing in a daughterly relation to God, whom, on one occasion, with the licensed audacity of rebelliousness characteristic of her manner, she addresses as "Papa above." The rules of the world are laid down by masculine beings and the point of many of her poems lies, as in the present one, in the opposition of the feminine creature to the masculine authority, which usually delights her even though she addresses it in irony or protest.

There are two speakers in the poem. They are of opposite sexes and they are half a world and some twenty-five centuries apart. When Emily Dickinson wrote, she could count on a prompt appreciation of what "message" it is that begins "Go tell it. . . ." Most readers of the nineteenth century knew the story of the Spartans at Thermopylae—how the huge Persian army under the great king Xerxes moved to conquer Greece; how the small Greek army took its stand at Thermopylae, where, between the precipitous mountain on the one side and the sea on the other, there was a pass so narrow that only a few soldiers could enter it abreast; how, when the Greek position was betrayed, the greater part of the Greek forces withdrew, leaving only the Spartans under their king Leonidas to hold the pass; and how the Spartans, some three hundred in number, were exterminated. Upon the spot a monument was erected which bore this inscription: "Go, stranger, and tell Sparta that here, obeying her commands, we fell." What a message indeed!

The feminine voice—and perhaps we should say the modern feminine voice—questions the basis of the Spartans' act even though the message says unmistakably what that is: obedience. The feminine mind wishes to understand the heroism as an impulse, specifically as an impulse of love. The language used is that of erotic attraction—the poet speaks of the heroic deed as having been a response to "a Lure—a Longing"; she sees it as instinctual, rising out of Nature. And across the centuries the men of Thermopylae refuse her interpretation of their act. They address her by the name of the principle she has invoked, speaking to her as if she were Nature itself, and, brushing aside the idea of their having responded to a "Lure" or a "Longing," assert that it was not Love but Law that moved them.

Yet the feminine voice is not to be silenced. In the very act of reporting how it is refuted and rebuked, it asserts itself in the peculiarly feminine epithet by which it characterizes the great event— "sweet Thermopylae," it says. And the men of Thermopylae seem suddenly to assent to the feminine understanding of their sacrifice— the salute which they send to Law is a kiss. The striking inappropriateness of applying the adjective *sweet* to the grim heroic battle is matched by the inappropriateness—almost comic—of the men of Thermopylae sending a kiss to the Law of Sparta, the most rigorous the world has known. The imperturbable soldiers have been beguiled into taking the feminine view of their action, and Law and Love are made one.

Sailing to Byzantium

WILLIAM BUTLER YEATS
1865-1939

O NE OF Hans Christian Andersen's best-known stories tells of an Emperor of China in whose garden lived a small brown bird. It was a nightingale, and the beauty of its song was a chief delight of the Emperor's life. But one day the court jewelers presented their master with an artificial bird which they had contrived with great artistry and ingenuity. It was made of gold and set with gems, and by means of a clockwork mechanism it was able to sing. The Emperor was captivated by the wonderful toy and quite forgot the nightingale of flesh and blood, who, in sorrow over his neglect, flew away. Time passed, the unvarying song of the nightingale of artifice palled on the Emperor, who was now old and near death, and one day the clockwork gave out. The Emperor, lonely on his deathbed, longed for the comfort of the real nightingale's singing. He spoke his longing aloud, the bird appeared at his window and sang for him, and the Emperor died happy.

We cannot be sure that Yeats knew Andersen's story, although anyone who had been a child in a literate home in the late nineteenth century was likely to have been acquainted with it. But whether he did or not, the story is pertinent to "Sailing to Byzantium" because it gives simple and memorable expression to an attitude which the poem controverts. For most people the word "artifice" and the adjective derived from it carry an adverse connotation. They imply something false; "nature" and "natural" suggest the real and true. Much of the force of "Sailing to Byzantium" derives from the heresy, as we might call it, of its preference for "artifice" as against "nature." The poet expresses the wish to be "out of nature," to be, exactly, a golden nightingale, a work of artifice.

The shock that the expression of this desire is calculated to produce is made the more intense by the reputation of the city that Yeats makes the comprehensive symbol of the non-natural or even of the anti-natural. Byzantium—later known as Constantinople, now as Istanbul—was the chief city of the Roman empire of the East. Eventually it became the administrative and cultural center of the whole Roman world in its long Christianized phase and, in its luxury and magnificence, it surpassed the city of Rome itself. Its architecture, which drew upon a highly developed engineering skill, has never lacked for admiration. But the pictures with which the churches, monasteries, and palaces were decorated fell into disrepute in Western Europe after the early days of the Renaissance. The chief ground for the unfavorable judgment was the indifference that the Byzantine artists showed to naturalistic representation, especially of the human form. The personages in Byzantine pictures are always clothed, and their voluminous robes give no indication of the body beneath. Their postures are static, and we have the impression that although these people are accessible to certain religious emotions, they have no capacity either for worldly feelings or for physical movement. The personal inspiration of the artist is subordinated to the control of tradition and convention; his indifference to naturalistic considerations can by no means be ascribed to a deficiency of skill in representation but to a complex aesthetic, derived from an elaborate theology, which repudiated the body in favor of the soul.

To the taste of the present time, Byzantine painting makes a strong appeal. The development of modern painting has been away from naturalistic representation and we take pleasure in the very abstractness that once was thought uninteresting and even repellent. But this revision of judgment is relatively recent, and up through the early years of the twentieth century, Byzantine painting was not likely to be admired except by scholars and connoisseurs of unconventional taste. Byzantium figured in most people's minds as the very type of a formalized "lifeless" culture.

Yeats's interest in Byzantium began when he was advanced in middle age. This was far from being the first time that a past culture had seemed to him of momentous relevance to his own life—indeed, nothing is so characteristic of Yeats, from the start of his career, as his preoccupation with the quality of life of some epoch of the past. It was thus that he expressed his passionately adverse sense of the modern world, which he thought ignoble in its rationalism, materialism, and calculating self-interest. As an Irishman, he was especially inclined to ascribe the modern ignobility to England although he also directed his scorn upon his own countrymen for betraying their heritage of romantic magnanimity. Against the dull prudence of modern life, he set the irrational heroic passions of the legendary Irish past; against the vulgarity and disorder of the present he evoked the recollection of a past era closer at hand, that of the eighteenth century, when the proud elegance of an assured aristocracy and the rich intuitiveness of an uncorrupted peasantry made the conditions of a good life. Such were the historical-cultural fantasies of the young poet who believed that the culture in which he had his actual existence stood in the way of his desire for fullness of life. Advancing years made a very different past culture seem desirable—to the aging poet Byzantium spoke of immortality.

The established and scarcely debatable view of Yeats's development is that, although he was a gifted and interesting poet from his early youth, he did not become a great one until his middle age. He was nearly fifty before he began to write the poems that won him his high place in modern literature. A special interest of his later work derives from the new diction he taught himself to use: hard, downright, fierce in its directness, and, as we say, "unpoetic." It is a manner consonant with the characteristic matter of the later poems, which is an aging man's harsh resentment of an ineluctable circumstance of human life, that we grow old.

This matter, which is to be distinguished from a concern with the transience of youth or of all of life, is new not only to the poet but to poetry. Yeats may well be the first writer ever to make his own representation of himself as an aging man a chief element of his creation. The general human importance of this cannot be over-estimated—it might even be said that Yeats added a whole stage of life to man's existence: by his impassioned resentment of it, he made the world know that old age may be as sentient and significant a period in a man's life as his youth. Hitherto old age had been represented wholly from the outside: the aged or aging person was made the *object* of understanding or sympathy; it is someone else, not the poet, who experiences the aging process. But Yeats, perhaps because he so feared and hated his old age, refused to let it make him into a mere object; he claimed it and proclaimed it as his experience, he imposed his imagination upon it—and thus remained a subject.

It is, then, as an aging man, with the prospect of actual old age before him, that Yeats takes leave of "nature" and seeks refuge in the permanence of "artifice"—of art, not as it refers to life in its shifting cycles of joy or pain, but as it suggests fixity and timelessness. His hope is much the same as that of Professor Cornelius, the historian of Thomas Mann's "Disorder and Early Sorrow," who sees in the unchanging orderliness of the past a means of escaping from the pain of the living present of youthful desire. But one need not be a man of middle age, like Professor Cornelius, or a man on the threshold of old age, like Yeats, to entertain the imagination of beautiful permanence. Keats was only twenty-four when he wrote "Ode to a Nightingale," the theme of which is not unlike that of "Sailing to Byzantium"; his "Ode on a Grecian Urn" is yet closer to Yeats's poem in the complex opposition it makes between beauty in nature, with its susceptibility to mutability and deterioration, and beauty in the permanence of art.

But we cannot read the first stanza of "Sailing to Byzantium" without being made aware of the poet's ambivalence toward nature, of how deeply Yeats loves what he says he has rejected. The beings that "commend" the natural cycle of existence, the life of generation, birth, and death, win from the poet the commendation of his scarcely disguised envy. And when he imagines his existence in "artifice," as the golden bird, it is not of timeless abstractions that he tells us he will sing but of nature and time, or nature *in* time—the triad which describes the burden of his song, "what is past, or passing, or to come," echoes the triad of rejected things in the first stanza, "Whatever is begotten, born, and dies." This has to be seen as a contradiction, and a moving one. And perhaps equally moving is Yeats's choice of the form of artifice in which the poet would wish to have his existence—not a great, still monument of the soul's magnificence but a minuscule creature of gold and enamel, a little toy of a bird.

The Waste Land

THOMAS STEARNS ELIOT
1888–1965

"THE WASTE LAND" is the most famous and influential English poem of our time, the most elaborate and highly wrought, and the most ambitious in its scope, for its subject is nothing less than the nature of modern life, which it represents as the ground of personal desperation. There is no question but that it is a difficult poem. As such, it has engaged the study of many scholars and critics. Their work, and the passage of time, which to some extent domesticates all that is strange and unapproachable in art, have considerably reduced the resistance which "The Waste Land" offered to our understanding when it first appeared in 1922. But it still remains difficult, it still demands a more than usual effort of comprehension. It requires a knowledge of its conventions and assumptions and a degree of familiarity with the recondite lore to which it refers.

The difficulty of the poem and the necessity of dealing with it in a rather special way were recognized by the poet himself. After its first publication, Eliot—perhaps with some irony—provided a series of notes to help set the reader on the right path. These notes appear at the end of the poem.

Yet acquaintance with "The Waste Land" is best begun, not with the confrontation of any of the poem's manifest difficulties, but rather with a response to that element of the poem which is not at all difficult to appreciate, its music. "The Waste Land" is a poem in which the voice plays a definitive part. This is not to underestimate the importance of its visual imagery, but if we can speak of the order in which our impressions of the poem are gained it is its voice—or voices—that we are soonest aware of. Our first experience of "The Waste Land" should be that of hearing it, whether by listening to a recorded reading or by saying it aloud, and quite without any special effort to discover the precise significance of what we hear.

This is not an evasion of what the poem communicates but a first happy step toward it, and the poet himself has given us ground for believing that it is the right first step to take. In one of his later critical essays, "The Social Function of Poetry," Eliot speaks of his pleasure in reading poems in a language he does not know well, so that he is more aware of the sound of the poem than of its exact meanings; and in another essay, "The Music of Poetry," he tells us that when he composes a poem what often comes first to his mind is a certain rhythm or tune which later, as it were, acquires words. The first experience of "The Waste Land" might well be likened to an experience of actual music—what we hear has meaning for us (although not in a denotative way), we know that the meaning of one passage or movement is different from that of another, we perhaps find one *more* meaningful than another, and yet we cannot say *what* the meaning is. If a particular piece of music initially seems difficult to "follow" or "understand," greater familiarity will lead us to a sense of more thorough comprehension. A reader will have much the same experience of "The Waste Land" if he merely listens to it, without questioning the intention of any one line, or figure of speech, or allusion.

This is by no means to say that close study of the poem is not profitable. The opposite is true. But studious reading should come only after one has responded to the poem in those of its elements— they are many—that are to be apprehended readily.

And it is well to know from the outset that even when all the details of the poem will eventually have been mastered, when the recondite references are understood, and all the subtle interrelations of the pattern are traced, the poem still will not be mastered: it will always have some measure of mystery; it will hold back from us some secret of its existence. This element of mystery or secrecy—as I have said of other poems less difficult than this—is not a negative but a positive quality of "The Waste Land" and of our response to it. The poem's continued resistance to our best efforts of comprehension is a sign of its vitality and an invitation to our continued interest.

If we are introduced to "The Waste Land" by listening to it, inevitably we are struck by the large variety of its vocal modes, its many different kinds of utterance—we hear speech that is sometimes grave and simple, sometimes lyric and tender, sometimes hysterical, sometimes toneless, sometimes querulous, sometimes awed; and the utterance may be song, or exhortation, or prayer. From whom do these various utterances come? The answer—or at least a first answer —is simple enough. The poem is largely dramatic in form, in the sense that it is not one voice that is heard but many voices, of many persons or characters, some of whom are in relation to one another. It is confusing that some of these utterances are set off by quotation marks and some are not. We are inclined to suppose that the passages that are not punctuated in this way are spoken by the poet himself. But we soon perceive that this is not possible, that of the several speakers in such passages the poet himself is only one and that although now and then he speaks in a manner which does seem to refer to his actual personal existence and emotions—as, for example, in the opening lines and in the passage about the Hyacinth garden —his voice is often merely that of a narrator or of a puppet-master introducing his characters. And at all times the voice of the poet is likely to change without warning into the voice of someone else.

And even our sense that we have now and then heard the poet speak in his own person is challenged by Eliot's note (to line 218) about Tiresias, who, we are told, "although a mere spectator and not indeed a 'character,' is yet a most important personage, uniting all the rest. . . . What Tiresias *sees,* in fact, is the whole substance of the poem." But Tiresias does not see as other men see—this most famous of the ancient Greek seers is blind. Of his legend the note tells us only the circumstances of his having for a time been transformed into a woman, and of how he came to be blind and a prophet; Eliot relies on the reader to remember his role in the *Odyssey* (Odysseus descends into Hades to consult his prophetic wisdom) and in two of Sophocles' plays, *Antigone,* which is about the burial of the dead, and *Oedipus Rex,* in which Thebes is a land made waste, deprived of fertility of every kind. No human figure in Greek literature was regarded with as much awed respect as Tiresias, and his presence in the poem gives rise to large conceptions—of the distant past which in some form is still alive in the present; of the future which, by Tiresias' foreknowledge, also exists in the present; of the dark powers in control of human life which are inaccessible to human reason although not to the prophetic mind. If the poem is difficult, if its matter is often inscrutable, if its order is not in accord with the expectations of the ordinary human mind, this is because its "whole substance" is contained in the mind of Tiresias.

Tiresias does not identify himself until the third section of the poem, but the theme of ancient prophecy has been announced well before that, and, in fact, before the poem actually begins—in the epigraph, which refers to the Sibyl of Cumae, one of the most famous of the ancient prophetesses. The epigraph is integral to the poem and a summary of its import. The great Sibyl hung up for show in a cage epitomizes the idea of degeneration and deterioration which informs "The Waste Land," just as the horror of her fate epitomizes its chief emotion—the dread of a life that is no life, that is a life-in-death. And no less significant is the nature of the person who tells of having seen the Sibyl in her cage. He is Trimalchio, one of the characters of Petronius' great novel of Roman life in the time of Nero, the *Satyricon.* Trimalchio is a millionaire, ignorant, ostentatious, boastful. His ascendancy in contrast to the degradation of the once great Sibyl points to another leading theme of "The Waste Land," that in modern life vulgarity has triumphed over the ancient pieties.

These pieties are religious, but of no specific creed. Eliot was later to become a devout Christian of the Anglican communion, and certain elements of "The Waste Land" make this not surprising. But at the time of writing the poem he had not made his religious decision. "The Waste Land" draws upon the traditions of Jewish, Christian, and Indian religion, especially as these faiths conceive of despair and the possibility of salvation. Christianity is indeed salient, but Buddhism is of almost equal authority, and for the climax of the poem Eliot uses a Brahmanic devotional text.* Even more important than the part played by the highly developed regions is that of primitive religion. Eliot makes this plain in the first and most general of his notes in which he speaks of his indebtedness to Jessie Weston's book, *From Ritual to Romance,* and to the more famous and comprehensive work of Sir James Frazer, *The Golden Bough.*

The concerns of primitive religion were not spiritual, in our meaning of the word, but utilitarian. The purpose of ritual was to secure the good will of a deity who was in control of one or another of the material circumstances of life; the fertility of the earth, upon which human life depends, was a matter of especial religious anxiety. The highly developed religions preserve the vestiges of this concern in their language about the spiritual life—religion as we know it has much to say about hunger and thirst, about water and green pastures, about bread and wine. But what is now metaphorical was once literal. The elaborate rituals to which Miss Weston and Frazer refer had once the practical intention of insuring the success of the crops and the fecundity of the flocks and herds, and also, what is of central importance in "The Waste Land," human fertility.

To many men, from the nineteenth century on, this primitive relation of human beings to the processes of nature has come to seem increasingly desirable, in itself a source of life. They feel that the rational processes of the intellect, which have grown in authority in recent centuries, have resulted in a dryness and deadness of feeling, in a loss of the vital power of the primitive imagination. Of the poems commented on in this volume, "The Waste Land" has its

---

* In his first version of the note on the word with which the poem closes, the thrice-repeated "Shantih," Eliot could write, " 'The Peace which passeth understanding' is a feeble translation of the content of this word."

closest historical affinity with "Dover Beach"—what Eliot says through complex dramatic symbolism, Arnold says in a single explicit utterance. When Arnold speaks of the ebbing of the sea of faith, he has in mind not primarily faith in a doctrinal religion but "animal faith," the sense that the energies of men are continuous with and supported by the energies of the world, which are in some way divine. It is true that the conceptions of doctrinal religion are always in the offing of "The Waste Land," but Eliot too is primarily concerned with the cultural circumstances that are the cause—and the result—of man's loss of belief in his old organic relation to the world. This connection is made by the imagination rather than by the intellect and provides a basis for the ability to experience life immediately and intensely, and, as we say, with meaning.

Miss Weston's book deals with the legend of the Holy Grail, the subject of numerous medieval romances in the cycle of stories about the Arthurian knights. The Grail itself was the cup in which the blood of Christ was received at the Crucifixion; the bleeding lance that figures in the story is the weapon that wounded Christ upon the Cross. The legend tells of a Fisher King—one of the symbols of Christ is a fish—who has received a wound that will not heal, by which he has been made sexually impotent. His condition has its effect upon the land over which he rules, so that it has lost all its fertility and lies sere and waste. The cure of the King and the consequent redemption of the land depend upon the right action of a perfect knight, usually Parsifal, who, led to the Waste Land by a vision of the Grail, which is in the possession of the King, must overcome certain trials of temptation and then ask certain questions about the Grail and the Lance which he beholds carried in ceremonial procession. We can scarcely fail to see that the Christian elements of the story are combined with those that are manifestly pagan, and it is Miss Weston's theory that the story is derived from the vegetation mysteries of India, and that the Cup and the Lance were originally sexual symbols in these rituals. The Wounded King brings the story into obvious connection with the many ancient stories of young men or young gods dying, often of a wound that is sexual in nature, and of being restored to life. Such stories formed the basis of the cults which Frazer deals with in *The Golden Bough.* To these ritual myths, many of which associate the dying and resurrected god with a tree and some of which represent him as being hanged on a tree, the story of the crucified and resurrected Christ has its manifest analogy.

Although Miss Weston's speculations on the origins of the Grail cycle were so important in the conception of Eliot's poem, the specific elements of the story are by no means obvious. The Fisher King is refererd to in a shadowy way in line 189, and it would seem that in Part V the long passage beginning with line 231 refers to Parsifal's journey through the Waste Land to the so-called Chapel Perilous that figures in the story (the "empty chapel" of line 389). But Parsifal himself appears only once and by rather recondite reference (see line 202 and Eliot's note on it), and there is no overt reference to the Grail or the Lance. The Waste Land itself appears chiefly as an emotional condition, especially as this is demonstrated by the failure of love which most of the characters of the poem experience and acknowledge.

The theme of sexual failure is proposed first, and rather gently, in the opening of Part I, "The Burial of the Dead," in the speech of the aristocratic German lady who can recall the joy of her girlhood but whose maturity or middle age is exiled and solitary. The song of the sailor quoted from the first act of Wagner's *Tristan and Isolde,* fresh, gay, and impudent, suggests the love-passion which the opera represents and celebrates, but it is echoed by the deathly negation of the line from the last act of the opera, which speaks of the vacant desolate sea. The poignant words spoken by the "hyacinth girl" are addressed to a love who does not—cannot—respond, being "neither / Living nor dead." In Part II "A Game of Chess," the failure of love is presented dramatically, almost sensationally, first in the scene of luxurious and elegant life, then in the scene, in a pub, of lower-class life; in both instances the failure of love has led to despair and boredom. Part III, "The Fire Sermon," is largely given over to the representation of loveless love-making, and also of homosexuality. The description of the Thames on a holiday makes use of the refrain from Spenser's "Prothalamion," in which the poet celebrates his approaching marriage and the beauty of the idea of married love; its presence here is obviously ironic—it brings to mind the deterioration both of the ideal of love and of the beauty of the river which was invoked by the poet in the famous refrain of his marriage song. Also serving the purpose of irony is the reference to Elizabeth and Leicester on the royal barge, symbolic of a vanished age of energy and glory; the irony is compounded by the unfulfilled and tragic sexual relation of the two great personages. The concluding passage, a quotation from *The Confessions of St. Augustine,* refers to the saint's unregenerate days and his conversion, and by implication—in reference to "Carthage" and "burning"—to the funeral pyre of Dido, the legendary queen of Carthage who slew herself when she was deserted by Aeneas.

With Part III the direct representation of sexual defeat ends. The brief fourth part, "Death by Water," speaks perhaps not only of death but of baptism and regeneration. Throughout the poem, water figures as the life-giving element, fire as the destructive element. Phlebas, the drowned Phoenician sailor, is commemorated in a brief elegy which may be intended to bring to mind the cool, sad commemorative verses of the *Greek Anthology,* perhaps also the drowning of Lycidas and the elegist's affirmation that Lycidas is not dead, "Sunk though he be beneath the watery floor," for he is "mounted high, / Through the dear might of Him that walked the waves." There is also striking reference to *The Tempest* in the second and third parts of the poem; its themes of the rightful lord dispossessed and restored, of rescue from the sea, of repentance, purging, and reconciliation, are much to the poem's purpose.

The scene of Part V is an actual waste land, stony and sun-parched, and since Eliot tells us in his note that the journey of the two disciples to Emmaus is one of the themes of the beginning of this part, we may bring to the aid of our visual imagination what we know of the harsh landscape of Palestine. ". . . The third who walks always beside you" may well be the resurrected Jesus, who (as the story is told in Chapter 24 of the Gospel according to St. Luke) joined the two disciples on the road and spoke with them without being recognized until he identified himself. The "murmur of maternal lamentation" may be the mourning of Mary but more likely it refers to the prophecy of catastrophe that Jesus utters in Chapter 23 of Luke, which tells of his condemnation and crucifixion: "And there followed him a great company of people, and of women, which also bewailed and lamented him. But Jesus turning unto them said, Daughters of Jerusalem, weep not for me, but weep for yourselves and for your children. For, behold, the days are coming, in which they shall say, Blessed are the barren, and the wombs that never bare, and the paps which never gave suck. Then shall they begin to say to the mountains, Fall on us; and to the hills, Cover us." It is a vision which manifestly accords with the poet's vision of the cultural and political decay of Europe, which in his notes he documents by a quotation from Hermann Hesse.

In the Vedic text known as the *Brihadaranyaka Upanishad*, the god Pragāpati speaks in the voice of the thunder, uttering three times the sound "Da," the initial syllable of the Sanskrit words *"Datta, Dayadhvam, Damyata,"* which mean, as Eliot's note tells us, "give, sympathise, control." He who has given, sympathized, and controlled may achieve regeneration, a new birth of the spirit. With the utterances of the thunder, which promises the relief and renewal of fertilizing rain, the sexual theme comes again to the fore. The lines following *Datta* and *Dayadhvam* are ambiguous, they may or may not refer to sexual conduct. But those following *Damyata* are plain enough—the control that is meant is not, as we might at first expect, self-control, but the lover's beneficent control of his beloved in the act of love. Perhaps nothing in the poem is more directly affecting than the lines that begin "The sea was calm," with its perhaps conscious reminiscence of the opening lines of Matthew Arnold's "Dover Beach," and that go on: "your heart would have responded / Gaily, when invited, beating obedient / To controlling hands"; the comparison of the beloved's heart to a boat well managed is consummated in the word "beating," which applies not only to the action of the heart but to the progress of a boat by tacking into the wind. The heart that would have responded gaily when invited had not been invited, and that word "gaily" emerges from the passage with a terrible pathos, suggesting how simple—how "human," as we say—is the quality of life that this elaborate poem mourns for.

The last passage of the poem, after a recapitulating reference to the Fisher King, proceeds to the conscious incoherence of a desperate mind. But even in its desperation it cannot refrain from repeating the thunder's three words of regeneration and from uttering, as a "formal ending," the word that means "The Peace which passeth understanding."

Perhaps something should be said about the quotations, direct or indirect, that figure so prominently in "The Waste Land." Some readers are offended by them and regard their presence as an affectation, even a pedantry. A sympathetic view might take them as additional "voices" that haunt the poem, or the poet's mind in his making of the poem.

Neither Out Far Nor In Deep

ROBERT FROST
1874–1963

THE power and charm of this poem lie in the discrepancy between, on the one hand, its tone and ostensible subject, and, on the other hand, its actual subject. The tone can be described as minimal, flat, even pinched, and perhaps as fatigued. The ostensible subject, an observation of the behavior of people at the seashore, is scarcely of great consequence and might even be thought rather trifling. The actual subject is the response of mankind to the empty immensity of the universe.

The discrepancy becomes manifest in the last line of the poem. Up to that point what "the people" do by the seashore is denoted by the word "look." This is perhaps our most commonplace and neutral verb for the act of seeing. It is the verb that least *dignifies* the act, for in itself it carries no implication of purpose or of any intensity, as do, for example, such verbs as "gaze," "view," "stare," or even "see." In everyday speech it is often linked with the minimizing or depreciating word "just"—"I'm just looking," or "I'm just looking at. . . ." Of course, linguistic circumstances can endow the word with one or another degree of force. Used by itself in the imperative —"Look!"—it is intense indeed. To "look for" something is very purposeful; but to "look at" something may or may not convey the idea of intention, and it may even, as I have suggested, indicate an entire lack of purpose, a mere idleness, as it seems to do in the first stanza of the poem.

Yet as the word is reiterated through the poem, it grows in meaning and force. It is used five times, and the mere repetition is somehow impressive, as if the poet were obsessed by the idea of mere looking. The first time it is used, "the people" simply "look one way" —we are not even told that they are looking *at* anything. There is a degree of intensity implied by the phrase, "They look at the sea all day," but the looking is still idle enough. By the third stanza, however, the word becomes very intense indeed. This is partly because the looking is suddenly—startlingly—associated with a very large question, "Wherever the truth may be," and partly because "the people" seem forever fixed in their looking: the last two lines of the stanza seem to say that just as it is a fact of nature that the water comes ashore and will come forever, so it is a fact of nature that "the people" look at the sea and will look forever. The last two uses of the word, in the last stanza, deny or limit the effectuality of the looking—

> They cannot look out far,
> They cannot look in deep—

but by doing so they suggest that the looking, which first seemed idle and then seemed almost a trance, was after all not without some purpose. And this suggestion is fully and forcefully confirmed in the concluding two lines:

> They cannot look out far.
> They cannot look in deep.
> But when was that ever a bar
> To any watch they keep?

The word "look" has suddenly yielded to the "watch they keep"— the minimal word is replaced, and explained, by a phrase of great dignity and richness of meaning. It implies a strong intention, and the activity of the mind as well as of the eye. And the activity of the heart as well as of the mind. It is a phrase that may suggest the idea of danger, or of hope, or of solicitude, or of loyalty. What is more, it has an archaic character; it is not a phrase that we use casually or lightly in ordinary speech, and its effect in the poem, the language of which is in general colloquial and flat, is solemn and ceremonial. The people who keep the watch are doing what soldiers do, warders of the coast, or what the shepherds at Bethlehem did. They await some significant event.

The small observation which is the poem's ostensible subject first presents itself to our minds as a speculation in psychology or aesthetics. If the land varies more than the sea and is therefore presumably more interesting, why do the people at the shore turn their backs upon the land to look at the sea? Why do the solitary objects that break the monotony of the sea—the nearing ship, the gull reflected in the wet sand—hold the attention so firmly? But the psychological or aesthetic speculation gives place to another of a more momentous kind. Partly because of the word "truth" in the third stanza, but not only because of that, we come to know that "the people" are looking, and waiting, for *something*. We are not told what they hope to descry on the vacant immensity of the sea, and they themselves seem not to know, but we do not doubt that the object of their silent expectation is of transcendent importance.

We are often told that poetry deals with the particular and the concrete, that this is its very essence. If this is so, how shall we account for the peculiar effectiveness of the word "people"? Surely it is the most general and abstract word possible, yet it has, as used here, a strange pathos. Is it because its generality proposes to us the ultimate generality of mankind: all people, all over the world, at all times ("When was that *ever* a bar . . . ?")? For some readers, it will have a reminiscence of the effect of naive simplicity with which the word is used in the Bible, as, for example, "Where there is no vision, the people perish." The word imputes a kind of humility: "the people" all "look at the sea" at the behest of something instinctual or innate, not at the behest of intellectual curiosity; there is something dumb, something of the animal, in the accord with which they turn their gaze in the one direction and keep it there. This imputation of an animal-like humility before the power of instinct is anything but contemptuous; on the contrary, it is tender. And the quiet anonymity which is suggested by the phrase "the people" is matched by the unnamedness of the thing they watch for.

The poem does not affirm that what is watched for will appear. It says no more than that it is the nature of "the people" to keep watch, whether or not there is anything to appear.

My Father Moved Through
Dooms of Love

E. E. CUMMINGS
1894–1962

IN OUR elementary schooling we are—or used to be—taught the "parts of speech" and how to distinguish one from another, only to discover that they all incline to be interchangeable, their nature being protean, and determined not by definition but by use. *Walk* is a verb until we take a walk, when it is a noun. *Clear* is an adjective until we clear the snow from the sidewalk, when it is a verb. *Further* is an adverb, but we further our sense of how English works when we confront the fact that nothing requires this word to be permanently adverbial. *Beyond* is a mere preposition, but we have no trouble in understanding that in The Great Beyond it rises to the substantive status of a noun.

The tendency to this kind of interchange among the parts of speech is very strong in English and seems to accelerate. But it does not make its way without resistance; we respond to some instances of it with more dubiety or surprise than we do to others. *Yonder* is an adjective—"Yonder peasant, who is he?"—or an adverb—"You can easily find out by walking yonder a way and asking him." And it can, under light duress, be made to serve as a noun; as in the Air Force song "The Wild Blue Yonder." But the phrase startles us a little; we recognize it as a more or less successful effort to manipulate the language in an interesting—a poetic—way, and as such we accept it, but it is not possible that any of us will make the same use of the word in ordinary speech. We are more startled, and likely to be pleased, when Gerard Manley Hopkins exclaims over a falcon in flight, "the achieve of, the mastery of the thing!" The phrase has much more energy and verve than if it had read "the achievement of, the mastery of the thing!" Yet there is but little chance that *achieve* will replace *achievement* in common usage.

A considerable part of the interest of E. E. Cummings' poem comes from our surprise over its use of parts of speech in ways that we are not accustomed to and are scarcely likely to adopt, although we can understand the mode of their use if we make the effort to do so. To say of the father that he moved "through sames of am" is to speak of the integrity of his being; he was always, as we say, himself. "Haves of give" recalls the statement of Jesus that "it is more blessed to give than to receive"; it says that for the father this was true in the most literal sense possible: for him to give was to have. His relationship to people is exemplified by the effect he has on three of them, a where, an if, and a why—the "motionless forgetful where" who turned at the father's glance "to shining here" is, we may suppose, a young man who, until touched into activity, had been lost in a passive self-absorption, not easily to be reached by actuality, not even his own, since that had not yet come into being. The "if (so timid . . . ?)" would seem to be another young man, distrustful of life and of his own powers, who under the father's vivifying influence undergoes metamorphosis and is transformed from a nonpersonal being, a "which," into an actual personal self, a "who," like a butterfly emerging from its chrysalis. The weeping "why" of the next stanza is manifestly a woman or a girl whose being, at the moment, is defined by her bewilderment or resentment at some pain inflicted upon her.

"Most poetry," a critic has said, "is on commonplace themes, and the freshness, what the poet supplies, is in the language." Cummings' theme may be said to be commonplace enough—how often have we heard the praise of integrity and sincerity, how often have we been asked to be aware of the beneficent power of sympathy and unselfishness! Often enough, surely, to make the virtuous qualities that are praised seem as dull, abstract, and imprecise as the words that are used to denote them. But when the old words are translated in ways that startle us and that require some little effort of energy on our part to perceive the equivalence, the virtues being praised shed their commonplaceness and shine with the freshness of invention.

Yet the novelty of Cummings' language cannot claim all the credit for the poem's engagingness, which in some part comes from the poet's conception of the best kind of goodness, that which is spontaneous, natural, and arises from and moves toward joy. The father is represented as being virtuous rather than moral or ethical, which would suggest a state of being arrived at by intention and effort. His virtue is to be understood in the old sense of the word, which meant power—he has a natural power of goodness that makes its effect less through what he does than through what he is. And this power is represented as being analogous with the beneficent workings of Nature; the instances and images that Cummings finds appropriate to his father, who was a Unitarian clergyman, might serve as well for some pagan fertility god. The poet touches upon the existence of his father in each season of the cycle of the year, but he makes spring his characteristic time, his characteristic action being, in Lucretius' phrase, to bring living things into the borders of light.

In Memory of Sigmund Freud
(d. Sept. 1939)

W. H. AUDEN
1907–1973

A MONG the first acts of the Nazi party after it came to power in Germany in 1933 was the suppression of the teaching of psychoanalysis in the medical schools and a ceremonial burning of the works of Sigmund Freud. This was in part a response to the fact that the founder of psychoanalysis was a Jew, for one of the axioms of the Nazi ideology was that the Jews were the cause of all the misfortunes of the German people and the source of all that was bad in the Western world. It was also a response to the actual content of psychoanalysis, especially to its theory that many disorders of the personality have a sexual etiology and can be traced to the patient's experience of the family situation in early infancy.

Freud, living in Vienna, was naturally much distressed over the turn of events, but he persuaded himself that the hostility of the Nazis would not come closer home. He was, of course, mistaken—in 1938 Hitler sent his troops into Austria and united that nation with Germany under his rule. Freud was forbidden to carry on his work and he and his family lived under the threat of the concentration camp. Before the invasion actually took place, he had resisted all suggestions that he leave Vienna, and even now he was reluctant to think of leaving the city in which he had lived all but two of his eighty-two years. Eventually, however, the counsels of his friends and colleagues prevailed and he consented to emigrate, but it was only after prolonged negotiations with the Nazi officials and the payment by his friends abroad of a large sum of money in ransom that Freud was permitted to leave Austria and, with his family, was brought to England, a country which he had held in affectionate admiration since boyhood and which now received him with great honor. He settled in London, and, although much enfeebled by the illness which had made existence a torture for many years—cancer of the jaw, necessitating innumerable operations—he resumed his habits of arduous work, seeing patients and pupils and carrying forward the composition of a new book. He died a year later, three weeks after the beginning of the Second World War.

Freud had never concerned himself directly with politics but the therapeutic psychology of which he was the inventor had social and ultimately political implications of great moment. If these had ever been obscure, they became manifest upon the violent Nazi opposition to psychoanalysis and they constitute the informing theme of Auden's commemoration of Freud.

The theory of psychoanalysis is enormously complex, but at its heart is the quite simple idea that the individual human personality is formed, and in all too many instances malformed, by the interaction of the biological impulses or "drives" with the controlling authority of the family, which is continuous with the authority of society and the state. The individual in the course of his development incorporates this authority into his emotional system, in both its conscious and its unconscious parts. If the authority thus internalized is excessively strict—as it may be either because it mirrors the actual repressiveness of the parental control or because the individual for some reason imagines the external authority to be more exigent than it actually is—there will result a malfunction of the instinctual life, inhibiting the healthy development of the personality and causing great emotional pain. The malfunction begins in earliest childhood, though it may not manifest itself until a later time, and Freud's method of therapy is to lead the patient to bring into the light of consciousness the particular circumstances, actual or fancied, that may serve to explain where his emotional life went wrong, why the "internalized authority" is devoted to causing pain. As Auden's poem puts it, Freud

> . . . told
> The unhappy Present to recite the Past
> Like a poetry lesson till sooner
> Or later it faltered at the line where

> Long ago the accusations had begun,
> And suddenly knew by whom it had been judged . . .

"Accusations" and "judged" are the crucial words—neurotic suffering may be ascribed to the patient's having instituted in his unconscious mind a juridical process in which the prosecuting attorney accuses too fiercely, the judge condemns too readily and sentences too sternly, and the jailer carries out the imposed punishment too eagerly.

By the time the Nazis banned it in Germany and Austria, psychoanalysis had won a considerable degree of acceptance, but only against a stubborn and often bitter resistance. The physicians who criticized its theory seldom did so in a spirit of disinterested scientific objectivity; they were likely to share the moralizing fervor of the many laymen who denounced it as a threat to society. The therapeutic goal of psychoanalysis is scarcely subversive and nowadays it is even said by some to err in the direction of social conformity, for it undertakes to make it possible for the patient to live in reasonable accord not only with himself but with his society. Yet even from the little that has been said here about the basic theory of psychoanalysis, it will be plain that it is antagonistic to authoritarianism, though not to rational authority. What Auden's poem aptly speaks of as Freud's "technique of unsettlement" cannot really be said to have overtly and explicitly foreseen "the fall of princes," but it nevertheless did bring the very idea of arbitrary rule into question. It is therefore not surprising that it should have incurred the hatred of "the ancient cultures of conceit."

At the present time the judgment on psychoanalysis is divided.

Many still regard it uneasily or hostilely, yet it has established itself as part of the substance of modern thought. Its influence is especially strong in the United States, where its premises and conclusions are taken for granted by many who have never read any of the works in which its theory is expounded. For many Freud is indeed

> . . . no more a person
> Now but a whole climate of opinion . . .

Writing not long after Freud's death, Auden naturally made the large public aspects of Freud's thought salient in his commemoration. With totalitarianism in the ascendant, the aspects of psychoanalysis that might well seem of first importance were those that bore upon politics, such as the opposition it offers to "the Generalised Life" and "the monolith / Of State." But the poem does not fail to take account of the effects that the technique of settlement may have upon the personal and private life, and not only in situations of extreme pathology, among "the Lost People," "the injured" who "Lead the ugly life of the rejected," but also among those who are not so grossly afflicted and who yet live less freely than they might, immobilizing themselves behind "a set mask of rectitude," having less courage, simplicity, and power of responsive emotion than it is within their capacity to have.

The last quatrain brilliantly expresses the paradoxical nature of Freud's thought. By ancient convention, rationality and impulse are believed to be at hopeless odds with each other. But Freud put his "rational voice" at the service of impulse, seeking its liberation. It may be questioned, however, whether the last two lines, fine as they are, represent Freud's thought with entire accuracy. It is certainly true that Freud was in avowed alliance with "Eros, builder of cities," the love that makes the family, society, and civilization. But nothing in his work affirms the beneficence of "anarchic Aphrodite," the irresistible, heedless love that we call passion.

The poem claims much for the intention of Freud's science, much for its achievement. Yet this large optimism is qualified by the tone in which it is asserted. One may hear a note of reserve in the large positive statements as though the recognition of Freud's purpose and achievement went along with the sense of how much is still to be accomplished for human happiness and with the awareness that any celebration of human advance must be of a muted kind when uttered at the beginning of a war that promises to be long and terrible. The restrained, slightly dry tone is in part an effect of the diction, which is determinedly plain. It is also, and perhaps to an even greater extent, an effect of the stanzaic form, which seems to have been consciously modelled on the so-called Alcaic strophe of Greek and Latin poetry. In this strophe the first two lines are of eleven syllables, the third of nine, the fourth of ten, and Auden conforms quite strictly to the pattern; there are only a very few quite minor departures. Unlike the Alcaic strophe, Auden's form has no set metrical pattern within the fixed number of syllables for each line, nor, indeed, any metrical pattern at all; but the rhythm of each line is controlled and made more or less homogeneous with that of its matching lines by the fixed number of syllables. One has the sense of prose that is always at the point of becoming metrical, or at least markedly cadenced, and always being prevented, falling back to its prose tone. And this effect of an energy continually checked, even if continually asserting itself, is supported by the interplay between the lengths of the lines of which the stanzas consist, the ranging first two lines with which each stanza begins, the sharply curtailed third, the fourth that a little recoups what its predecessor had lost.

For the Union Dead

ROBERT LOWELL
1917–1977

I N 1863, the third year of the Civil War, Governor Andrew of
Massachusetts commissioned a new regiment, all of whose
rank and file were Negroes although its officers were white
men. The formation of the first Negro fighting unit had been undertaken only after considerable hesitation. It was felt by many that
the war should not be exclusively a white man's war, that Negro
citizens of the North should be allowed to take part in the liberation of their race. In addition to this principled consideration, there
was the practical one that the Northern forces were in need of more
fighting men. But the antislavery sentiment of the North was by no
means unqualified and the considerable feeling against the war and
against Negroes had to be taken into account. Such Negroes as
might wish to bear arms in the fight against slavery had no military
tradition, no one knew how they would perform as soldiers, and it
would be a severe blow to the antislavery cause were they not to
acquit themselves well.

The event proved that the doubts were quite groundless. Only a
few months after it had been formed, the 54th Massachusetts took
part in the assault on Fort Wagner, a Confederate stronghold on the
South Carolina coast within sight and cannon shot of Fort Sumter;
it is said to have been one of the strongest earthworks ever built.
The 54th arrived on the field weary and hungry. It had previously

given a good account of itself in minor engagements and now the field commander of the Union forces offered the regiment the honor of leading the attack, which its Colonel accepted. It charged the terrible guns and penetrated the outer defenses of the fort. Before it was withdrawn an hour later, nearly half its men were killed within the fort or before its walls. The question of Negro soldierliness had been answered forever. "Wagner still defies us," a Union publicist said, "but prejudice is down." Before the end of the war 180,000 Negroes were under arms; President Lincoln said that they tipped the balance in favor of Union victory.

At least one Confederate officer gave the 54th its due measure of praise. "The Negroes fought gallantly," Lieutenant Iredell Jones wrote after the engagement, "and were headed by as brave a Colonel as ever lived." The Colonel was killed at the beginning of the attack. When he fell from the parapet into the fort, eleven of his men leaped after him and were cut down by the defenders. Although the Confederate burial-parties followed custom and interred the other dead Union officers in separate graves, the Colonel of the 54th was buried in a trench with his men; when, at a later time, an effort was made to recover his body from the common grave, his father forbade it— his community in death with his Negro men, intended as an indignity, could be nothing but an appropriate honor for Colonel Shaw.

Robert Gould Shaw was twenty-five years old when he died. The only son of a wealthy and distinguished Boston family, he had, as the phrase goes, everything to live for; he was later to be remembered as "the blue-eyed child of fortune upon whose youth every divinity had smiled." In 1863 he was serving as captain in the 2nd Massachusetts Regiment, having risen to the rank from private; he had seen action at Cedar Mountain and Antietam. When the 54th Massachusetts was being formed, the Governor offered him its command because of his military record, his personal character, and his accord with the strong and well-known antislavery commitment of his parents. Shaw hesitated to undertake the arduous responsibility of the post, in part because he doubted his abilities, in part because he loved the regiment with which he was serving. Indeed, his first decision was to refuse the Governor's invitation, but second thoughts led him to believe that it was his duty to accept; it was he whom Emerson had in mind in writing the once-familiar lines:

> When Duty whispers low, *Thou must,*
> The youth replies, *I can.*

An intelligent and enthusiastic soldier, he won the devotion of his men and trained them thoroughly, to what effect their conduct at Fort Wagner makes plain.

The death of the young Colonel was deeply felt in Boston, and a year after the end of the war a committee was formed to erect a memorial to him. "The monument," it was said, "is intended not only to mark the public gratitude to the fallen hero, who at a critical moment assumed a perilous responsibility, but also to commemorate that great event, wherein he was a leader, by which the title of colored men as citizen-soldiers was fixed beyond recall." It was not, however, until 1897 that the monument was erected on Boston Common and dedicated at exercises held on Memorial Day in the Boston Music Hall. The work of Augustus St. Gaudens, the most notable American sculptor of the period, it is a large bronze stele which depicts in high relief the 54th Massachusetts marching in column, its flags furled, a boy drummer at its head; the young Colonel on a superb charger, his sabre unsheathed, rides beside his men; a symbolic female figure in flight over the column beckons it forward with one arm and holds in the other the palms of glory and the poppies of death. The faces of the men are set in calm, stern determination; their stride is long and vigorous; Shaw on his reined-in, slow-stepping great horse is erect and inflexible; his movelessness at the center of the composition, its fixed and still point, emphasizes the forward-thrusting energy of the marching column. The virtuosity with which a wealth of naturalistic detail is executed does not diminish but rather enhances the heroic aspect of the work.

The demeanor of Robert Lowell's poem about the memorial of his kinsman is significantly unlike that of the monument itself; the

salient characteristic of the poem is its air of acknowledged fatigue.
The units of utterance are fragmented and small, their movement
is never of a forward or an upward kind; the diction is dry and
sparse. At only one moment does the voice of the poem move with
something like happy energy, at the lines:

> He is out of bounds now. He rejoices in man's lovely,
> peculiar power to choose life and die—

The recollection of Shaw's dying for the liberty that alone makes
mere existence into what may rightly be called "life" arouses the
tone of the poem from its sad discouragement to a moment of
affirmation. A moment only; the dry minimal tone returns, to continue to the end, and we must read the poem as a lament for the
death of the monument itself—this memorial has lost its power of
awakening memory and "sticks like a fishbone / in the city's throat."

The poem tells us that William James was present at the dedica-
tion exercises, but it does not tell us that the famous philosopher was
one of the speakers of the occasion. James's sense that he "could almost hear the bronze Negroes breathe" was expressed in the course
of the speech he made—in praising St. Gaudens' work he said,
"There on foot go the dark outcasts, so true to nature that one can
almost hear them breathing as they march." Another passage from
the speech finds its way into the poem, which, when it speaks of "a
thousand small town New England greens" on which stand "the
stone statues of the abstract Union Soldier," echoes a sentence of
James's about "the abstract soldier's-monuments . . . reared on
every village green." These small particular references that the
poem makes to the speech do not comprise the whole of the relation
between what Lowell is saying and what James said. So artful a poet
as Lowell would not be likely to have read the speech as part of his
preparation for writing the poem without being aware of the difference, and the significance of the difference, between the nature of
James's utterance and of his own. Of the five speeches that were
made on that Memorial Day of 1897, one was called a "report" and
three were called "addresses," but James had been designated the

"Orator" of the exercises and his speech was listed as an "oration." He had been asked, that is, to speak of Colonel Shaw in a certain way, with elevation and eloquence, to the end of affecting and "inspiring" the audience. He met the demand handsomely, and to the fluency and freedom of James's oration, which are consonant with the qualities of St. Gaudens' relief, the minimal fragmented style of Lowell's poem stands in a contrast that was surely intended.

If the orator of 1897 could speak in a freer and more open voice than the poet of 1963, it was because he spoke from more confidence in the possibility of social virtue than the poet can feel. In his eulogy of Shaw, James first praised his military courage, but went on to call it a courage that was "common and gregarious" and to set above it "another courage," which was Shaw's best glory. "That lonely kind of courage (civic courage as we call it in times of peace) is the kind of valor to which the monuments of nations should most of all be reared, for the survival of the fittest has not bred it into the bone of human beings as it has bred military valor; and of five hundred of us who could storm a battery side by side with others, perhaps not one would be found ready to risk his worldly fortunes all alone in resisting an enthroned abuse." And as James drew to his conclusion, he said, "The republic to which Robert Shaw and a quarter of a million like him were faithful unto death is no republic that can live at ease hereafter on the interest of what they have won. Democracy is still upon trial. The civic genius of our people is its only bulwark, and neither laws nor monuments, neither battleships nor public libraries, nor great newspapers nor booming stocks; neither mechanical invention nor political adroitness, nor churches nor universities . . . can save us from degeneration if the inner mystery is lost."

The orator was not wholly without apprehension about the outcome of the trial of democracy, but he could be of good cheer, as the poet cannot be. In Lowell's view, the "mystery" is already lost. His commemoration of a memorial of the struggle to free some men from the servile condition imposed upon them ends with the perception of the "savage servility" which has become the general condition, freely chosen. Of this the symbol is the "giant finned cars"; the "underworld garage" that is being constructed for them makes the circumstance that beleaguers and shakes the monument. Memory, or faith, has so far failed that "there are no statues for the last war here," only the inglorious memorial of the "commercial photograph" of a safe that survived the atomic bombing of Hiroshima. "The drained faces of Negro school-children" belie the promise that might once have been seen in the firm gaze of Colonel Shaw's "bell-cheeked Negro infantry."

The bitter sadness over the decline of public life from a better state in a former time—it is one of poetry's ancient sadnesses—begins with the evocation of the poet's own lost past. And the Aquarium of his childhood, now dismantled and forlorn, is the source, as it were, of an extended series of associations, having chiefly to do with fish, which makes a thematic line easy to trace but hard to explain. The Aquarium's deteriorated "bronze weathervane cod" is of course immediately appropriate to the purport of the poem, for the cod is the official emblem of the Commonwealth of Massachusetts. The "cowed, compliant fish" introduce the idea of servility and point toward the "savage servility" which is associated with the "giant finned cars" that "nose forward like fish," almost explicitly sharks. But a connection between the passive and the active servility is not readily apparent. Then, although one can understand that a despondent man might sigh "for the dark downward and vegetating kingdom / of the fish and reptile" as representing the comfortable passivity of childhood, other dark and downward things in the poem cannot well be the objects of nostalgia; these include the "underworld garage" and the burial "ditch" which is said to be "nearer." And if it is reptiles that are sighed for, they are at hand in the steam-shovels, which are likened to dinosaurs. What relation the "fishbone / in the city's throat" has to the other fish references is not plain. In an effort to understand the "bubble" upon which Colonel Shaw is said to ride, some readers will recall Jaques's speech about the seven ages of man in *As You Like It,* in which the soldier is said to seek "the bubble reputation / Even in the cannon's mouth";

this reading has the advantage of seeming to explain why the Colonel "waits / for the blessèd break"—because it would release him from his public symbolic existence to the privacy for which "he seems to . . . suffocate."* But the bubbles of the fish that the boy's "hand tingled / to burst" come in to make this interpretation difficult, as does the simile of the "balloons" which is used to describe the faces of the Negro school-children on the television screen. In short, although a rather tight system of associations is manifest in the poem, its syntax is difficult.

The epigraph of the poem is derived from an inscription on the face of the monument, *"Reliquit Omnia Servare Rem Publicam."* The Latin sentence, which may be translated "He left everything behind to serve the nation," is the motto of the Society of the Cincinnati, whose members are descendants of American officers of the Revolutionary War; Robert Shaw was himself a member.† By changing the canonical form of the sentence to make it say, *"They* left everything behind to serve the nation," Lowell has given his epigraph a reference beyond Shaw himself; it now includes the rank and file of Shaw's regiment and all the Union dead. It is possible to read the variant as an implied criticism of the choice of the inscription.

---

* In a letter to his brother Henry, William James, who had known the colonel in their youth, wrote of "poor . . . Robert Shaw," who had been "erected into a great symbol of deeper things than he ever realized himself. . . ."

† Cincinnatus was the legendary Roman hero who, at a time of military crisis, was chosen to be dictator of Rome; the legend is that the emissaries of the Senate found him plowing in his fields, that he left the plow standing and returned to it sixteen days later, having defeated the enemy and resigned the dictatorship. Because membership was hereditary and confined to the descendants of officers, the Society at its inception was denounced as an aristocratic organization, a charge that has since been repeated.